Architecture and
the Environment

BIOCLIMATIC BUILDING DESIGN

Architecture and the Environment

BIOCLIMATIC BUILDING DESIGN

DAVID LLOYD JONES

CO-ORDINATING RESEARCHER

JENNIFER HUDSON

The Overlook Press

WOODSTOCK & NEW YORK

First published in 1998 by
The Overlook Press, Peter Mayer Publishers, Inc.
Lewis Hollow Road,
Woodstock, NY 12498

Library of Congress Cataloging-in-Publication
Data

Jones, David Lloyd, 1942-
Architecture and the environment - contemporary
green buildings /
David Lloyd Jones
p. cm.
Includes bibliographical references and index.
1. Architecture--Environmental aspects.
2. Architecture, Modern--20th century.
I. Title.
NA2542.35.J65 1998   720'.47--dc21
97-27423 CIP

Printed on acid-free paper
Printed in Hong Kong / China

ISBN 0-87951-819-7

9 8 7 6 5 4 3 2 1

Contents

To Linda

Acknowledgements

I gratefully acknowledge the contribution that Susannah Hagan has made to this book. Her advice and encouragement were invaluable and her comments on drafts of Chapters One, Two, Three and Five assisted both in focusing and conveying the message of the book. Susannah Hagan is a senior research fellow at the School of Architecture and Interior Design, University of Brighton, and a visiting lecturer to the Architectural Association, London.

The forty-four projects illustrated in Chapter Four were selected from over one hundred buildings. These were gathered from all parts of the world for assessment in London. I am grateful for the assistance of Dr Deo Prasad, Patrina Eiffert Taylor, Commissioner Atta Tahir, Dr Sajila Haider Vandal, Prof. Rodney Harber, Tamiko Onozawa and Yasuyuki Hirai in researching projects in, respectively, Australia and New Zealand, the United States and Canada, Pakistan and India, South Africa, and Japan.

I am grateful for all those who submitted projects for inclusion in the book and for their work in providing descriptive information, data and illustrations. I am also grateful for the help of four experts who prepared the commentary and performance data for a number of projects illustrated in Chapter Four: John Pletts covered the Vice Chancellor's Office, Académie des Antilles et de la Guyane, the Seed House and Forestry Centre, Eastgate in Harare and the Viaduct Refurbishment in Paris. Akira Koyama covered Tokyo Gas 'Earth Port', Matsushita Electronic, Akira Kusumi's Guest House,

Toyo Village Mason Museum, Sea Folk Museum, Museum of Wood, Water Temple and Yasuda Academia. Sue Woolf covered the John Menzies Headquarters, Palmetto House, the Women's Humane Society Animal Shelter, the Center for Regenerative Studies, Westminster Lodge, Spring Lake Park Visitors Center, Barclaycard Headquarters and the BRE Office of the Future. Sebastian Wormell covered the J Walter Thompson Headquarters, the EDF Regional Headquarters, the Library and Cultural Centre, Herten, the Science Park in Gelsenkirchen, the Apartment Building in Biel, the RWE AG Headquarters, the City Gate, Düsseldorf and the Commerzbank Headquarters. Sebastian also wrote the single paragraph introductions to each of the six building categories comprising the projects illustrated in Chapter Four. I am also grateful for comments and advice on particular sections from Dr William Bordass, Crispin Matson, David Nicholson-Lord and John Field.

I have drawn extensively from many publications and printed papers. These are listed in the Bibliography. Of recent publications, I am particularly indebted to the late John Farmer's (and colleagues') Green Shift, published by Butterworth Architecture in association with WWFUK. This particular perspective of the 'Green Idea' as it developed through recent architectural history was formative in developing my own point of view. Caroline Constant in her article 'From the Virgilian Dream to Chandigarh, Le Corbusier and Modern Landscape', served as the source for the analysis of Le Corbusier's plan for Chandigarh; Sophia and Stefan

Behling's ethnographic and meteorological overview from Sol Power (Prestel); Nobert Kaiser's analysis of energy use from Solar Energy in Architecture and Urban Planning (Prestel), Nigel Howard's work in numerous papers on embodied energy; and Bill Bordass' and Adrian Leaman's post-occupancy studies, energy-use analyses and work on building control systems were all prime sources for various sections of the book, for which I am grateful. I have also drawn from the pioneering work of Amory Lovins, Brenda and Robert Vale, Dean Hawks and Robert Lamb in particular, and many others in general. I am grateful to John Lobell and Shambhala Publications Inc. for allowing me to reproduce in the Preface a passage from Louis Kahn's writings taken from the book Between Silence and Light.

My fellow directors, Andrzej Kuszell and Cezary Bednarski, and all the members of Studio E Architects have put up with a degree of grumpiness and petulance over the last year as a consequence of early morning and late night work on the book. I thank them for their tolerance. Finally, I thank Nathalie Moore for typing the whole thing up and the copy editor, Christine Davis, without whose painstaking work the narrative would be that much more incoherent.

David Lloyd Jones

Foreword

Tadao Ando

The whole world today harbours feelings of misgiving over the crisis facing the global environment and the general loss of our spiritual culture. Now more than ever, it is time to return to our point of origin, to deepen our understanding of the environment and to correct our ways of mishandling the earth's forests and woodlands which play such an important role in shaping and developing the human spirit.

The cities of the twentieth century were built on a basis of function and rationality. Technological innovation and changes in social structure have caused an excess of people and things to become concentrated in urban areas. The entire world has generally shared the common belief that an economy-led society is the ultimate and desired direction. Driven by consumption, mankind has generated tremendous amounts of dynamic power, never before seen in our history, by converting the planet's irreplaceable fossil fuels and, in doing so, we have also released massive volumes of by-products into the air and the seas. We have also produced many non-biodegradable chemicals not found in Mother Nature.

The result of our attempt to use resources which have been the products of billions of years of solar energy within what is relatively a mere instant has been, conversely, to spew more substances and energy into the environment than the planet is capable of digesting, and this has thrown the entire global ecosystem out of balance.

All over the world we are finally beginning to recognize the threat that abnormal weather and pollution in the air, water and ground are posing to civilization. Economic development that wastes limited resources and destroys the environment brings only momentary prosperity; it lacks sustainability and threatens the very existence of future generations. Now is the time to change our consciousness in this regard and, focusing on solar energy, to come up with the appropriate means of utilizing our resources such as wind, water, and so on.

In the process of changing our ways, we should focus on the natural cleansing effects and the power of self-regeneration found in the world's woodlands and rivers. Though it is easy to chop down a forest, it is difficult and extremely expensive to reforest and restore the ecosystem. We must re-evaluate the blessings brought to mankind by the forces of Mother Nature found within thick, foliated woodlands and learn to use these limited resources carefully under the guidance of the earth's ecosystems.

Though it is troublesome to make biodegradable goods and to utilize natural energy in our present ways of life, it is not impossible. We have already developed sufficient technologies to effectively utilize Mother Nature while sustaining her unspoiled beauty, and now is the time for the entire world to awaken to the limits of our materialistic ways and to change society as a whole.

Preface

'The formation of the first earth being a piece of divine architecture' Thomas Burnett: *The Theory of the Earth*, (2 vols, 1684–90)

Some have said that architecture is the Mother of the Arts, thereby claiming for it both maternal and aesthetic ascendancy. If this is so, the matriarch in architecture holds in balance the well-being of another mother figure: Mother Earth, while the art in architecture, uniquely, has to meet the complex demands of use as well as transport-ing the senses. It is on the relationship of these two roles – architecture as an art of function and architecture as an environmental custodian – that this book is focused.

The current preoccupation with green-ness has been brought about by the recognition that our planet is in a precarious state. In general, 'Green' architecture is seen as a reaction to the predicament of environmental depredation in much the same way as 'organic' farming is a reaction to the dominance of intensive, chemically based agriculture. It is perceived as worthy but dull and positioned on the fringe of the mainstream. An alternative view, conceived largely in academic circles, recognizes the ameliorating agenda of Green architecture, but maintains that it has attained the maturity of a distinct movement and seeks to endow it with the perquisites of an 'ism: a manifesto, a style and a focus for esoteric deliberation. This categorization again separates and marginalizes it.

It is true that the environmental crisis which currently faces us has focused attention on the impact buildings have on the environment. People who have taken an interest in the subject now know that buildings in the Western world – their construction and use – are responsible for 50 per cent of the deleterious emissions which are causing the planet to overheat. They also know that the goal of radically reducing energy use (and thereby carbon dioxide and other 'greenhouse' gases) has been broadened to include the goal of sustainable equilibrium in the use of resources, a state whereby that which one generation uses is replaced in kind or value for the benefit of the next. However, it is also true that the dialogue between architecture and nature is as old as architecture itself. It is only in recent history – say since the Second World War – that this happy interaction has been extinguished. Until then, both aesthetic and functional attributes of architecture were inextricably linked to nature. Seen in this light, Green architecture represents an overdue return to, and a broadening of, this innate and continuing exchange. It lies squarely in the mainstream of architecture and is neither expedient reparation nor arcane cult.

Architecture, as much as any other design activity, is dependent on a satisfactory reconciliation of the intuitive with the rational. A building has to be both poem and machine. Few buildings achieve this felicitous equipoise. Those that are sensually stimulating often lack sound construction technique, or fail to fully meet operational requirements; and those that successfully answer practical needs often fail to generate an emotional charge. Many fall short on both counts. Axiomatic to arriving at an inspirational balance between sense and sensibility are two relationships – that of building to site, and both of these to nature itself.

Implicit in the creative thought process of every architect is the conviction that transcendental qualities derive from an apt conjunction of building and site. A successful rapport between the two may derive from a predisposition to satisfying either the emotions or the intellect. Modernists, for example, invariably sought to capture the *genius loci* – the quintessential character of a chosen site; that content which makes it special and distinctive. Classicists of the Enlightenment, on the other hand, preferred to treat the site as a *tabula rasa* on which they could impose their own artful schemes; schemes which, through careful deliberation, harmoniously combined idealized building with idealized nature.

The relationship of building and site to the wider natural environment is again subject to the intuitive and the rational. Market towns and native villages expand organically following successive subjective and pragmatic decisions. Conversely, the peoples of ancient civilizations, such as the Pharonic in Egypt and the Mayan in the Yucatán, selected sites by divination and disposed buildings on them in accordance with the rights and rituals of their deities' earthly representatives. The art of architecture, therefore, has to embrace both the inspirational and the analytical, and architectural response to our environmental predicament will also reflect this dichotomy.

'In doing a memorial I started with a room and a garden. That was all I had. Why did I choose a room and a garden as a point of departure? Because the garden is a personal gathering of nature, and the room is the beginning of architecture.

The garden has to do with nature as it applies to a place that has been chosen by man and is developed for man's use in a certain way. The architect becomes the advocate of nature, and makes everything in the deepest respect for nature. He does this by not imitating it at all, and not allowing himself to think that he is a designer – if he imitates how, let us say, the bird plants the tree. But he must plant the tree as man, a choosing, conscious individual.

The room is not only the beginning of architecture; it is an extension of self. ... The large room and the small room, the tall room and the low room, the room with the fireplace and the room without, all become great events in your mind. You begin to think, not what are the requirements, but rather what are the elements of architecture that you can employ to make an environment in which it is good to learn, good to live, or good to work.

Also marvellous in a room is the light that comes through the windows of that room and that belongs to the room. The sun does not realise how wonderful it is until after a room is made. A man's creation, the making of a room, is nothing short of a miracle. Just think, that a man can claim a slice of the sun.'

Louis Kahn. From *Between Silence and Light* by John Lobell, © (1979). Reprinted by arrangement with Shambhala Publications, Inc., 300 Massachusetts Ave., Boston, MA 02115.

Commentators on Green architecture have generally reacted to global depredation in terms of remedial mechanistic measures: technological innovation, rational planning, appropriate specification of materials and effective building systems management. However, an examination of buildings that have a feeling for nature, as distinct from the more specific concern with assaults on global bio-systems, shows that an intuitive response can be as profound and elevating as one based on careful analysis and measured application.

A sustainable architecture appropriate to the demands of the next millennium will not materialize solely through applying the remedies of revivifying building physics to the architecture of the last decade. The relation-ship of building to environment is after all not just a recent concern; it has been a vital force throughout history, and the precise nature of the relationship has varied widely to reflect the preoccupations of each era. The distinction of this period is that the traditional discourse between building and nature could turn into a valediction. An enduring sustainable architect-ure will emerge and convey the multifarious concerns of our time. It will both reflect deeply intuitive impulses of our cybernetic age and express the rigour of operational analysis. It will also be informed and stimulated by the range of measures formulated by government bodies and others to give greater protection to our habitat. The challenge is to reach a point where Green architecture is indistinguishable from good architecture.

Architecture and the Environment sets out to examine and illustrate examples of notable

Green architecture of the last decade. What was striking when selecting the buildings was their diversity. Could all these buildings, which were clearly strongly influenced by their relationship to nature, really be Green, and, if so, against what sort of criteria of green-ness? In the first instance, it seemed sensible to look at the relationship of buildings to nature and their setting through the span of history, particularly recent history leading up to the current environmentally conscious era; and, in the second, to set down the principles upon which a contemporary environmentally conscious building might be conceived. The book, therefore, begins with a historical overview, albeit from the viewpoint of a practising architect, not a historian. This is followed by a review of design principles for sustainable architecture.

The body of this book reviews, illustrates and provides data, in dossier form, on forty-four recent buildings which, one way or another, address environmental issues and nature in a cogent and imaginative manner. This section is preceded by a chapter which looks at influences leading up to these designs and is followed by another which examines what could develop in this field in the immediate future. The appendix contains a table which, in summary, relates the principles of environmentally sound architecture to the various climatic regions of the world.

The results of all this confirm me in my view: Green architecture is a catholic province of the discipline and, at its best, transcends any environmentally based ethic to become, not just good, but great architecture. Gustav

Metzger, the veteran architectural critic, stated at the 1996 symposium on sustainability at the Architectural Association:

First we had nature. And then came the Environment. Environment is the smoke humanity has put on nature: the people who used Latin had no word for environment – they only knew natura.

Coherent discussion of the subject is hindered by deficient terminology. Both the words 'environment' and 'Green' mean numerous and different things; they have lost any precision they might have had when coined. I use 'environment' to mean the external conditions in which plants or animals live and which tend to influence their development and behaviour; the word 'nature' to mean the whole system of forces and events of all physical life that are not directly controlled by man.

I have tried to avoid the use of the word 'Green' in describing a type of architecture as it has become such a portmanteau concept; I use the more building-specific term 'bioclimatic', by which I mean an approach to design which is inspired by nature and which applies a sustained logic to every aspect of the project, focused on optimizing and using the environment. The logic covers conditions of setting, economy, construction, building management and individual health and well-being, in addition to building physics. A glossary on pages 248–249 defines the more technical terms.

David Lloyd Jones

The Roots of
Green Architecture

The two buildings illustrated on this page and opposite were both completed in the 1990s. Their architects both espouse bioclimatic principles, claiming these to be the motivation and determining force of their design. And yet it is difficult to conceive of two modern buildings so far removed from each other.

Westminster Lodge at Hooke Park, near Dorset, UK, is the latest in a series of back-to-basics home-grown buildings commissioned by the Parnham Trust. Founded and directed by John Makepeace, the Trust teaches bespoke furniture design and has over the years embraced the Green movement and adopted a commitment to environmental sustainability. The recent and enlightened commissioning of new buildings at Hooke Park follows in the line of country estate patronage passed down from the seventeenth century. Westminster Lodge, designed by Edward Cullinan Architects in 1996, provides accommodation for those visiting the school in the seclusion of a wooded tract of the park.

In plan the lodge has a doughnut-ring shape, with a circle of rooms around a glass-roofed communal space. The structure uses timber thinnings, and apart from the glass is almost entirely constructed from natural materials. Its appearance is self-consciously vernacular. It evokes a tree-house in the woods, nest-like in the sylvan landscape.

Menara Mesiniaga is a headquarters building in Malaysia for an electronics and business machine company, designed by Ken Yeang and completed in 1992. The building is one of a series of towers designed by Yeang for corporations and developers in the densely populated cities of the Far East. Within an environment of exponential economic growth and runaway consumer consumption, where simple homespun technology and New Age philosophy hold little sway, Yeang's approach is to ride (superficially at least) the prevailing materialist bandwagon. He uses a combination of technical innovation, luxuriant vertical planting and consummate design flair to convince his clients – and those who occupy his buildings – that an ecologically based approach can also be commercially sound. The building is 15 storeys high and circular in plan. Without reservation, it incorporates all the industrialized materials – glass, aluminium and steel – that represent contemporary construction. Glossy and high-tech in appearance, it looks like a Cape Canaveral launch pad.

Westminster Lodge and Menara Mesiniaga exemplify the polarization in attitude that currently exists towards the design of environmentally sound buildings. The two attitudes reflect two profoundly opposed philosophical approaches to protecting the planet. For some, salvation can only be met through a radical change in social and cultural values, with economic growth ceasing to be the panacea for prosperity and well-being, and with the family and community taking precedence over the individual. These people look to simple community-based lifestyles for their model, where materials and labour are obtained locally, and where everything that is taken from the world's limited supply of resources is returned, one way or another, in useful form. Although they believe that

^
02

01> Westminster Lodge, Hooke Park, Dorset, UK (1996) by Edward Cullinan Architects (see page 194).

02> Menara Mesiniaga, Selangor, Malaysia (1992) by Ken Yeang (see page 232).

Chapter One / The Roots of Green Architecture

solutions are vested in the locality, their view is global. They deplore the capitalism of the free market, which they hold responsible for the enormous gulf in living standards between the industrialized nations and the Third World.

Others see salvation by way of a technological fix. They believe that ecological disaster can be avoided if we learn to harness technology in an 'appropriate' manner. This will allow us to overcome the problems associated with our profligate age, such as pollution and resource shortages. They consider that scientific understanding and invention are bound to follow their inexorable course, constantly feeding on the latest achievements. Scientific enquiry may be guided, but it cannot be made to stop in its tracks or change course. This group is more interventionist in approach. Rather than looking to existing or past models, they prefer to coerce society to form new structures and communities. Their architecture is assertive, glossy and of-the-moment.

Between these extremes there are many shades of view. Of course, neither extreme will prevail. The question we are faced with is how to find a coherent strategy from the middle ground; a strategy that, by degrees, will take us towards environmental equilibrium at a sufficient pace not to be overcome by catastrophe on the way.

Protection of the globe through radical re-evaluation of the way buildings are designed and constructed reflects the concerns of the Green movement generally. The major impact that building design,

construction and management has on national energy consumption began to be widely recognized in the early seventies with the threat and subsequent rationing of oil supplies to the West by the OPEC countries. The crisis confronted politicians with the vulnerability of their oil supply, and underlined the dependence of industrialized countries on the few exporting countries, many of which had politically volatile regimes. This led directly to the search for alternative sources – which were usually more costly – and to the consideration of measures to reduce consumption.

At the same time, the 'drop out' society of the sixties had grown into the 'alternative' society of the seventies, absorbing along the way the doctrines of radical philosophers and scientists. From these and other influences, and from the worrying results of the first scientific studies monitoring conditions on Earth, the Green movement was born. Governments, meanwhile, adopted a somewhat piecemeal approach, moving in fits and starts in response to each forecast of calamity and each statement of reassurance. The response of architects in industrialized countries to warnings of the dangers of wasteful design was at first sceptical. This changed when the consequences could no longer be denied, but their approach generally confined itself to the practical aspects of building design.

The issue of energy conservation provides a good example. In the seventies and eighties, energy conservation was promoted by governments via a series of recommendations,

in the same way that they might wish, for example, to encourage access for the disabled. In Europe, governments sponsored a series of research programmes which, in time, were formulated into guides, codes of practice and, sometimes, government legislation. This did indeed lead to the introduction of sound environmental practice into the construction industry. Fundamentally, however, attitudes remained entrenched. The fact that it was government bodies promoting the measures meant that environmental issues, to most architects, were seen as practical aspects of design that had to be faced up to and incorporated within a pre-existing design philosophy. Accordingly the radical implications on building design heralded by these new concerns were overlooked by the majority of architects.

By the early nineties, Green issues had begun to command a higher profile on the international agenda. In 1996, the Intergovernmental Panel for Climatic Change confirmed that the planet is, indeed, warming up as a consequence of rising carbon dioxide levels in the atmosphere caused by the burning of fossil fuels. Finally, architects were forced to re-evaluate the impact that environmentally sound measures could have on their buildings. Gradually it became evident that such measures could contribute in a positive way to a building's design; that considerations of orientation, natural ventilation, daylight, solar control and thermal capacity could result in potent form-finding building elements. Taken together, they could trigger a new architectural language. In a desire to find new expression which could overcome the sterility of much architecture of the eighties, this stimulus was very appealing; moreover it had the aura of altruism and the promise of seductive and innovative technologies. Not surprisingly, the last decade has seen leading international architects, not formerly noted for their concern for environmental issues, wholeheartedly espouse the cause and appropriate with enthusiasm the more expressive elements of Green design. Other less visually inspiring (and more problematic) measures, such as the issues of recyclability of materials, embodied energy (the energy consumed in the manufacture and delivery of materials and components) and the treatment of waste, have not been adopted with the same alacrity.

'Green architecture' is an unfortunate appellation. It implies something based purely on empirical and pragmatic tenets, separate from the architecture of the mainstream. Moreover, because the Green movement, politically and intellectually, has tended to be assigned to the fringe, Green architecture is accorded the same peripheral status.

The design of any building derives from considered responses to climate, technology, culture and site. Architecture is born when, through intellectual deliberation, an inspired and appropriate balance between these four constituents is reached and a singular physical entity is created. Considerations of global sustainability and energy conservation bear directly on these four issues and therefore go right to the heart of architectural design. As a consequence, bioclimatic architecture – that is, architecture deriving from a

consciously formulated agenda to combat environmental depredation – does not stand distinct in its own right, nor is it peripheral. The evaluation, elaboration and incorporation of environmental measures is as important as issues of planning, structure, services, space and form – and indeed it has an effect on the final shape of all these. Green concerns, therefore, are intrinsic considerations in the design of any building and are critical to determining the elusive 'fine balance' of inspired architecture.

Since consideration of environmental issues is innate in all building design, although generally not satisfactorily realized or overtly expressed, it is difficult to argue the case for a Green aesthetic in the same way that one might recognize post-modernism, deconstructionism or any other 'ism'. Furthermore, a heightened environmental approach to architecture involves, as we shall see, a sensitivity to nature which may be manifest in ideology, physical form and detail, or in symbolic content. It does not, however, address aesthetic issues *per se* – issues such as space, light, mass and proportion – unlike Gothic, Baroque, Modernism or any other fully developed architectural movement.

As architects begin to recognize the importance of incorporating Green measures, there is a tendency to translate these measures overtly as expressive elements in a building's design. (In many cases, the Green element cannot be other than physically apparent – for instance when using photovoltaic solar arrays.) However,

the expressive incorporation of a functional element or combination of elements does not in itself create an architectural aesthetic or movement. They are merely the outward manifestation of an underpinning philosophy; one which has to embrace comprehensively social, environmental, cultural and spiritual needs.

Since issues of climate, technology, culture and site are the essential constituents of architecture, and since designing to protect the planet involves a particular slant on just these issues, it follows that environmentally conscious building design should be inherent in the creative process. Environmental concerns are nothing new; our relationship with nature (or with the natural environment) has been a defining factor throughout architectural history – albeit without today's critical life-preserving edge. Bioclimatic architecture, therefore, has a robust and discernible lineage.

Being Green generally involves understanding that our planet is under threat and taking precautions (where possible) in an effort to avert the environmental disasters predicted by pressure groups and pundits. For most people, this means taking trips to the bottle bank, fitting catalytic converters, selecting lead-free petrol, sorting rubbish into colour-coded bin liners, using both sides of copy paper, and sending an annual subscription to Friends of the Earth or Greenpeace. In reality, of course, far more profound and comprehensive measures will be needed if we are to change the direction of civilization in a way that will ensure the

survival of the planet. These involve scientific advancement, physical planning and rural development; they touch national economies, politics and society at large. In other words, they affect every aspect of our way of life. The direction that each of these aspects must take has to be agreed and orchestrated on a global scale if the goal of sustainability and survival is to be reached.

Architecture's response to these perils needs to be similarly comprehensive. It must both reflect and support the changes required of society. The solution lies not merely in energy efficiency and the specification of appropriate materials and components; a more 'holistic' – all-embracing – approach has to be adopted.

A GREEN PERSPECTIVE ON ARCHITECTURAL HISTORY

In the beginning there was shelter. Shelter was provided by primitive buildings constructed by the people who were going to occupy them; they used the materials that were immediately to hand and employed basic construction techniques which were passed from one generation to the next, changing little in the process. As with artefacts also in day-to-day use, such as pottery and rugs, in many instances the surface and form of these shelters would be appropriated as 'canvases' for decorative and symbolic expression.

Vernacular or folk buildings, such as those shown here in Nigeria and the Alps, remain with us in the less developed parts of the world. For many years such buildings were more or less ignored by the architectural

establishment. It was not until Bernard Rudofsky's influential exhibition 'Architecture Without Architects' at New York's Museum of Modern Art in 1964 that vernacular architecture began to be given its due. As Rudofsky points out in his book accompanying the exhibition, architectural history in the West has traditionally concerned itself with only a few select cultures; moreover it has generally been confined to looking at the evolution of architecture in its late phases. (This, in Rudofsky's opinion, is as arbitrary as dating the birth of music with the advent of the symphony orchestra.) He also draws attention to architectural history's social bias, declaring that 'it amounts to little more than a Who's Who of architects who commemorated power and wealth; an anthology of buildings by and for the privileged – houses of true and false gods, of merchant princes and princes of the blood – with never a word about the lesser people.'

The reason why architectural historians have generally dwelt on buildings for the powerful and wealthy is that it was the combination of power and wealth that created architecture as distinct from construction; that is, building based on intellectual and aesthetic considerations in addition to those of practical necessity. When communities became more structured, mobile and prosperous, they were able to build with increasing elaboration and monumentality. They built palaces and tombs for their rulers and temples and shrines for their gods. These buildings were intended to impress and endure. Wealth and organization allowed them to use a greater range of materials and more human (often slave)

resources. They were able to transport materials from further afield and refine and process them to greater technical effect. New techniques were developed to increase internal comfort and to provide the means for washing, excreting and bathing without leaving the building. These processes required dedicated specialists; constructional processes became divorced from the site and professional consultants were introduced. Thus commenced the cycle of extraction, processing and, in due course, pollution which has ultimately led to the critical condition of our planet. Another consequence of this cycle has been the distancing of the user of the building from those involved in its construction; this, in turn, has caused a degree of antipathy and incomprehension between the two.

Rudofsky was right to bring our attention back to the simple indigenous buildings that still provide much of the building stock of the world. He is not, of course, the first to do so. Le Corbusier took inspiration from the native architecture of North Africa and Greece,

03> Primitive indigenous building on the Jos plateau in Nigeria.

04> Decorated primitive building, Zaria, Nigeria.

05> Log cabins, Lugano, Switzerland: simple, opportunist and effective vernacular structures.

06> Wind towers on traditional homes in Baghdad. The towers direct air into the heart of the buildings.

07> Katsura detached palace, Kyoto, Japan, incorporating open screens and sliding panels to allow the passage of air.

15

C. F. A. Voysey and Baillie Scott from the cottages of the English countryside, and Mies van der Rohe from the grain silos of the mid-west plains in the USA.

It is not an exaggeration to say that primitive and vernacular building and the natural setting in which it exists forms the backdrop, indeed the leitmotif, of architectural history. Looking back over its epochs and movements, it is possible to trace a trail of architectural responses and reactions to this common folk heritage, where architecture, at critical stages of social and cultural change, has

been invigorated by day-to-day construction and inspired by natural forms; a continuing dialogue between architecture and nature. Within this dialogue the strands that today comprise a Green sensibility can be identified.

Architecture and environment are inextricably linked and their relationship complex and multi-faceted. In order to trace the history of Green sensibilities in architecture, therefore, it is helpful to examine different strands in turn. Firstly, consideration will be given to responses to natural climatic forces: sunshine, wind, rain and snow. Then resources, the

means with which buildings have been constructed down the ages, will be assessed. Finally the historical relationship between architecture and the environment, and the meanings that have been attributed to nature, the cosmos and the primitive in this context will be reviewed more extensively.

Climate

Climatic forces have been an important factor ever since man first constructed shelter. Throughout architectural history, local builders have used great ingenuity in providing the most comfortable internal conditions possible within the exigencies and constraints of local climates. In hot regions, evaporative cooling is induced by accelerating airflow through and across spaces; temperatures are reduced by ensuring that direct sunshine cannot penetrate the building; and the thermal capacity of massive structure is used to insulate and take up heat during the day and release it at night when it is cooler.

In cold regions, the insulating quality of materials is exploited and solar heating encouraged. Building designers have found ways of enhancing and manipulating daylight, and contriving shelter from cold winds. In temperate regions, buildings tend to employ a combination of these measures, the particular mix tuned to suit local climatic characteristics.

Thus we have the wind towers of the Middle East, built to cool internal spaces; gigantic marine engineered canopies to protect the Roman public in the Colosseum; *mushrabeyeh*

Chapter One / The Roots of Green Architecture

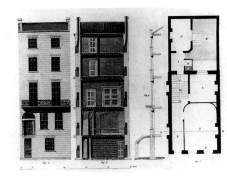

^
11

to shade the interiors (and protect the women from view) in Cairo; screens and sliding shutters to allow traditional Japanese homes the benefits of good ventilation and internal flexibility; and in China the roundhouse which protects not only against the elements but also against marauders. As these examples illustrate, the problem faced by a building designer is never purely that of how to maximize internal comfort; there are always other pressing concerns. In the case of the Colosseum, for instance, large numbers of people had to be accommodated in a manner reflecting the hierarchy of Roman society, all with good views of the spectacles held in the arena. With Chinese roundhouses, protection from bandits was paramount so as to provide for a complex, fully sustainable community. Each solution is a balanced response to climate, culture, technology and site.

Not all buildings gave such importance to climatic factors. Larger buildings, those with a complex function and those imbued with high symbolic content tended to give less importance to harnessing natural forces to provide comfort. This is true of sacred architecture, where the overriding objective was to heighten the spiritual rather than the corporal experience, and is also true of palaces, where ceremonial display and the need to enhance the prestige and standing of the owner or ruler was paramount. It can also be seen in today's more complex, multifunctional buildings – such as shopping centres and airport terminals – where recourse is made to technological rather than natural forces, to provide comfort for the occupants.

Resources

As with the issue of climate, that of resources is also bound up in the differences between vernacular and monumental building. In the past, in vernacular building, there was little option but to use local resources and to use them sparingly to maximum benefit. As the wealth and power of rulers and society increased, builders and architects were able to call on greater resources – intellectual, human and material – and bring them from further afield. Throughout history, wealth and influence has always determined the scope of resource available to any building project. The construction of a terrace of houses in Georgian London exemplifies the effective use of resource. The land was used efficiently, employing narrow frontages and with the larger houses rising to four storeys above a basement. The site would have been excavated in such a way as to create basement, garden, mews and street without having to cart away spoil. Plans and detailed design were based on pattern books, and construction was standardized. Since there was no local stone, walls were constructed in brick which would have been excavated, moulded and fired at the nearest suitable clay beds in Bedfordshire. The same basic pattern applied to houses for the artisan and the nobleman, varying only in size and elaboration.

By contrast, establishing an English country seat in the same period, where the display of wealth and accommodation and entertainment of royalty and their retinues was required, involved the construction of elaborate buildings spread over many acres. Marble would have been imported from Italy, craftsmen from the Low Countries, and the surrounding natural landscape may well have been completely rearranged.

The recycling of materials is not only an important aspect of today's need to conserve resources; it is also a historic phenomenon. The Pyramids in Egypt were stripped of their outer casings to construct Ayyubid and Mamluke Cairo; the Forum in Rome was quarried to construct subsequent city building; and North African Greco-Roman temples were pillaged to build mosques.

The processing of early building materials was limited in scale. Bricks were usually dried in the sun, and the husks and stalks of harvested crops were often used to fire them. Limestone and chalk were baked for cement and gypsum plaster. Iron and other metals were employed in limited quantities; if used more extensively, this was generally for embellishment. This situation changed in the nineteenth century, with wide-scale

^
12

08 > The structure of the canopies used to shelter Roman spectators in The Colosseum.

09 > Roundhouse, Xiamen, south China. The three-storey dwelling surrounds a temple and outbuildings.

10 > Second rate Georgian townhouse from *The New Improved Practical Builder and Workman's Companion*, Peter Nicholson (1823).

11 > Kedleston Hall, Derbyshire, UK (1758) by Robert Adam.

12 > The base of the central kiva at Pueblo Bonito, one of the Anasazis' 'cities' at Chaco Canyon, New Mexico.

13 > Aerial view of Chetro Ketl in Chaco Canyon, another of the Anasazis' 'cities'.

17

^
13

industrialization bringing techniques which greatly improved the performance of construction materials. Industrialization also meant widespread social hardship, pollution and waste.

As architects Robert and Brenda Vale have pointed out, the failure to link 'true' architecture with a concern for resources dates back to the origins of architecture (*Green Architecture,* 1992). The architectural historian J. J. Coulion suggests that monumental architecture, that is buildings intended to impress and endure not just perform a function, made its appearance in the Greek world in the seventeenth century BC (*Greek Architecture at Work,* 1977). From the start, this architecture was an exploration and perfection of a structurally unsophisticated system: 'The basic system remained a post-and-lintel structure executed in large, carefully dressed stone blocks. This structural conservatism is probably inherent in the Greek conception of architecture as it was concerned primarily with external form rather than internal space.'

Although the Greeks understood the principle of the arch, they did not use it in their architecture except in cellars and underground vaults, even though its construction used less stone to create any given size of enclosure. Subsequent epochs, in particular the Romans in their secular buildings (but, interestingly, not in their sacred ones), Romanesque and Gothic all exploited the structural and spatial potential of the arch and vault. In their case, however, the motivation for doing so was not so much for economy of means, but for aesthetic and symbolic effect.

Most building is constrained in its use of skill, labour and materials by budget and is, accordingly, relatively efficient in its employment of resources. When architecture is used to convey symbolic content, however – whether sacred or profane – consideration of economy of means is entirely subjugated to the nature of the expression being sought. This is as true today as it was in ancient Greece or in Medieval times.

Man and Nature

The third strand of Green sensibility has to do with the meanings attributed by society to nature and natural phenomena, and the effect these attitudes have had, throughout history, on buildings, settlement and landscape. This is broadly taken in chronological order.

Early societies lived close to nature. Their lives were ruled by the seasons; they depended on benign aspects of the seasons, augmented by their own endeavours, for survival. Nature had both a practical and supernatural influence. The Anasazi Indian settlement at Chaco provides a good example of such a community.

The Chaco civilization, occupying the San Juan River basin in the north-west corner of New Mexico, flourished for a relatively short period – about 300 years between 900 and 1200 AD. Within that period a complex and sophisticated society emerged, representing the first integrated experiment in social, political and economic cohabitation in the American south-west. The Anasazi Indians were not a self-contained society. The community's size and wide-ranging needs necessitated trade with the outside world. Communication with other societies may have been one of the factors which led to their cultural, scientific and architectural sophistication. The community comprised 13 'cities' each, typically, with an outer shell of multistorey stone-constructed living accommodation facing south with its back to the north cliff of the river valley. The living cells fronted on to a 'square' within which were located semi-sunken circular 'kivas'. The citizens made best use of climate, topography, local materials and, judging by their ability to calculate the seasons precisely through astrological observation and from archaeological finds, had a dynamic and inspirational relationship with the cosmos, the climate and the landscape.

This close, intuitive communion between society, nature and the supernatural is fundamental to all the early epochs, from Egyptian and

^
14

Mesopotamian to Byzantine and Gothic periods. One of the most developed manifestations of this relationship is Feng Shui.

This is an ancient Chinese science used to identify building sites, and to decide the most auspicious deployment of buildings on the site, and the form and character of the buildings themselves. Judgements are made on the basis of natural characteristics, such as topography, the effect of wind and the presence of water, and on the metaphysical – the intrinsic qualities of form, shape and setting. The practice of Feng Shui continues to this day in the Far East, but in Europe the symbiotic relationship between nature, culture and building was brought to an end by the Renaissance.

The Greek philosopher Protagoras wrote that 'Man is the measure of all things'. This observation sums up the spirit of the Renaissance. It celebrated the primacy of man; his intellect and physical prowess. Religion ceased to be the intrinsic and all-pervasive influence of daily life. It became both aestheticized and secularized and had to take its place alongside the realms of state, science and trade.

The age of humanism revived the Classical language of architecture, recognizing its potent civilizing attributes and its intellectual lineage. Its foundation in mathematical proportion, order and harmony clearly expressed the spirit and aspirations of the period. Classical architecture evolved to express, in the first instance, the omniscience

of deities and, later, the power of the state and the potency of statesmen and generals. It developed from smaller and simpler structures which may well have been constructed, at least in part, in materials other than stone. Literal interpretation by Classical, and now Green protagonists, of Abbé Laugier's *Essai sur l'architecture* (1753) regarding the evolution of Classical architecture from the 'primitive hut' misses the point. Laugier's essay is a discourse on aesthetics and the development of an architectural language, not a treatise on the physical evolution of that language.

Classical architecture's foundation in mathematics and geometry, rather than natural form, set it apart from nature and the organic. While the symbolic significance of location and site were extremely important in Greek and Roman times, the natural setting was only of significance in the manner in which it could present and enhance the building. The Classical tradition relies on a contrast between what nature is, and what man can make. Its aim is to find the point of balance between the two and create harmony. Renaissance architects, taking their cue from the Classical tradition, sought to tame and manipulate the natural setting to create a harmonious, integrated and awe-inspiring man-made entity. The desire to rearrange and enhance the landscape was taken still further in the Mannerist, Baroque and Rococo periods.

The Classical tradition reinforced the split between architecture for the privileged and building for everyone else. While the latter

^
15

was, necessarily, concerned with the best use of resources and acknowledged this dependency in the functional expression of its parts, Classical architecture expressed its independence from such considerations, despite its adoption as the architecture of the age of humanism. The Renaissance was primarily confined to the court – focusing on Florence, Urbino and Mantua – and touched relatively few people. It flourished on learning, harmony, good manners and understatement (made possible, however, by the less refined activity of extensive trade and expropriation). These attributes are particularly represented in its architecture. It adjusted the monumental Greco-Roman Classical tradition to that of reasonable human necessity. These few modest, elegant buildings are an assertion of the dignity

14> Pazzi Chapel,
S. Croce, Florence
(1429–) by Filippo
Brunelleschi.

15> *The Tempest*
(c. 1505, Venice) by
Giorgione. This unlikely
scenario is the outcome
of using nature and
natural phenomena as
a context and deploying
figures and buildings
to create a balanced
composition.

16> Arc-et-Senans
Saltworks, France
(1775–9) by Claude-
Nicolas Ledoux. The
heavily articulated
façade evokes the
natural rock from which
the salt is mined.

17> Newton's Cenotaph
(1784) by Etienne-Louis
Boullée. The section
shows how the night sky
would be reproduced
with minute openings in
the gigantic dome.

∧
16

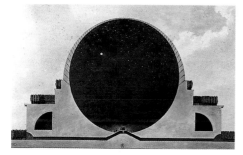

∧
17

of man, but distance man from nature.
Renaissance ideals were taken a stage further
in the seventeenth and eighteenth centuries
in Europe. Divine authority gave way to the
results of experience, experimentation and
observation, and also to mathematics. In this
so-called Age of Enlightenment, scientific
thought and invention experienced a
resurgence, this time based on Cartesian and
Newtonian rationalism. The decline of the
Christian Church as a creative force and
religious focus prompted the development
of a new morality. It was based on natural
law, justice and tolerance.

Like the Renaissance princes, the philosophers
of the Age of Enlightenment looked back to
the antique Classical era, but this time drew
their inspiration from the stoic morality of
the Roman Republic. Unlike the Renaissance,
however, this new morality was intended to
encompass all citizens and the natural world.
Rousseau elevated common man as the
embodiment of virtue, believing immersion
in nature to be the means whereby our identity
can be lost in the whole, and our gain,

accordingly, a more intense consciousness
of being. Nature, in Rousseau's terms, might
be defined as those parts of the visible world
not created by man which can be perceived
through the senses.

It was at this time, in the late eighteenth
century, that ideas such as harmony with
nature, care for the rights and well-being
of the individual and the efficacy of
technological development came to the fore.
With tenets like these, it seems clear that
the seeds of the Green movement, as we know
it today, must lie in this era. However, few
at the time realized that these technological
developments would lead to the problems
we face today – of industrial sprawl,
pollution and despoliation.

The interesting consequence of the shake-up
engendered by the industrial revolution was
that the old division between monumental
buildings intended to impress and endure,
and the remainder of building constructed
locally with materials that were to hand (and
often inadequate to needs), became eroded.
The new prosperous bourgeoisie required
buildings to suit their status and purse.
These buildings, in trading cities like Bruges,
Amsterdam and London, were spacious, light
and comfortable, yet built with relative
economy of means. Apart from houses, the
new middle class required town halls, schools,
clubs, theatres, markets and trading halls.
All of these needed surveyors, architects,
builders and craftsmen. This body of building
grew to dominate construction. Today it is
the focus of pressure for environmental
awareness.

Eighteenth-century architects did not just
concern themselves with pragmatic housing
for the new middle class, however. They
speculated on what sort of dwelling Rousseau's
'noble savage' might occupy and how it might
have metamorphosed into the style of the
Classical temple. Ironically, the effect of
speculation about the primitive in the
eighteenth century was to make the revivals
of earlier Classical styles more popular, in
particular the Doric order, which complemented
society's espousal of the austere values of the
Roman Republic. It also produced a fashion for
'primitive huts' which were built at focal points
in the parks and the gardens of the wealthy.
These were variously used as hunting lodges,
hermitages and shelters from inclement
weather. The grotto also made a comeback.
The use of untrimmed rocky surface, of
stones piled up as in nature, came to signify
a reminder of the elemental, the raw state
of things, against which artefacts of human
invention could be juxtaposed.

The visionary French architects Claude-
Nicolas Ledoux and Etienne-Louis Boullée
could hardly be further removed from this
fashion for 'primitive huts'. But, in their own
way, they played a pivotal role in determining
the development of a Green sensibility in
architecture. They, more than any other
architects, expressed in architectural terms
the spirit of the Enlightenment. Neo-classicism
stripped Classicism of its Baroque accretions
and found a revolutionary expressive power
to reflect new scientific ideas about the nature
of the cosmos as envisaged by Newton. The
idea of an architecture *parlante*, in the sense
of a building's forms symbolizing its function,

19

was true to Enlightenment ideals. This idea anticipated the Modernist maxim of form following function, where the forms of the building more literally expressed its use and construction. Indeed French Neo-classicism is viewed by many as the precursor of the puritanism of the Modern Movement.

The philosophy of the Enlightenment, therefore, influenced succeeding generations in different ways. One strand led directly to the foundation of Modernism, another continued the notion of buildings set in a rural idyll. This line continued from the 1790s to the 1860s and developed from one-off constructions to adorn the estates of royalty (the hamlet for Marie Antoinette at Versailles) and landed gentry (John Nash's Dairy at Blaise Castle, near Bristol, UK) to, particularly in England, cottages for estate employees constructed by altruistic and modern-thinking landlords (Nash's Blaise Hamlet and Lord Ongley's housing at Old Walden, Bedfordshire, UK).

These buildings always related, however perversely, to a real or imagined vernacular with essentially functional design, and used local building techniques and materials. They were picturesquely sited, highly decorative (the cottage orné), and clearly related to the world of nature in their asymmetry, use of natural materials and their siting within the landscape.

A more profound view of man's relationship to nature can be found in the work of the American writer Henry David Thoreau. He described in lyrical detail the two years

that he spent alone at a cabin he built on Walden Pond at Concord, Massachusetts, where he had retreated in order to 'solve some of the problems of life, not only theoretical but practical'. The construction of the cabin is described in practical terms (unlike Abbé Laugier's description of the primitive hut, which was purely an aesthetic exercise) and one can clearly recognize the sensibility towards nature and natural materials with which environmentalists identify today. He claimed that 'true art is but the expression of our love for nature'. His views had a significant influence on the development of a home-based American architecture, and this architecture, particularly in the refined form of Frank Lloyd Wright's work, influenced the rest of the world.

In Europe in the mid-nineteenth century, industrialization was gathering pace. Discoveries in science by Darwin, Lyell and others were extending and reshaping human understanding of nature. Significant advances were also being made in building and construction technologies, particularly in the use of steel and glass, and in the development of heating, artificial lighting and sanitation. John Ruskin was one of the first people to foresee the inherent dangers of uncontrolled industrial development. The reforming propositions Ruskin put forward for the arts and then for society were, besides much else, the first systematic reaction of a kind we would now call Green. 'God', wrote Ruskin, 'has lent us the earth for our life; it is a great entail. It belongs as much to those who are to come after us, and whose

names are already written in the book of creation, as to us; and we have no right, by any thing that we do or neglect, to involve them in unnecessary penalties, or deprive them of benefits which it was in our power to bequeath' ('The Lamp of Memory' from *The Seven Lamps of Architecture*, 1849). Ruskin's advocacy lay in both moral and aesthetic spheres. He championed the crafts and respect for artisans. He analysed industrial ills, pressed for social change, and carried out practical experiments in cleaning up pollution. He promoted Gothic architecture, in part because he felt the style to be more

18 > Cottage in Marie Antoinette's hamlet, Versailles, France (1782).

19 > Cottage Orné, Houghton Lodge, Hampshire, UK (c.1800).

20 > Oxford Museum, Oxford, UK (1855) by Benjamin Woodward. John Ruskin championed this building more than any other new building of his time. Composed of a mélange of European Gothic sources, it is notable for its lace-like cast-iron structure and handcrafted construction. The building represents a secular, science-based equivalent of a Medieval cathedral, with biblical iconography replaced by representation of natural form.

21 > North-west corner of the Crystal Palace, Hyde Park, London (1850–1) by Joseph Paxton.

22 > Blackburn House, Little Thakeham, Sussex, UK (1902) by Sir Edwin Lutyens

23 > The Red House, Bexley Heath, London (1859) by Philip Webb.

^
21

^
22

^
23

artists and friends could congregate and where creative work and the home life could coexist harmoniously alongside each other and with nature. The architecture of the Arts and Crafts movement was almost entirely confined to the house and domestic living. It was grounded in the practical study of folk traditions of construction, and the use of local materials and techniques. It represented a quiet revolution against the assumption that the products of industrialism were superior to hand-crafted goods, and that technology offered the only possible way forward. In the hands of Raymond Unwin, C.F.A. Voysey and Baillie Scott, and incorporating the planning principles of Ebenezer Howard, the movement offered an attractive and life-enhancing alternative to the dehumanizing back-to-back housing of the expanding cities.

Its influence was widely felt: in California where Greene & Greene produced their spacious Japanese-inspired houses; in Australia where architects such as Walter Burley Griffin produced timber-framed villas in the suburbs; and across Europe to Austria and Germany in the artists' colony at Darmstadt. The movement's ideas pervaded the socio-economic spectrum, resulting in residences for upper- and middle-class capitalists, designed by the likes of Sir Edwin Lutyens and Norman Shaw, as well as social housing for artisans in the garden cities and early corporation housing by the London County Council and others.

Though rooted in an essentially nostalgic view of nature, the Arts and Crafts movement was a potent precursor of the iconoclasm to come.

attuned to reflect the natural world in its use of materials and in its embellishment (because of its darker, more ambiguous and accommodating character), and because in his opinion it suited northern climes better than the Classicism born of the Mediterranean.

Ruskin failed to understand, however, that economy of means and appropriate technological development could also assist in achieving his goals. His contemporaries – Brunel, Telford and Paxton in Britain, and Bogardus in the United States – all saw the

potential in the new scientific discoveries, particularly the processing of iron and its capacity to transform structural design. Romantics and moralists such as Ruskin, Gray and Wordsworth saw technological development primarily as a product of industry, a product of hard, demeaning labour and a cause of social deprivation.

If John Ruskin was the first individual overtly to express Green objectives and concerns, the Arts and Crafts movement in Britain was the first group to do so. The Arts and Crafts pioneer William Morris shifted the ideas of Ruskin from the critical and theoretical to the practical. He also moved away from the ponderous historicism of mainstream nineteenth-century architecture to a plainer, more 'organic' architecture – one that celebrated regional form, detail and materials and allowed setting, not axial planning, to influence layout and massing. The Red House, designed by Philip Webb for Morris, embodied not only this freer approach to architecture, but a manner of living where

24 > Victor Horta House Museum, Brussels, Belgium (1898).

25 > Park Güell, Barcelona, Spain (1900–14) by Antoni Gaudí.

26 > The Glass Pavilion, Deutscher Werkbund Exhibition, Cologne, Germany (1914) by Bruno Taut.

∧
24

The Modernism of the Bauhaus, although seemingly at odds with Arts and Crafts ideals, owes much to the movement's philosophy. At the turn of the century, as the influence of the Arts and Crafts movement was being more widely felt, a number of idiosyncratic styles flourished which were directly inspired by nature and natural forms. Art Nouveau rediscovered the delight and fluidity that could derive from embellishment inspired by plants, animals and geology. Unlike eighteenth-century Rococo, where such inspiration was largely confined to the interior elaboration of box-like buildings or, at most, the embellishment of an entrance façade, Art Nouveau used natural form to shape and mould entire buildings and structures. Victor Horta and Hector Guimard were the great exponents of this approach.

In Secessionist Vienna, architects such as Otto Wagner also called upon nature to articulate and embellish their buildings. In Scotland, Charles Rennie Mackintosh referred constantly to plant forms. The inspiration that these architects drew from nature was, however, essentially decorative. They recognized its life-enhancing exuberance, but the buildings themselves remained static and four-square. It was Antoni Gaudí, following a little later, who translated nature in all its florid abundance – sylvan, anthropomorphic, verdant and filigreed – into amazing architectural fantasies.

The German Expressionist architects, particularly Bruno Taut, took their inspiration not so much from organic life, but from geology and the Earth's crust. Their

<25

22

^
26

fascination with geometric order was stimulated by contemporary interest in the exploration of crystalline forms. The regularity of crystal structures, the diversity of forms possible with a limited range of shapes, and the geometric laws which seemed to govern their formation, reinforced the Expressionists' ideas that nature was best reflected by man through geometric order. The discovery that continents move, that mountains rise and that geological formation was an ongoing process seemed for the Expressionists to blur the boundaries between the organic and the inorganic, the animate and the inanimate.

Alongside developments in metallurgy (whereby cast iron could be transformed into high-performance steel) and the invention of ferro-concrete (a versatile composite that combined the tensile properties of steel with the compressive properties of concrete), architects began to realize the potential of glass and glazing technologies. Taut was one of the first to exploit this, with his Glass Pavilion for the Cologne exhibition of 1914, which replicates crystalline forms. In due course the Modern Movement was to employ glass as a way of dissolving the division between inside and outside.

MODERNISM AND NATURE

Modernism is generally considered to be antithetical to nature, the natural world and regional distinctions, being wholly occupied with a purist and universal response to technology and socialism. This may be true of the more mechanistic and 'classically'

focused practice of architects from the Germano-USA axis (pioneered by Walter Gropius, Mies van de Rohe and Marcel Breuer, continued by Philip Johnson, Skidmore Owings and Merril and other large American corporate architectural practices, and finally debased into a ubiquitous international vernacular, in the same way that the Arts and Crafts house became debased into the formulaic cherry-lined ribbon development housing of the suburbs). However, it does not apply to the more intuitive, individual and organic approach of Le Corbusier, Alvar Aalto and Frank Lloyd Wright, or the expressionism of Eric Mendelsohn and Taut. Indeed, parallel Green strands of sensibility to nature and reference to the vernacular can be found in much Modern Movement architecture – albeit embedded within a complex architectural language and set of relationships. To cover these complexities comprehensively would in itself fill a volume. However, it is possible to look briefly at four of the giants of the Modern Movement and identify in their separate approaches to architecture distinct strands of a sensibility which, taken together, go some way towards providing the backdrop to the contemporary Green movement in architecture.

Le Corbusier

Le Corbusier (1887–1966) is perhaps the most bountiful exponent of the Modern Movement. His genius encompasses the dialectical, the poetic and the artistic. His architecture is a product of all these sources.

In Le Corbusier's writings, nature is a prevalent theme, often imbued with semi-religious overtones. He sometimes invoked it as a force antithetical to the works of man, equivalent to chaos or the Romantic notion of the sublime; at other times he portrayed nature in its essence as a system, of which man is a part, and as an embodiment of order. The latter mode of thinking reflected the Rationalist in him, the same side of him that described a house as being a 'machine for living' and led him to revere the imagery of contemporary technological marvels such as the ocean liner, the automobile and the aeroplane.

The theme of nature was also central to his social aims. Echoing Ruskin, whose work he had read at college in Switzerland, he considered nature an agent for the moral regeneration of mankind, capable of rekindling the humanitarian values lost to industrialized society. In *The Radiant City* (Paris, 1967) he declares: 'Man is a product of nature. He has been created according to the laws of nature. If he is sufficiently aware of those laws, if he obeys them and harmonizes his life with the perpetual flux of nature, then he will obtain [for himself] a conscious sensation of harmony that will be beneficial to him.'

However, Le Corbusier also declared: 'There is no such thing as primitive man; there are [only] primitive resources. The idea is constant, in full sway from the beginning.' For Le Corbusier, the primordial, the beauty which derives from adherence to rational law and the humanitarian were

23

Chapter One / The Roots of Green Architecture

^
27

all inextricably interrelated. In invoking these three aspects Le Corbusier infused modern Rationality with primeval symbolism and thereby sought to endow his architecture with universal and eternal value.

Le Corbusier's early search for a modern architectural language developed from intellectual considerations and away from more instinctive, metaphysical feelings. His theoretical principles, conceived in reaction to Beaux-Arts academicism, inverted the traditional relationship of building to landscape while retaining the same separation of one from the other. His early villas bore the same relationship to landscape as, say, Palladio's did – white, independent and distinct – using the setting as a foil to heighten the architectural experience (and by association, in the case of Le Corbusier's villas, the machine age experience). However, instead of employing a rusticated base, terracing and subsidiary buildings (farm buildings sometimes in Palladio's villas) to ground the building and mediate between the formality of the residence and the disarray of the countryside, Le Corbusier elevated his villas on pilotis to provide a continuous ground plane. An example of this is the Villa Savoye at Poissy (1929–31). The natural landscape, isolated from the building volume, becomes an object for contemplation from within the internal spaces and from the roof; and the building, viewed from a distance, appears as an alien machine poised for lift-off. The 'garden' is transferred to the roof and placed in a room open to the sky.

In Le Corbusier's urban dwellings, dramatic roof terraces provide a combination of detachment and engagement with landscape, similar to that of his rural villas. They are compelling explorations into designed landscape, demonstrating his quest for primordial values, that led him to transcend radical theory. It would seem that the opportunity for freer design afforded by this less polemically charged element of the building, the roof garden, allowed Le Corbusier to indulge in sculptural effect, wit and metaphor, and provided the conduit for the tendency towards eclecticism and spirituality that manifests itself more fully in his later work.

Later, Le Corbusier rejected the concept of an actual garden on the roof, since this countered his aim of reintegrating man with nature. In the Unité d'Habitation at Marseilles (1947–52), he uses the roof space to suggest archaic values, employing primal forms, the deliberate ambiguity of which amplifies the other-worldliness of a platform suspended in the sky. The parapet enclosing the terrace blocks the city from view to become a substitute horizon, collapsing foreground and background. By visually eliminating the middle ground, Le Corbusier isolated the roof terrace from its immediate environs. The effect is to recover the sense of integration with nature, a quality he so admired as a young man in the Acropolis at Athens.

The shift from idealistic preoccupation with void and solid contrasted with nature, to a more poetic concern with natural forms

^
28

and integration with landscape, was quite probably accelerated by the subconscious effect of the Second World War. The memory of intensive city bombing and the threat of nuclear catastrophe must have had a bearing on the way Le Corbusier replaced his pre-war white, floating, machine-like buildings with monolithic protective structures in chromatic hues with rough-cast surfaces. The Maisons Jaoul (1954–6), the Unité and the monastery of Sainte-Marie de la Tourette (1957–60) combine the celebration of reinforced concrete not as a means of freeing space from the confines of load-bearing walls but as a heavy, rough, crude material conveying a sense of security and durability, with the now carefully continued and controlled introduction of daylight and sunshine to interior space.

These buildings evoke vernacular antecedents, albeit subsumed into an architectural language that draws on diverse sources. The vernacular vies with the technological capabilities of reinforced concrete, steel and plate glass and is transmuted to serve the spirit and aspirations of another time and

^
29

^
31

^
30

27> Villa Savoye, Poissy, France (1929–31) by Le Corbusier.

28> Villa Saraceno (1560/66) by Palladio.

29> La Tourette (south façade), near Lyons, France (1957–60) by Le Corbusier.

30> Model of Chandigarh, India (1951–6) by Le Corbusier.

31> Model for the Governor's Palace, Chandigarh (1953) by Le Corbusier.

culture. Nevertheless, the fecundity of earth, the warmth of the sun and the delight in day-lit space is manifest in Le Corbusier's later work in form, detail, colour and texture. Le Corbusier's first design for the capital complex at Chandigarh in northern India, executed towards the end of his life, may be the modern era's most convincing testimony to the integration of architecture and landscape on an epic scale. Influenced by the symbolically explicit model of a Mughal paradise garden, he accomplished this synthesis by transferring the mythopoeic treatment of the rooftop landscape back to the ground plane. At Chandigarh, he distinguishes three scales of landscape: the pragmatic landscape of the residential city, the monumental landscape of the capital complex, and the more intensely symbolic landscape of the Governor's Palace.

Le Corbusier's grid plan, relieved by the irregularity of the river and strips of public park, is quite conventional and surprisingly Beaux-Arts in its conception. The capital complex is centrally located, but is separated visually and physically from its surroundings by a roadway, a canal and a series of artificial mounds. The mounding, in the

form of ha-has, has the effect, like the parapets of the roof terraces, of eliminating the middle distance, reinforcing the separation of the capital plateau and providing a building plane for elaborate, highly charged, symbolic artifice and imagery.

Throughout the complex, Le Corbusier uses references to the cosmos to affirm the unity of nature and human consciousness. Many of Chandigarh's monuments and its hieroglyphs cast in concrete surfaces refer to the sun, its daily path and radiance. Like ancient cultures, Le Corbusier recognized the sun as a primal force ruling all life, an emblem of harmony between man and nature.

Le Corbusier's design for the Governor's Palace sees a return to the tradition of a building rooted in landscape and he employs every means to emphasize the interrelationship of the two. The Palace was designed to be square. Three floors rise from a larger base floor and are crowned on the roof with an upturned crescent, silhouetted against the Himalayan foothills and serving simultaneously as viewing platform, shading device and trough to catch the monsoon rains. It cradles the sky, while suggesting both a crescent moon and horns of the sacred ox. Gardens were set out on all four sides. Their form and disposition, like that of the architecture itself, draws on many sources: the Chahar bagh or paradise garden of Mughal creation; the other-worldliness of his roof terraces; and the evocation of archaic sites through excavation and sculpting of the ground plane. By fusing Mughal symbolism with primal imagery, archaic ritualistic

space with Classical architectural principles, Le Corbusier sought to conflate the traditional Indian concept of the sacred with a modern metaphysic, the cultural with the universal.

Le Corbusier's work was profound, contradictory and inspiring. The intuitive mythologizing and poetic aspects of his work, those which addressed the relationship of man with nature, were devalued and ignored in the subsequent unifying efforts to make from Modernism's creative diversity a homogeneous and consensual architecture; what came to be known as International Style. Only now is the complexity of his work, in its multiplicity of sources and, in particular, the inspiration which it drew from nature, being recognized and its influence felt by a new generation of practising architects.

Alvar Aalto

The work of Finnish architect Alvar Aalto (1898–1976) is similarly the product of a unique and personal view of the relationship between man, technology and nature. Aalto's approach was more particular, lyrical and self-effacing than that of Le Corbusier. Although espousing Modernist principles of functional integrity, he eschewed the ideology of reductionist abstraction, and found inflexible dogma alien to his psyche.

Having emerged on the architectural scene a little later than the founding masters of Modernism, Aalto avoided the Calvinistic proselytizing for purity of thought and expression that characterized the movement

32> The Tuberculosis Sanatorium, Paimio, Finland (1929–33) by Alvar Aalto.

33> Villa Mairea, Noormarkku, Finland (1938–9) by Alvar Aalto. The house epitomizes Aalto's humanist and regional interpretation of Modernism. The white walls are limestone washed brickwork and the porch is supported on tree-like groupings of thin timber columns.

34> Hall of Residence at the Massachusetts Institute of Technology (MIT) (1949) by Alvar Aalto. The building is characterized by its undulating façade facing the Charles River, giving every student an oblique view of the only significant natural feature on an otherwise bleak campus.

∧
32

in its early phases. The Modernist language of architecture – standardization, new methods of construction, and a new conception of space that was fluid and unpredictable – was fully developed by 1930 and lay at the disposal of anyone capable of using it. At this time the artists Joan Miró and Paul Klee, whose work was bound up with the organic and irrational, were coming to the fore.

In Finland, a similar event took place in architecture. Aalto dared to move from the rational-functional to the irrational-organic. This development was not so much a reaction to Modernist principles, rather an expansion and enriching of them: the elaboration of intrinsic attitudes already enshrined in its ideology. In the same way that Mannerist and Baroque expression grew from early Renaissance architecture, a broadening of language and a loosening of precepts took place in the development of certain Modernist practitioners. By this time, however, the Western world had expanded through Europe and across the Atlantic, and issues of regionalism – culture, climate and technology – had become a factor, too.

Finland was to Aalto as Spain was to Picasso and Ireland to James Joyce. It provided him with an inner source of energy that is evident in all his work. Materials, imagery and architectural character all flow from stimuli that are particular to his native country. Finland had been something of a backwater during the passage of cultural and scientific advancement that had taken place in Europe and the East. The region was covered by glaciers for longer than most during the

Ice Age, and the advancement of civilization reached this country later than most of Europe. Unlike the Vikings of Norway, the Danes in medieval times and the Swedes in the seventeenth century, the peoples of Finland never became an imperial power, and for most of the country's history it was dominated or ruled by neighbouring countries, often finding itself a pawn in other people's power games. Finland has an elemental character; a country of vast dimensions and solitudes, with its vast network of lakes and forests, it evokes images of the Creation, when water and earth were first separated. Metals, timber and fish are its principal resources, indeed Aalto's forebears were foresters. It is perhaps because of its isolation, its primeval vastnesses and the stoicism of its people that, through Alvar Aalto, Finland marked Modernist expression so indelibly.

Aalto's early masterpiece is generally considered to be his Tuberculosis Sanatorium at Paimio (1929–33). This is an elegant, white, six- to seven-storey complex set sensitively amongst birches and pines, and in its formal resolution and humanitarian concern it adheres closely to the precepts of Modernism. Widely regarded as one of the seminal buildings marking the rise of the Modern Movement, it also signals a turning point in Aalto's architectural development. Despite his greater international recognition and his acceptance of a professorship at the Massachusetts Institute of Technology (MIT), Aalto's subsequent work increasingly encompasses a regionalism and individuality particular to his country and his personal preoccupations.

Aalto's work following the Sanatorium is characterized by its sinuous irregular curves, its multiplying and diverging planes, and its fluid bunching and spacing of elements. These may appear antithetical to the orthogonal and regular requirements of industrialization, but he was nevertheless fully aware of the economies of rationalization and standardization, and employed this discipline whenever expedient. These forms, shapes and rhythms were clearly a response to the Finnish landscape, with its curvaceous lakes, its glacier-smoothed outcrops of rock and its vibrant forests. They also derive from the exigencies of placing buildings on the folds and spurs of an undulating countryside. That Aalto could construct these shapes and forms economically was largely due to his extensive use of timber. The Modern Movement had discounted timber as a structural material, since it did not offer the performance of steel and ferro-concrete and was imbued with hand-crafted, folk connotations. In Aalto's hands it was transformed into a versatile, flexible and high-performance material providing infinite variety of expression and a humanity and warmth alien to industrialized products. Not only did he employ it in all elements of his buildings, but he also used it in laminated form to create simple classic furniture that is still marketed today.

As well as introducing a regional sensibility into Modernist ideology, Aalto's designs and town planning are notable for the sensitivity they show towards practical and spiritual human needs. Without denying the precepts of Modernism, Aalto's buildings display

33

34

a humane modesty of execution and a lyrical lightness of touch that bring delight and a sense of equanimity. Where Le Corbusier would place his buildings on the highest point where they could be admired, in silhouette, from afar, Aalto would place them below the crest where they would meld with the landscape and where the natural environment could remain dominant.

Aalto, therefore, while intellectually a Modernist, drew inspiration in shaping and constructing his buildings from the particular part of the world where he was born, was raised and worked. This sense of being tied to, and cherished by a singular climate, culture and economy is an essential aspect of Green thinking in architecture today.

Frank Lloyd Wright

The American architect Frank Lloyd Wright (1869–1959), born and brought up in Wisconsin, was unconstrained by the tenets of European Modernism. He forged his own path, drawing on the sources and thinking

of his particular locality. The architecture he evolved is often referred to as 'organic'. 'Organic' is a problematic term, and one that has been used by different commentators at different times to encapsulate a mood in architecture as much as a physical presence. Wright himself explained it thus in 1914: 'by organic architecture I mean an architecture from within, outward in harmony, with the conditions of its being as distinguished from one that is applied without'. It also implies passage of time. Louis Sullivan, Wright's employer and mentor, said: 'Organism is not. In organism it is becoming'. Wright adopted the term 'organic' and made it his own, imbued with a distinctive meaning. As an inveterate writer, speaker and proselytizer, he attempted on many occasions to explain what he meant by it.

An organic approach to architecture, therefore, suggests the idea of an intuitive and poetic response to nature, augmented by the passage of time. Gothic cathedral architecture can be seen as organic in form and expression – in part because of its relatively free compositional possibilities as opposed to the symmetrical rules of Classicism, but more importantly because these cathedrals took many decades to build and, in most cases, were the outcome of many minds. Traditionally, architecture that appears most organic is that which has evolved, changed, grown or shrunk through time. A building, down the years, does not only change its shape, form and internal arrangements, it somehow seems to become settled into the landscape. This integration into a setting can be both the result of

familiarity – a building becomes, in the subconscious, a feature in the recognition or the recollection of a particular place – and of physical absorption: materials submit to weathering, vegetation grows up, neighbouring buildings are introduced and accommodated, and borders are redefined.

In recent decades the pace of change and adaptation has grown exponentially. Unless frozen in time as a result of finding itself in what is deemed to be a setting of 'heritage' value, or a victim of its own architectural success, condemned to 'listed' stasis, a building is more likely to be demolished and replaced before its time than it is to grow old and die a natural death. This tendency has prompted a certain kind of organic response in architecture, one which anticipates and accommodates further change and which is capable of evolving and adapting without undermining original precepts. A particular example of this approach are modern bioclimatic office buildings, several of which feature later in this book. In Wright, however, the tendency for buildings to have a limited life span prompted quite another response.

Wright's architecture is not obviously Modernist. It is not white, cubic or transparent; there are no pilotis, no steel structural frames and no underpinning social manifesto. Superficially, it is more akin to the British Arts and Crafts movement of Voysey, Shaw, Webb and, particularly, Mackintosh. The reason Wright is considered to be a master of the Modernist school and not an imaginative and forceful exponent of

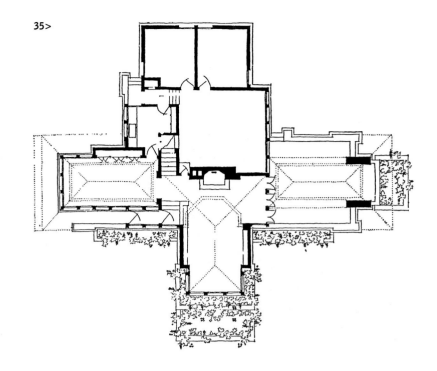

Chapter One / Architecture and the Environment

^
37

35 > Plan for Isabel
Roberts House, River
Forest, Illinois (1908)
by Frank Lloyd Wright.

37 > Falling Water,
Bear Run, Pennsylvania
(1937–9) by Frank
Lloyd Wright.

36 > Taliesin West,
Scottsdale, Arizona
(1938) by Frank Lloyd
Wright.

the Arts and Crafts movement is primarily due to the manner in which he handles space. His house plans are not made up of the hall, the parlour and the billiard room of the 'Cluedo' board as are Arts and Crafts houses. Wright's plans are predicated upon the assumption of a single space which is often articulated and manipulated around a central hearth. On this one attribute his assignment to the Modern Movement seems perverse. There is no doubt he was innovative in the design of buildings, in the manipulation and enhancement of light and in the free-flowing treatment of space. On the other hand he had an aversion to cities and was unhappy when constrained by city grid planning. In the suburb or the countryside the dictates of setting were less severe. The sobriquet 'Prairie Architecture' does not so much allude to the long horizontal lines of his residential architecture as to the sense of openness and space that they need to inhabit.

Pioneer of the Modern Movement or not, Wright certainly sits foursquare within the tradition of architecture deriving stimulus and rationale from nature and setting. As an architect born and raised in the mid-west of the United States, he was not burdened by European culture and history. He inherited the notion of European home, but had the perception and inquisitiveness to look further afield. The early influence of Japanese architecture and, in particular, the traditional Japanese house was seminal in the development of his own architecture. This not only encompassed the sense of spacial fluidity but reverence for materials and veracity in their use. He took up elements arising purely

from their utilitarian use, and discovered in the raw materials employed in meeting this use their hidden expressiveness and secret potentialities. This empathy with 'natural' materials is, of course, a strong characteristic of contemporary sustainable design.

Wright's native landscape and archaeology was a major source of inspiration. From pre-Columbian sites he derived a sense of integration with nature, of a building growing from the earth – not separated, hovering over it on pilotis – and a sense of man's innate harmony with nature and the seasons. Falling Water (1937–9), the weekend house he designed for the Pittsburgh millionaire Edgar J. Kaufmann, is often held up as the epitome of Wright's drive towards the integration of built form and natural setting. Hovering over the cascades of a Pennsylvania stream, Falling Water pits smooth horizontal and interlocking planes against the rugged terrain. The building's impact derives from the contrast between the man-made and the natural, not the symbiotic melding of the two. The wooded and boulder-strewn setting acts as a foil for the daring cantilevered composition in reinforced concrete hovering above them. In this respect it is true to the spirit of European Modernism where new technological capabilities and clean lines are set in juxtaposition to nature.

At Taliesin West, Wright's own house and studio in the Arizona desert, a very different spirit prevails. The building crouches within a hostile landscape strewn with stones and punctured with cactus; its form is subservient to the wide desert panorama. It appears to

grow naturally from the ground, its boulder walls petering out into the randomness of the landscape while its oversized, upstanding timber beams appear stark as a sand-scoured skeleton, bleached and baked by the desert sun.

It is significant that when one describes Wright's buildings, without noticing it, they become animate; they 'inhabit' space, they 'hug' the landscape, they 'solicit' attention and 'seduce' one's senses. This feeling for the anthropomorphic was an in spiration to his immediate followers and is a line that flows directly to today's bioclimatic architecture.

Richard Buckminster Fuller

The fourth pioneer of Modernism whose work, at least in hindsight, similarly influences bioclimatic architecture, is Richard Buckminster Fuller (1895–1983). Something of a maverick, Fuller was a latter-day Renaissance man of vision and genius whose significance has only gradually been understood outside the academic fraternity. He has not traditionally been regarded either as a leading light of the Modern Movement, or as an important contributor to the development of sustainability in architecture. His work covered design, art, science and the humanities, a pluralist vision which allowed him to make the interdisciplinary connections that those working in a single field could not. The cross-fertilization between these specialisms resulted in a series of mould-breaking projects, including the Dymaxion House, Car, Bathroom and World

29

38 > Geodesic Dome, 'Climatron' Botanical Garden, St Louis, Missouri (1960) by Richard Buckminster Fuller.

Map, and the Geodesic Dome, and in a succession of inspirational pronouncements and theories.

Most notably he drew our attention to the minuteness of Earth in its cosmological setting and stressed the interdependency of global systems and society. His One Town World Plan anticipated Marshall McLuhan's 'Global Village' by more than 35 years. He had the vision to see that with international conglomerates accumulating wealth and power far exceeding those of most countries, with the growing speed of travel and with the coming of worldwide instantaneous communication, the planet Earth would no longer be encompassed by elaborately prepared expeditions, regions would no longer develop in relative isolation along a path of their own choosing, and communities would no longer be confined to arts, culture and education of their own singular creation.

Fuller's first book, *Nine Chains to the Moon* (the idea being that if the peoples of the world all stood one on top of another the height of the human 'chain' would be equivalent to nine times the distance of the moon from Earth), published in 1938, expounds upon aspects of interdependency, diversity and harmony. His method, via a series of elliptical essays and discourses, is to examine the particular and draw out the universal. The local, regional and unique only held his interest insofar as it informed the development of a strategic view. He was not, therefore, a man of nature as, say, Thoreau was. He advocated a technology-led response to issues of

∧
38

population growth, urban regeneration and domestic convenience. While he never quite pinpointed the impending ecological crisis, it is clear that he would have looked to technology to mitigate or avoid it. He can be seen as the first world citizen. It is this overview of a more efficient and equitable use and distribution of resources that developed into the ideas of global sustainability and consciousness of the world as a finely balanced eco-organism.

Fuller's aim to 'accomplish prototyped capabilities of doing more with less' calls to mind Mies van der Rohe's dictum 'Less is more'. Whereas Mies refers essentially to

an aesthetic approach, however, Fuller saw this reductionism strictly in scientific and engineering terms. His inventions and constructions were all based on an engineering approach which, through geometry, calculation and the imaginative use of materials, pared down to an absolute minimum the resource required to manufacture, assemble and operate them.

Perhaps Fuller's most innovative work was the development of a structural system known as 'tensegrity'; structures, whereby compressive and tensile forces are accommodated in a geometrical arrangement of struts and strings, enabling superimposed loads to be taken on what appears to be ephemeral and insufficient support. His most enduring invention is clearly the Geodesic Dome, in which a similar geometrical balance is achieved but with standardized struts and connectors which accommodate both tensile and compressive forces, depending on how the structure is loaded at any particular time.

As Fuller foresaw, the construction industry, with its tradition of low investment and labour-intensive, trade-segregated, constructionally imprecise practice, was not in a position to adopt the highly engineered, interactive approach that he advocated. It was in other spheres – the boat-building, aeronautic and aerospace industries – where performance was more demanding and refined, that the do-more-with-less approach was embraced and developed.

Despite the difficulties of introducing his ideas into conventional construction, Fuller's influence was felt and nurtured by the architectural and structural engineering professions more than any others. It inspired exponents such as Jean Prouvé (1901–84) and Frei Otto (b. 1925) and their innovative work in, respectively, lightweight prefabricated and membrane structures. He is also revered by high-tech adherents such as Sir Norman Foster and Jan Kaplicky who find in his work a justification for their technology-led response to environmental depredation and social dysfunction. Architects of the Modern Movement, then, were not exclusively preoccupied with social engineering, industrialization and the distillation of techno-aesthetic credos.

As this overview of the ideologies espoused by four key masters shows, the architectural response to environment and setting that had manifested itself in various forms in preceding epochs was not sidelined; indeed one might argue that this period saw not merely a continuity but an intensifying of the dialogue between man, built form and nature.

Looking again at the work of just four pioneers, we can see the roots of all the issues which have now become so critical in the current environmental movement in architecture, albeit in a very different context and not manifest in all-encompassing doctrine. In Le Corbusier's work we can sense a primordial and symbiotic interaction with nature, starting with the dispassionate and surreal and concluding with the profound and the mythic; in that of Alvar Aalto we see a clinical and doctrinaire architectural language gradually transformed by a subtle and elegiac expression of regional sensibilities; in Frank Lloyd Wright, respect for materials, place and a reciprocity with the primitive and vernacular is there from the start; and in Buckminster Fuller we find insight into the global predicament and the advocacy of appropriate and efficient technology and resources. A look at the 44 recent projects illustrated in Chapter Four clearly shows the influence of these aspects of their work on today's bioclimatic architecture.

Although the work discussed here was much admired and deliberated upon at the time, the architecture that evolved following the Second World War in a (Western) world of renewed trade and buoyant economies was one that was inherently incapable of embracing the poetic and intuitive, the ethereal and the mythic. Instead, new construction adopted the attributes of Modernism it could most expediently respond to, ones that would reflect accelerating urbanization and commercial exigencies. Materials were employed to enhance corporate prestige rather than be expressive or 'truthful'. These buildings are characterized by their use of grid planning, new structural techniques, industrialized components and a stripped-down, enigmatic aesthetic. It was the architecture of the displaced 'purists' of the Modern Movement – Walter Gropius, Mies van der Rohe and Marcel Breuer – not those endowed with more regional and elemental sensibilities, whose work was most appropriated in order to create a Modernist vernacular. This debased brand of Modernism had scant regard for place, economy of means, sensitivity to setting and symbolic relationships between built form and nature. It was exported around the world and, even now, is constructed as totemic evidence of civilized urbanism by arriviste cities and states. It has taken a series of energy crises, and the incontrovertible confirmation that humankind is indeed affecting the climate on Earth to the detriment of its people and its ecology, to finally question this offspring of a movement that was founded in social concern and creative interaction with nature.

Principles of
Bioclimatic Architecture

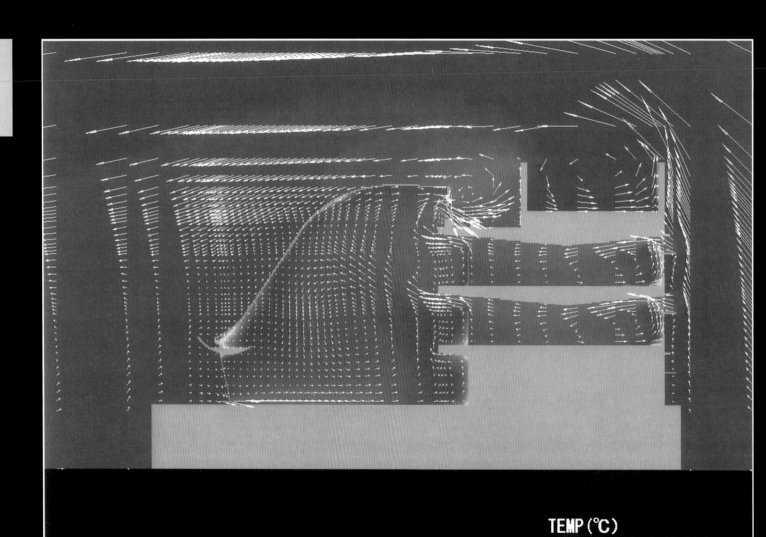

01> Predicting temperatures and air flow. Computational fluid dynamic (CFD) plot through the Tokyo Gas 'Earth Port' (see page 67).

02> Nefertiti adoring the sun. Limestone stele from Tell el Amarna, New Kingdom, 18th Dynasty Egypt.

The sun's beneficence is most pervasive and obvious as a provider of warmth and light. There is little that is more sensuous and relaxing than feeling its warmth on your back as you read, write or paint; and it is the light falling on the book, writing pad or canvas that allows you to do so. More than this, however, the sun is the source and sustenance of every aspect of life on this planet. The Earth was born of the sun and survives only as long as it survives. The sun is the ultimate power source; a nuclear reactor which is many millions of times that of the largest man-made reactor. Paradoxically, it is relatively small and insignificant compared to other stars in the universe.

The sun is made up of layers of hot gases, predominately helium and hydrogen. At its core its temperature is fourteen million degrees Celsius; at its surface six thousand degrees. Its energy is a product of nuclear fusion whereby nuclei of hydrogen combine to form helium. The process releases a massive amount of energy, in the form of heat and light. It takes about eight minutes for light and heat from the sun to reach the Earth.

About half of the sun's energy and a high proportion of damaging radiation is scattered or absorbed by the Earth's atmosphere. More than 90 per cent of the energy that does reach the Earth is absorbed by the oceans and organisms that live on the Earth's surface; the bulk of the remainder is absorbed by plants through the process of photosynthesis. The amount of solar energy used directly by man, by comparison, is infinitesimal.

Conditions on Earth, over its two thousand, eight hundred million years of existence, have followed a pattern of continuous evolution. The commingling of matter and gas led to a primordial 'soup' which in turn created an environment which allowed micro-organisms to flourish. The micro-organisms prompted further change which fostered more complex forms of life; these, over time, led to the conditions we currently enjoy.

Solar radiation falling on Earth is responsible for the major elemental forces manifest on its surface. Sea and land take up and release heat at different rates and, due to the planet's spherical shape and the fact that it rotates, different parts reach different temperatures at different times. These erratic temperature differentials are transferred to the atmosphere that encases the Earth, causing complex patterns of air movement which we know as wind. Precipitation is caused by the confrontation and interplay between air masses of contrasting temperatures.

Plants, algae and some bacteria are all sustained by the sun. Through photosynthesis, they convert solar energy into stored chemical energy. Plants are part of a sustainable cycle as most have a positive carbon dioxide balance – meaning that they take up more carbon dioxide than they release when they decompose. Coal, oil and natural gas absorbed their carbon dioxide millions of years ago, but, through extraction and combustion, are releasing it now. This creates an imbalance in the carbon cycle – the accumulation of carbon in the biosphere.

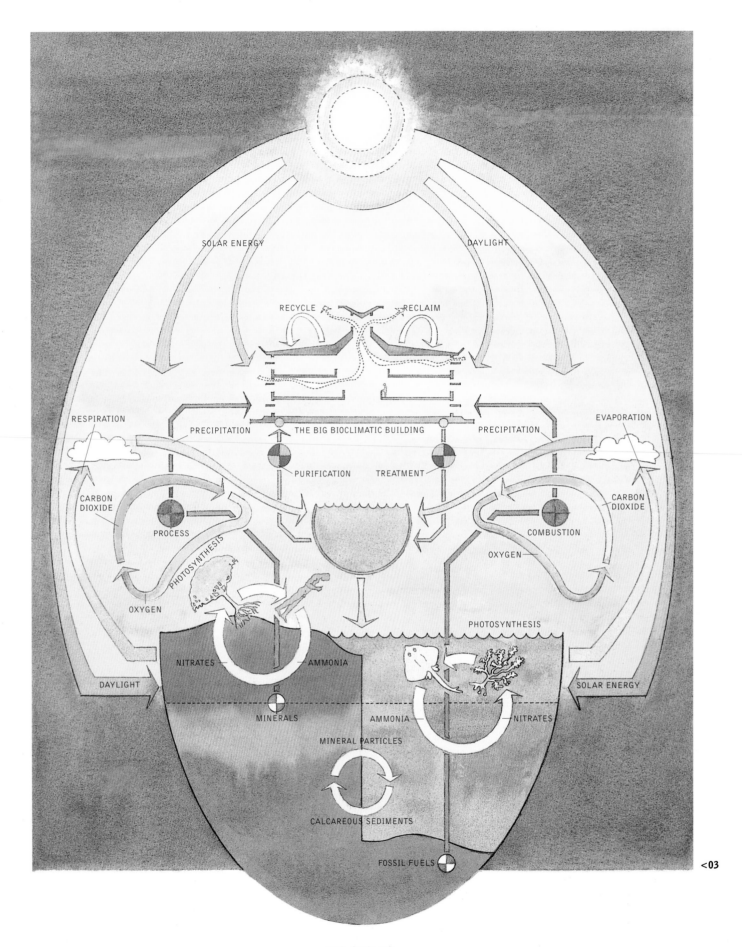

SOLAR ENERGY

DAYLIGHT

RECYCLE RECLAIM

RESPIRATION

PRECIPITATION THE BIG BIOCLIMATIC BUILDING PRECIPITATION

EVAPORATION

PURIFICATION TREATMENT

CARBON
DIOXIDE

CARBON
DIOXIDE

PROCESS

COMBUSTION

PHOTOSYNTHESIS

OXYGEN

OXYGEN

PHOTOSYNTHESIS

DAYLIGHT

NITRATES AMMONIA

AMMONIA NITRATES

SOLAR ENERGY

MINERALS

MINERAL PARTICLES

CALCAREOUS SEDIMENTS

FOSSIL FUELS

<03

BIO-CYCLES

03>Bio-cycles. The Earth is governed by interrelated 'bio-cycles' which at any one time should be broadly in balance, but over periods of time do evolve and change. The bioclimatic building recognizes these cycles and is designed to support rather than undermine them over the course of its life.

Our ecosystem is composed of three nutritional groups: producers, such as plants; consumers, mainly animals; and decomposers, bacteria and fungi. By a process of synthesis, producers provide organic materials which are fed on by the consumers. The decomposers release and convert materials from the dead bodies, faeces and other waste matter of the producers and consumers, thereby ensuring a continuous supply of raw materials for the producers. The biosphere is composed of many bio-cycles which at any one time are (or should be) broadly in balance, but over long periods of time do evolve and change. Population growth, the intensity of human activities, and the pace of change that these activities are now enforcing on natural biorhythms, are the causes of the depredation that we now face.

The sun's shortcomings, so far as our convenience and comfort are concerned, are its discontinuity and inconsistency. It goes out at night and, with irritating unpredictability, when there is cloud cover. In most parts of the world, for long periods, it is either too hot or too cold. With the help of suitable clothing humans can tolerate a considerable range of temperature, but we are most productive within a fairly small band. It is this discontinuity and inconsistency which has led to increasingly sophisticated substitutes and mediators in the form of artificial heating, lighting and cooling. In order to fuel this demand for extensive and exacting comfort (and to provide transport and answer the needs of industry) we are extracting and exhausting – within a minute span of cosmic time – the finite fuel resources that have been stored in the Earth's crust for millions of years. We use these resources to generate power in a highly profligate and destructive manner to provide for our comfort; to process, refine and transform non-replaceable natural materials into complex components, assemblies and appliances; and to transport goods, food and ourselves around the globe in gas-guzzling conveyances.

Human activities have now started to turn the benign effects of the sun into those of debilitation and destruction. We are frightened even to sit in the sun's rays for fear of melanomas, and within a decade or so, unless there is a radical change in our approach to the use of energy, global warming and rising sea levels look set to cause disaster on an unprecedented scale.

It is clear that this degree of dependence on fossil fuels is a glitch, albeit a destructive one, in the overall development of human energy-use. Until the industrial revolution, people's needs were met entirely by solar-derived energy, whether it was by combustion of biomass (organic matter such as timber, straw and animal waste), by wind power, or by hydropower. Although the fossil fuel era might extend further than many predict, due to new discoveries and greater energy efficiency, in time, all of the profitable areas of extraction will be used up. As these sources diminish, and before we learn how to harvest solar energy in space and beam it to Earth (or create a form of nuclear fission or fusion that is safe, economical and socially acceptable), terrestrial use of solar power is bound to be reintroduced extensively and with greater efficiency and sophistication. Early signs of this are already apparent.

This brings us to the notion of bioclimatic architecture – that is buildings which are inspired by nature, which have a clear strategy for minimizing environmental depredation and which encourage a sense of well-being. The issues that must be addressed in the design of contemporary bioclimatic buildings and settings are essentially threefold: energy; health and well-being; and sustainability. Each of these issues will be looked at in turn.

Uses and Forms of Energy

There are two aspects to the issue of energy in building design: how it can be used efficiently, and what form it should take. Energy conservation is as much about choosing the appropriate form of energy at the appropriate time, as it is about saving that energy. In modern buildings, energy usually takes the form of electricity, conventionally supplied by the national grid and generated by fossil fuel combustion, hydro turbines or nuclear fission, or gas supplied directly from natural reserves or as a product of fossil fuel combustion. With the exception of nuclear and hydro power, all of these sources are dependent on the extraction of fossil fuel – with the conversion process releasing excessive quantities of carbon and sulphur dioxide into the atmosphere.

Solar energy, even in its converted form, is largely non-polluting; it is also available in unlimited quantity – it is therefore a renewable resource. Solar radiation can either be used

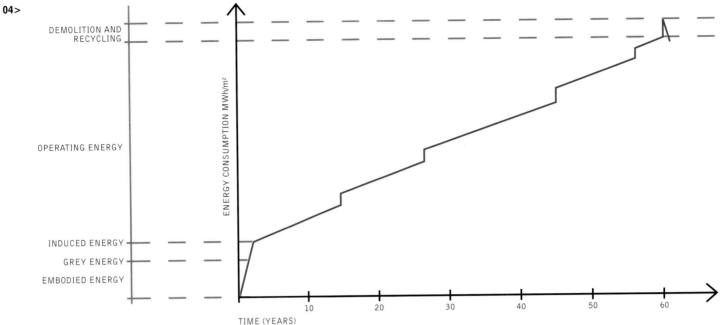

DEMOLITION AND
RECYCLING

OPERATING ENERGY

ENERGY CONSUMPTION MWh/m²

INDUCED ENERGY

GREY ENERGY

EMBODIED ENERGY

TIME (YEARS)

10   20   30   40   50   60

directly to create warmth in a building, or gathered in the form of heat, via thermal collectors, and in the form of electricity, via cells (photovoltaic modules). Solar radiation – in its naturally converted forms of biomass, wind, and water energy – is harnessed via human and technical intervention using processes such as combustion plants, turbines and heat pumps.

As regards the construction and occupation of buildings, parameters relating to the use of energy will vary according to location and political and economic factors. In Switzerland, a country largely powered by hydro-electric plant, and with a modest local manufacturing base, day-to-day energy efficiency may not be as important as the careful selection of materials and components, and the extent to which imported goods use energy in their manufacture and transportation. By contrast, in Japan, where power largely derives from imported fossil fuels, energy use at every stage needs to be minimized and alternative renewable sources introduced at all levels.

A building consumes energy in a number of ways: in the manufacture of building materials, components and systems ('embodied' energy); in the distribution and transportation of building materials and components to the construction site ('grey' energy); in the construction of the building ('induced' energy); and in running the building and its occupants' equipment and appliances ('operating' energy). A building also consumes energy in its maintenance, alteration and final disposal. An energy-efficient building looks to reduce consumption in all of these areas.

Since energy efficiency in the processing and manufacturing of materials reduces production costs, it would logically follow that this would support the commercial interests of the manufacturer. In practice, however, the equation is not quite so simple. While there has been considerable progress in introducing energy-saving measures to the factory floor, a number of other factors have slowed and sometimes reversed this movement. The capital needed to invest in new energy-efficient plant and procedures is often not readily available; measures to reduce waste and pollution, which have greater legislative bite than regulations encouraging the control of energy use, sometimes in themselves require greater energy consumption; there are often special discounted rates and tariffs for energy use in industry which give the impression that the company has 'struck a good deal'; and in some branches of the building supply industries, such as glass production, composites and curtain walling, the energy-demanding but alluring image of a highly honed, sophisticated and machine-produced product is an intrinsic part of the promotional package. Other considerations such as the ease and efficacy of eventually recycling the material and the amount of the material actually used in a building has to be taken into account. The overall trend in industry is towards higher efficiency but also towards more processing, and often to high transport energy pre- and post-manufacture.

The architect must weigh up a number of issues when considering measures to minimize this type of embodied energy use. First call must be to select materials that, in their

manufacture, use little energy. These are either materials that can be used close to their raw state, such as stone, timber and compacted earth; or recycled manufactured materials such as crushed brick and concrete, hardcore and reused steel joists, or waste materials from other processes. The latter might include pulverized fuel ash from power stations for blinding, and silicon wafers from the microchip industry for photovoltaic cells. With the exception of silicon, these materials imply fairly rudimentary construction and a reliance on traditional technology, rather than precision-designed, sophisticated techniques.

Thus we arrive again at the issue of design strategy, followed closely by that of style. The philosophical debate lying at the core of the Green movement in architecture is predicated on these issues: whether to design reductively and sparingly, down to a sustainable salvation, or whether to design ourselves inventively and sophisticatedly out of our predicament. This polarization is described in more detail in Chapter One. It is also demonstrated very clearly in recent buildings which lay claim to energy efficiency and environmental sensitivity. Those illustrated in Chapter Four show both extremes, but perhaps the most successful are those that find a careful and appropriate balance between the two.

Grey energy – that which is expended in transporting materials and components from places of extraction and manufacture to the construction site – can be minimized by support of local industries and the use of local materials. Where there are no suitable local resources available, careful account

04>Energy consumed in the life of a building.
The graph shows how energy is consumed over the
60-year life of a building. The flatter the incline,
the more energy-efficient the building.

needs to be taken of delivery distances and the
mode of transport employed. This is usually
a relatively straightforward assessment.

Induced energy, the energy used in the
construction itself, is normally modest in
comparison to embodied and grey energy,
and for this reason is not usually given much
attention. It is, however, an important aspect
of the overall management and running of
the site, as are efficient operation and health
and safety measures. The architect should
ensure, at tender stage, that the builder has
a comprehensive energy policy for site
operations, including waste avoidance
(currently 5 to 10 per cent of building
materials are thrown away unused), economic
use of water and eco-friendly disposal of
demolished materials, and that this policy
is acted upon during construction.

This is an area where legislation is making
some impact. In certain countries there are
noise and pollution constraints relating to
demolition – the level of noise is limited and
the period over which noise is permitted is
defined, and on-site burning of combustible
materials is prohibited. There are also
regulations relating to the disposal of
hazardous materials, such as asbestos, and
more recently, levies have been introduced on
spoil which is removed from construction sites.

In the end, the selection of materials and
systems for any one building project should
be the result of a balanced analysis of the
required performance of the building against
an assessment of embodied energy in the
manufacture and processing of materials and

components (in many cases useful information
on this subject is limited); an assessment
of grey energy consumption, covering
identification of the original source of the
materials and the energy costs involved in
transporting the materials and components to
the site; and what can be done in the field of
limiting, recycling and using waste materials.

Operating energy is the form of energy
that has been given most consideration by
researchers, designers and legislators. This
is the energy used in actually running a
building; this kind of consumption will
continue as long as the building stands and
is occupied – which could be for hundreds of
years. (Operating energy has also been a
focus because it is relatively easy to expand
existing construction codes of practice to
incorporate issues of energy restraint and
environmental conservation.)

Since energy use in buildings is closely tied
to the climatic conditions in which they are
located, the measures taken to minimize it will
vary from region to region. (See the Appendix,
page 244, for a summary of these measures.)
The basic requirements, however, are fairly
uniform. Most buildings will require seasonal
heating or cooling; and most will need good
light levels for the activities taking place
within them to be conducted satisfactorily.

A key aspect in designing a bioclimatic
building is determining its 'comfort criteria'.
This is not as straightforward as it seems.
Perception of comfort varies considerably
from individual to individual and between
ethnic groups who become more habituated

to local climatic conditions. It will also vary
according to the activities taking place in the
building – whether these are largely sedentary
or active – and according to the psychological
frame of mind of the occupants. In some cases,
such as museums or laboratories, the contents
of the building or the processes taking place
there will be more sensitive to environmental
conditions than the occupants, and the criteria
will have to be set accordingly.

The most effective way of conserving energy
is to design the building to exploit natural
forces – sunlight, wind and daylight – to best
effect. Harnessing the beneficial attributes of
the climate, without recourse to mechanical
systems, is known as 'passive solar design'.

Any building acts as an intermediary between
conditions on the outside which are often
widely changing, and the requirement for a
relatively stable interior environment. In order
to succeed, a bioclimatic design needs to bring
a number of factors into play. A building needs
to be carefully balanced to reduce excessive
solar heat when the weather is hot, whilst fully
utilizing solar radiation when the weather is
cold. It should also allow abundant daylight
to enter the building but guard against glare,
excessive solar gain and excessive heat loss.
Architects need to ensure that plenty of
natural ventilation is provided when the
weather is hot or humid, and that the building
can also be sealed but adequately ventilated
when it is being heated artificially. Finally,
the fabric of the building should be used to
absorb and release heat on a daily cycle
(when there is sufficient difference between
day- and night-time temperatures to do so),

05+05A>How energy
is used in office buildings.
A successful low-energy
office building will consume
between 70 and 80 kW/h/m2
in a temperate climate. The
histograms compare energy
consumption in different
types of UK offices with the
cost of that energy. (Data
provided by BRECSU.)

05>

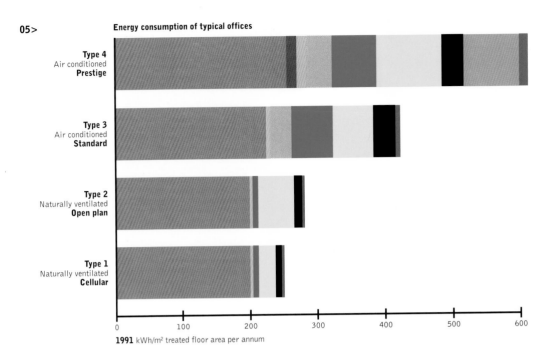

Energy consumption of typical offices

Type 4
Air conditioned
Prestige

Type 3
Air conditioned
Standard

Type 2
Naturally ventilated
Open plan

Type 1
Naturally ventilated
Cellular

0   100   200   300   400   500   600

1991 kWh/m² treated floor area per annum

whilst being sufficiently insulated to provide thermal stability.

The measures available to architects are those that have always been available, but that have largely been overlooked in architecture during the last century. They have to do with optimizing orientation; finding a balance between sun shading and sun trapping; installing windows that open (and open to greatest effect) but when closed are tightly closed; insulating well; and ensuring leak-free construction. They also involve understanding the thermal performance of materials, planning the interior to mitigate extreme thermal fluctuation, and landscaping to create complementary external conditions.

Only relatively modest buildings are able to rely solely on passive heating and ventilation measures. With buildings of intensive use, high occupancies, located in polluted settings or accommodating complex activities or processes, supplementary artificial ('active') measures are needed. The extent to which these have to be resorted to will depend on the degree to which the building environment will be 'stressed' by its location, use and occupancy. A building that combines the exploitation of natural forces with carefully conceived and orchestrated use of artificial measures to produce energy efficiency is known as a 'mixed-mode' building. All buildings require artificial lighting and most larger buildings will require a certain amount during the daytime. In non-domestic buildings without air conditioning the highest energy cost is usually that of lighting. A building that uses daylight effectively, whose layout and

specification of light fittings is efficient, and which incorporates simple, robust and easily understood controls, has therefore taken a significant step towards energy efficiency.

Many large buildings will need to augment the effects of natural ventilation and evaporation with artificial cooling. In its simplest form this can mean placing fans strategically throughout the building to ensure that there is sufficient ventilation and air movement on still, hot days. Natural or fan-assisted buoyancy, however, can only circulate air in a building at (or close to) the temperature of the air entering it; the sense of cooling is achieved by the evaporative effect of the air passing over the occupants. To significantly lower temperature in a building, the air needs to be passed across a colder surface. Once internal air has become colder than external, it becomes very precious, since considerable energy and cost will have been used to transform it to this state. It must not be allowed to leak away prior to carrying out its function of keeping temperatures to a comfortable level. Where buildings are artificially cooled, therefore, they have to be sealed – and a sealed environment makes temperature, humidity and air quality entirely dependent on mechanical systems the performance of which will, in turn, depend on maintenance, control and management. A weakness in any of these areas will provoke frustration amongst the occupants, a decline in performance and, ultimately, ill health.

Artificial cooling, while it is to be avoided where possible, is not in itself antithetical to energy-efficient, environmentally sound design.

It is the means by which it is provided and the extent to which it is employed that is important. Environmentally sensitive methods for introducing auxiliary cooling include fabric heat storage combined with night cooling; air cycle refrigeration; a reliance purely on mechanically circulating ambient air; and the use of natural cool stores such as aquifers, lakes and the sea.

When we think of energy consumption in a building, at least in temperate climates, we usually think of how it is heated. In the days of the open hearth, a fire was more of a ventilator than a heat source since most of the hot air disappeared up the chimney and in so doing drew in cold air from outside. Radiated heat was fierce close to the fire; further away the spaces were uncomfortably draughty. With the advent of 'central' heating, all spaces could be heated to similar and comfortable levels. Day-to-day use, in winter, was extended to all parts of the building. The concept of heat conservation, however, was relatively slow in following developments in heat distribution.

A building that is well insulated, and constructed to minimize leakage through its fabric, can be heated extremely economically. The main demand on the heating system will be when the building has to be heated from cold – for instance after the weekend in the case of a commercial building. The rest of the time the boilers will just be 'topping up' as heat gradually dissipates.

Like cooling in summer, heating in winter implies a sealed building, with double seals

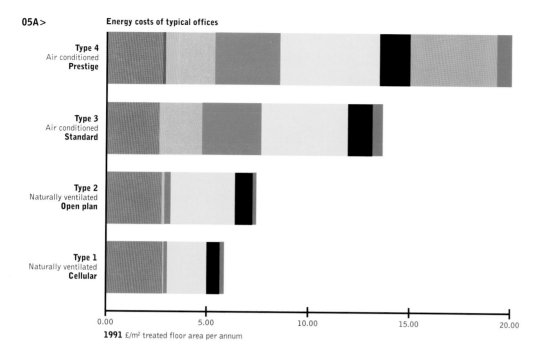

05A>

Energy costs of typical offices

Type 4
Air conditioned
Prestige

Type 3
Air conditioned
Standard

Type 2
Naturally ventilated
Open plan

Type 1
Naturally ventilated
Cellular

0.00　　5.00　　10.00　　15.00　　20.00

1991 £/m² treated floor area per annum

Key

■ Heating + HWS

■ Catering gas

▨ Catering electricity

▨ Refrigeration

■ Fans, pumps, ctrls

□ Lights

■ Office equipment

▨ Computer room

■ Other

around the window openings, draught lobbies and a construction that is leak-free. In such highly insulated buildings, some form of outside air ventilation will need to be introduced, ideally in a position where it passes over a heat source before circulating within the building. The test for the architect lies in providing fresh air in such a way that it is called on only when the internal air becomes stuffy or contaminated, and in quantities which do not make undue demands on the heating system.

Having reviewed the different forms of energy use and some specific ways of minimizing these, the building as a whole – how it can be conceived, designed and managed to ensure maximum energy efficiency – needs to be considered. Renewable sources of energy (ie the sun) can then be looked at. The adjective 'passive', as in the appellation 'passive solar design', is somewhat misleading. It is intended to describe an approach to the design of buildings whereby the innate attributes of climate are harnessed to secure comfort by means of a static disposition of architectural elements. A building only becomes active when it relies on electro-mechanical means to achieve the same, or similar, results.

The casual observer, however, might be forgiven for concluding that the 'passive solar' building was decidedly more active than the 'active' one. The latter conventionally comprises an intransmutable building shell containing an installation (albeit of moving parts) providing pre-programmed comfort. Usually the only active aspect of this type of building is the building manager's increasingly

desperate attempts to pacify its over-heated, under-heated, light-deprived or glare-dazzled occupants.

The 'passive solar' or bioclimatic building is not an inert assembly of materials and components; it has to have, or at least has to mimic, the attributes of an organism. Unlike a building that relies entirely on the skills of electrical and mechanical engineers for its viability, the very fabric of the bioclimatic building must be capable of constant adjustment. Dependent as the building is on utilizing climate, it must also accommodate the climate's capriciousness. Like all buildings, too, it must meet the fluctuating demands of its occupants and, to a greater or lesser extent, the needs of the future. But, unlike electro-mechanically dependent buildings, it must do all this without the support of sophisticated 'artificial' installations. It has to respond both cyclically and intermittently. It must cope with momentary, daily and seasonal changes in temperature, sunshine, daylight and air velocity; it has to respond to sparse occupation on some occasions and over-occupation on others; and it must assimilate both occasional changes in internal partitioning and servicing, and more frequent re-locations, replacements and additions of heat-producing equipment. Whereas satisfactory performance of the sealed and air-treated building relies on constant adjustment to the output of its systems and installations, the bioclimatic building relies on constant adjustment of the building envelope. The mixed-mode building is subject to both. In essence, adjustment of the

envelope means that around one-quarter of a building's wall surface must be capable of opening and closing, one-third be capable of introducing uninterrupted daylight, and a similar area must allow sunshine to enter at certain times but screen it at others – and screen it by degrees. What is more, the envelope has to be designed to do all this without interfering unduly with views to the outside.

The shift in emphasis from adjustment to plant output to adjustment of the building envelope has provided a stimulus to architectural expression of the façade and roof – elements previously confounded, respectively, by the blandness of the curtain wall and the necessity of accommodating on the roof the accumulation of plant that occasioned the blandness of the wall treatment in the first place. This shift has also acted as a fillip (not altogether recognized) to manufacturers of the components that comprise the building envelope – in particular glass, glazing and fenestration – to develop innovatory products that meet the challenge of variable adjustment and multi-function. Glass manufacturers have made considerable steps towards development of products which do not only allow visibility but also thermal insulation, solar control and spontaneous adjustment between different modes of performance. And there are signs that window manufacturers, instead of merely producing products for viewing and ventilation, are developing compatible systems of components that can be combined to suit particular circumstances. These include components for enhancing daylight, for glare and solar control, and for ensuring an

39

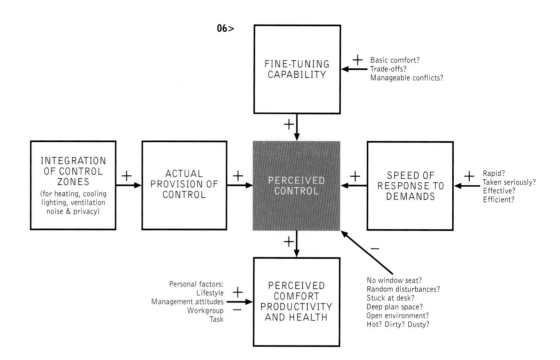

FINE-TUNING
CAPABILITY

+ Basic comfort?
Trade-offs?
Manageable conflicts?

INTEGRATION
OF CONTROL
ZONES
(for heating, cooling
lighting, ventilation
noise & privacy)

+ ACTUAL
PROVISION OF
CONTROL

+ PERCEIVED
CONTROL

SPEED OF
RESPONSE TO
DEMANDS

+ Rapid?
Taken seriously?
Effective?
Efficient?

Personal factors:
Lifestyle
Management attitudes
Workgroup
Task

+ PERCEIVED
COMFORT
PRODUCTIVITY
AND HEALTH

No window seat?
Random disturbances?
Stuck at desk?
Deep plan space?
Open environment?
Hot? Dirty? Dusty?

effective construction interface between window and opening – allowing them to be assembled and installed in accordance with façade orientation, façade construction, building use and project budget.

Some look forward to the day when adjustments in building fabric and services systems, in response to changing meteorological conditions and modes of operation, will be activated by the onset of change of climate itself or even in anticipation of it. When this happens, the 'intelligent' building will have truly arrived. This scenario does not necessarily wrest control in an adverse manner from the occupiers or, indeed, the building manager; it could, it is argued, bring to buildings a sophisticated level of control similar to that currently enjoyed by executives in their motor cars. Here, controls that are key to the overall performance of the car are conceived to be fully automated, out of sight, and subject to specialist maintenance on a periodic basis; while those that immediately affect the driver's individual comfort and well being – air conditioning, sound systems, sun roof, seat and steering wheel configuration, each with their bewildering array of functions – can be controlled, fine tuned and pre-programmed at will.

While many such developments, in the form of autonomous products or systems, may find their way into the second millennium building, the analogy between building and car cannot be sustained. Not only is the financial structure of the automobile industry

different from that of the construction industry, but cycles of obsolescence and replacement are also widely dissimilar. Whereas cars wear out, go out of fashion, and are traded and dumped, most buildings adapt, grow, are re-skinned, refurbished and, in essence, endure. The car is a consumer product while a home is home. In fact there is much evidence that occupants look for greater individual control over the performance of their building rather than less and that controls should be robust and forgiving rather than remotely located and unnecessarily precise.

As the shift from building management control centred on the plant room to the control of components distributed around the perimeter of the building has gathered momentum, designers and clients are presented with a choice: automated central control, or local operation by the occupants. Many of the most successful bioclimatic buildings are based on a control strategy that effectively combines the two.

It has been clear for some time that the conventional sealed, air-conditioned building breeds considerable frustration amongst those who live or work there. Occupants of this type of building are often positioned at some distance from a view of the outside world. If it is an office building, they may be largely sedentary and their work often repetitive or undemanding. They also have little or no control over the comfort of the space they occupy. The combination of sensory deprivation, unremitting routine and lack of influence in determining individual

environment ensures that a relatively small deviation from optimum comfort conditions will not go unremarked. Bill Bordass, Adrian Leaman and Steve Willis, pioneers in analysis of energy use and occupant behaviour, have pointed out that modern control and energy-management systems have the potential to improve individual comfort and reduce energy consumption at the same time ('Control Strategies for Building Services: the Role of the User', conference paper, 1994). Evidence now indicates that fully automated control is not the complete answer, however. Advanced control systems do not always stop building services running wastefully and unnecessarily; sometimes they become barriers, not aids, to effective building management.

Textbooks and guides imply that building service controls only need to be designed, installed and commissioned to prescribed performance levels to do the job properly, but the way in which buildings are run and operated needs to be seen from a broader, more empirical perspective. Account must be taken of the context in which the controls are used, the interaction between different types of control operating simultaneously, and the fact that occupants will inevitably want to alter the targets the building systems are set to achieve.

At the heart of this issue lies the matter of defining goals for individual comfort and convenience. This is notoriously difficult for an architect to do since people's comfort needs vary one from another, and perception of comfort varies between seasons and with the degree of control that individuals have in

40

^
07

06 > **Occupants' perceived control of internal comfort and its components.** Studies carried out by Bill Bordass of William Bordass Associates and Adrian Leaman of Building User Studies Ltd have assessed the physical and psychological effects on building occupants in relation to their perception of the extent to which they can control their own comfort. The diagram shows the components that contribute to this sense of control.

07 > **Public Library, Pompeu Fabra, Mataró, Barcelona, Spain, by Miguel Brullet i Tenas (1997).** This building incorporates photovoltaic modules on its south façade and its roof. Its goal was to find an optimum balance between the integrated solar energy system, energy savings, good internal comfort, and natural light and aesthetics. The photovoltaic façade and skylights will produce approximately 15MW/hr per annum, more energy than is needed for the library. Thermal needs of the building will be reduced by about 30% as a result of using the heat produced by the photovoltaic modules.

maintaining it. This last factor is particularly significant in the context of the bioclimatic building. Comfort may well be best defined as 'absence of discomfort'. It is curious, therefore, that building design tends to put more explicit emphasis on the elements of control intended to deliver comfort, than those which can speedily alleviate discomfort. Occupants of buildings will normally take action only when significant discomfort is reached, but when the action they do take proves to be unresponsive they swiftly object. Surveys have shown that those occupying buildings which provide them with effective and responsive controls over their comfort will carry out their tasks within significantly wider comfort tolerances than those without control. The reason for this is partly physical – being able to adapt and choose the best conditions by repositioning themselves, putting on and taking off clothing and so on – and partly psychological. The knowledge that you can, at any point in time, make adjustments to the environmental quality of the space you or your group occupy puts you 'in charge', and the unseen, baleful presence of corporate 'big brother' does not become an issue. Each occupant becomes necessary to the satisfactory operation of the building – and if it gets a little hot in summer, well it *is* summer after all.

The designers of successful energy-efficient buildings will have carefully considered control strategies for the operation of the building. They will have given individuals as much control of ventilation, heating, sunshine, daylight, glare and artificial light as is compatible with the overall energy and operational strategies of the building. Central

controls will be operated on a zone-by-zone basis and be focused on a robust strategy for the building as a whole. They will typically ensure that air quality is maintained, that ventilation paths are clear and coordinated in hot weather, that roof lights close at the onset of rain, that ventilation at night (when the building may be largely empty) is properly secured, and that artificial lighting is not used wastefully. The designers will have ensured, as far as possible, that the controls of separate systems do not counteract themselves and that they default to the most energy-efficient mode. They will have designed the system in such a way that the most effective control in a given circumstance is made the easiest (and the least effective, in the same circumstance, the most difficult) and that all control responses have a very clear and evident result.

The building manager here will be somebody who really understands the principles on which the building's operation, comfort procurement and energy strategy are based. This individual will be able to match output of plant closely to the demands of use and ensure that those demands are met to the optimum level; the building manager will also be counsellor, adviser and provider to the building's occupants in matters concerning their physical setting. However well designed the building may be, if it is not run effectively, the result will be disgruntlement.

A review of energy sources is outside the scope of this book. However, where energy is harvested or generated on site by means of the sun, it will have a significant impact on the design of the building and its deployment

on the site. Solar energy, in its broadest definition, comes in two forms: renewable and regenerable. The renewable form comprises the conversion of solar radiation, or the natural effects of solar radiation, by technical processes into electricity. These types of generation include photovoltaic systems, thermal collectors, wind and water power, and tidal energy. The renewable form also, of course, includes the use of solar energy directly and without any intermediary technology (except maybe to enhance it), such as sunlight warming up the fabric of a building.

The mode of generation that is currently causing most interest is photovoltaic systems. This process converts solar radiation directly into electricity. Prior to the development of photovoltaic technology for use in buildings, electric power could only be procured from solar radiation by means of turbines. Although they have enormous potential, however, photovoltaics have a considerable way to go in terms of product development if costs are to be reduced, conversion efficiencies increased and embodied energy minimized.

Regenerable solar energy comprises biomass in the form of regrowable raw materials, such as timber or waste from crops, which are converted to usable energy through combustion – as in the burning of timber for heat – or gasification – as in the decomposition of vegetation for methane. The carbon dioxide produced during combustion can be compensated for by replanting and the consequent photosynthesis process. The balance in energy use will vary

41

according to the regrowth time of the vegetation used to generate the energy. A field of sunflowers will compensate for the use of their oil in providing energy over a year (assuming a yearly harvest) whereas a plantation of trees might take fifty years to compensate for the use of their timber, but give the same result at the end of that time.

The regenerable form of solar energy normally takes place off site and it is, therefore, the renewable forms and the passive use of radiation that architects will need to concern themselves with in designing low-energy buildings.

Health and Well-being

The World Health Organization's definition of good health, given in 1961, as 'a state of complete physical, mental and social well-being' is broader than the generally accepted meaning of 'absence of disease'. Since living and working environments have a major influence on an individual's sense of well-being, this broader concept of health is particularly pertinent to the aims and objectives of building design. The concept of comfort – a primary aim of any building after the provision of shelter and security – is synonymous with 'well-being', and studies of 'sick buildings' have drawn a connection between poor comfort conditions and symptoms of ill-health in the occupants and users.

J. Mitchell, in his 1984 book *What is to be Done about Illness and Health,* sets out seven 'attributes of healthy life': a clean, safe environment; time for rest and recreation; a reasonable living standard; freedom from chronic worry; hope for the future; an additional level of self-confidence and autonomy; and having a worthwhile and fulfilling job.

Clearly the majority of these needs are influenced by society as a whole, but it is not difficult to deduce the role that physical setting and the built environment have to play. Prior to the industrial revolution, building design with regard to encouraging good health was largely based on common sense and traditional practice. The effects on health of bad drainage were easily observed, and the benefits of allowing sunlight and daylight to enter the building, and air to ventilate the rooms, were apparent to all.

In the nineteenth century, epidemics such as typhoid fever, running rife through the squalid, overcrowded neighbourhoods of burgeoning industrial towns, brought home the close link between disease and poor housing, polluted water supply and inadequate sanitation. The concept of public health was thus established, with its concomitant legislation.

The health consequences of today's accelerating technological revolution mirror those of the industrial age. We may be well on our way to eliminating many of the diseases caused by occupational exposure (such as mesothelioma from asbestos and lead poisoning from pipework) and those that can be traced directly to inadequate design, planning or building services (such as intestinal or respiratory problems), but we now face a host of far more insidious disorders. These result from our more complex social interrelationships and from the extensive development of chemically based technologies. Buildings can make a significant contribution to disorders and disease arising from our current situation. These disorders may result from unanticipated and unexplored consequences of aspects of design and specification – as with Legionnaires' disease, first identified in 1976, which is caused by contaminated water from air-conditioning cooling towers being inhaled in the form of a fine spray.

The causes of a disorder may combine with the social and psychological consequences of work practice or other activities taking place in a building. This can be seen in instances of 'sick building syndrome' where poor building design, bad selection of materials and debilitating work practice combine to create a work environment that is detrimental to health. For example, a building may be designed with deep floors, where views out are distant and control of the immediate environment is non-existent; the floor finish and furnishings may emit harmful contaminants; and the work may be repetitive, sedentary and focused on the VDU screen. This type of situation does not encourage good health, nor does it provide a productive and stimulating atmosphere in which to work. On the other hand, the effects of a building's operations may leave the occupants relatively unscathed but contribute to health hazards on a global scale. It is now an established fact that chlorofluorocarbons (CFCs) and other gases caused by chemical reactions in man-

42

made building and consumer products have depleted the protecting ozone layer, which in consequence substantially increases the risk of skin cancer and other illnesses caused by raised levels of radioactivity.

As we have seen, the stimulus for bioclimatic design arose initially from the necessity to conserve fuel and, then, to protect the environment. It is fortuitous that many of the measures advocated for this purpose are measures that one would wish to introduce to make a building a more healthy and stimulating place in which to live, work or enjoy oneself. The energy conservation requirements for controlled sunshine, good daylight, natural ventilation, individual control and materials of low embodied energy are, happily, all those that foster good health and well-being.

The health of the planet and the health of those who live on it – and, in the case of the construction industry, those who manufacture building products, construct buildings, or occupy them – are intrinsically linked. A successful bioclimatic building designer will take due consideration of both but, viewed in the context of our definition of well-being, it may not be enough merely to create a building that is both energy efficient and eschews installations, materials and components that are hazardous to health. The designer also has to find that elusive quality which marries occupant to building, and building to setting; a phenomenon which makes the occupant feel that the building, or a particular part of it, is their 'special' place, a place which provides harmony, order and the sense of unequivocal

rightness. This is well-being bordering on spirituality, but it is an experience to which a building can make a singular contribution. It not only provides for well-being, but for the inner being.

The sense of 'rightness of place' is almost impossible to pin down, but one knows it when one experiences it. The American architect Steven Holl calls the dynamic relationship between site and building 'anchoring'. The site of a building, for Holl, is not simply one aspect of its conception, but its very foundation: 'The resolution of the functional aspects of site and building, the vistas, sun angles, circulation, and access, are the "physics" that demand the "metaphysics" of architecture. Through a link, an extended motive, a building is more than something merely fashioned for the site. Building transcends physical and functional requirements by fusing with a place...' (*Anchoring,* 1989). At Louis Kahn's Salk Institute in La Jolla, California (1959–65), there is a time of day when the sun, reflecting on the ocean, merges with light reflecting on the rivulet of water in the trough bisecting the central court. Ocean and courtyard are fused by the phenomenon of sunlight reflecting on water; architecture and nature are joined in the metaphysics of place.

Towards a Sustainable Future

We have considered energy use in buildings and energy sources in so far as they have an impact on the design of buildings; we have also looked at the effects of buildings on health and well-being, and have placed all

this in the context of a relatively fragile global bio-system. This final section examines building construction from the broader perspective of world-wide industrial and economic development, and looks at how this might continue without bringing about the destruction of the planet.

Governments have been slow to embrace environmental issues and to act effectively to mitigate the most obvious debilitating practices. For many years a vocal minority has been pointing out the dangers of a wide range of activities that hitherto few had questioned. Over time, tacit (but notably little political) support came from the majority of citizens in industrialized countries.

Faced with pressure from voters and hard evidence from scientists during the 1960s and 1970s, politicians finally conceded that action on a broad front needed to be taken. In 1992 an Earth Summit was held in Rio de Janeiro, resulting in promises by the industrialized countries to level off 'greenhouse' emissions by the year 2000. A subsequent meeting was planned to take place in Kyoto, Japan, in 1997, to determine whether pollution levels can actually be reduced. So far, even the 1992 promises have barely been fulfilled. There are many reasons for this delay. Governments of developed countries are bolstered by a web of commercial interests which do not respond kindly to sudden change and the consequent risks to which their investment income and plans are subjected; governments of developing countries recognize that environmental legislation will introduce significant additional costs to their emerging industries, and do not

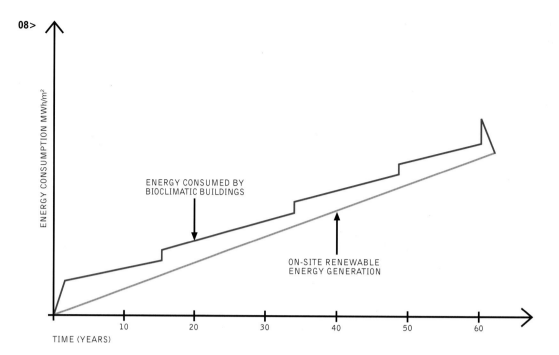

08

ENERGY CONSUMPTION MWh/m²

ENERGY CONSUMED BY
BIOCLIMATIC BUILDINGS

ON-SITE RENEWABLE
ENERGY GENERATION

TIME (YEARS)

concede that they should submit to constraints while Western countries have had many years of unfettered development; and governments of underdeveloped countries are wholly concerned with survival – survival by any means available.

Thus emerges a picture of persuasion and coercion, geared towards objectives couched in terms of damage limitation. But environmental and ecological salvation will not be found in such opportunist and piecemeal measures. As many have pointed out, any steps we take towards ensuring the survival of the planet and the well-being of its inhabitants must be made in the context of global sustainability. (This, indeed, was the underlying theme of the Rio summit.) The Brundtland Report of 1988 defined sustainability as 'Development that meets the needs of the present without compromising the ability of future generations to meet their own needs.' The report envisages a world where at every level the resources that are consumed are made up, in one way or another, by the introduction of new resources of a similar value and usefulness.

Implicit in the Brundtland definition is a requirement for coordinated action across all disciplines, including politics, economics, design and education, and across all nations; a complex system of 'trade-offs', whereby every resource that is used must be compensated for; and a time frame for doing this. This definition is somewhat problematic for the construction industry.

It is now generally realized that many of the resources once thought of as infinite will

within decades become exhausted or uneconomical to extract, and that human activities throughout the world have caused irreparable environmental and ecological degradation (and continue to do so). Faced with these facts, international institutes formulated the principles of sustainability. Sustainability, they believed, can operate at any level: from the extended family through the local community, the town and the city to the nation, continent and world. This might be a practical proposition if it were possible for a new society to be set up from scratch; but since we inherit a diverse, suspicious and heterogeneous society securely entrenched in particular ways of doing things, the road towards sustainability, at least at the outset, is going to be assembled in a piecemeal fashion.

The phenomenon of the global economy is now so entrenched and so much a part of our way of life and existence that it precludes viable self-sustaining communities in any socially and economically interconnected context. This is not to say that local communities cannot go some way towards sustainability or that they cannot put considerable pressure on local government authorities to go further; but to make an impact on the very real dangers we now face on a global scale, direction and leadership is needed from the top. This involves not only international organizations and national governments, but multi-national corporations, and since they are far less accountable than most governments, their cooperation may be more difficult to secure.

Similarly, designers, specifiers, manufacturers and contractors in the building industry should set up and follow principles for sustainability, and these principles should be clearly associated with and recognized by the industry. Their progress will be compromised and less effective, however, if other industries (agriculture and transport, for instance) do not do likewise. The construction industry will also fall short of its objectives if it finds itself operating in a world community which has not embraced and acted upon over-arching measures to secure global sustainability.

This is where the Brundtland definition proves to be inadequate. Within the construction industry operating on a building-by-building basis, each attempting to meet a complex commercial or social function, it is simply not practicable to design within a closed balance of sustainable gains and losses. A redefinition of sustainability for the construction industry, therefore, might go along these lines: 'Development that meets the needs of the present and is at least as valuable to future generations as the value of the environmental exploitation that results.'

This interpretation allows for the extraction and use of even very large quantities of resources provided they are renewable or demonstrably exist in sufficient quantities for all time. It permits waste and pollution levels that the planet is clearly able to tolerate and accommodate. It does not require everything to stay the same, and recognizes that development implies trade-offs within and outside the industry. It does not necessarily imply self-sufficiency and

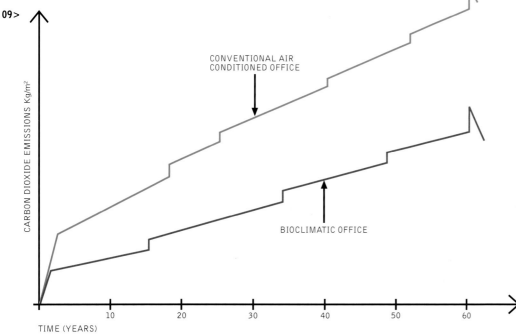

CARBON DIOXIDE EMISSIONS Kg/m²

CONVENTIONAL AIR
CONDITIONED OFFICE

BIOCLIMATIC OFFICE

TIME (YEARS)

10   20   30   40   50   60

08 > The profile of a zero energy building.
A sustainable building (in energy terms) is one that over its life breaks even or is in credit in respect to energy consumption. This is only possible if the building is designed to use minimum energy and incorporates on-site renewable energy generation (such as a photovoltaic array) powerful enough to generate sufficient energy to meet or exceed its lifetime consumption.

09 > Carbon dioxide emissions arising from profligate and efficient use of energy in offices.
A conventional air-conditioned office produces five or six times the carbon dioxide of a well designed bioclimatic office. The production of carbon dioxide correlates directly with the amount of centrally generated energy consumed and the type of fuel used (gas and electricity).

autonomy except within the context of the planet as a whole.

The challenge for the construction industry is to quantify and evaluate these issues. To do this it needs to clarify objectives; identify and list the different types of environmental impact that construction involves; and assign physical units of measurement to them. It has to understand the scientific principles governing sustainability – the characteristics of entropy, the modes, manner and extent of impacts, and the relationship between cause and effect – and assign monetary, or other, value to the effects on current and future generations, as well as interpreting the results over the life cycles of the buildings and their components.

This process is inherently complex, and entails much scientific and methodological uncertainty. It is further complicated by the lobbying of interest groups and by commercial and political secrecy. It is difficult to envisage an assembly of forces that could initiate an integrated and international undertaking to embark on this massive task. Maybe the best that we can hope for in the short term is for international coordination and legislation to mitigate the most immediate and dangerous causes of global depredation; national controls and legislation to mitigate those threatening countries and regions; incentives and disincentives to push communities towards sustainability; and explanations and demonstrations of 'good practice' to guide them in carrying it through. Even so, these measures may not be enough to halt the countdown to environmental disaster that we are currently experiencing.

Such measures may make the individual architect feel powerless, but it is through individual action and grass-roots agitation that progress will be made. Every study into sustainability that has been carried out stresses the key effect of energy use. If this one area could be satisfactorily resolved within a relatively short time frame, much of the rest would fall into place. Energy use is generally seen as most critical in the manufacturing and processing industries. The energy used in producing a building is approximately 20 per cent of its operating energy taken over its lifetime. This explains the importance given to reducing operating energy. But the problem with energy used in producing a building (embodied energy) is that it is being expended now – at a time when construction across the world, and in particular around the Pacific Rim, is at an all-time peak, and when measures to reduce pollution and carbon dioxide from power stations and to introduce renewable energy are in their infancies. Operating energy, on the other hand, is spread over a long period, and it must be hoped that more benign forms of energy production will be introduced during that period. The decisive factor, therefore, in our struggle to halt the destruction of the environment and to introduce sustainable practice is the energy expended today in the production process, which is fixed (subject to maintenance and alteration) for the duration of the life of its host product.

So how, then, should we design for a sustainable future? Carbon dioxide emissions are a direct consequence of power generation and, therefore, energy consumption. The

graph above shows carbon dioxide emissions projected during the life (say 60 years) of a conventional air-conditioned office building compared with that of a 'best practice', naturally ventilated, energy-conscious office. Clearly the latter represents a very significant improvement over the former, but the energy-conscious building only achieves a reduction in the angle of the graph, not a complete flattening. To achieve a zero energy building (or most realistically a close-to-zero energy construction programme), the issue of energy generation itself has to be addressed. And this means a rapid change from fossil fuel-generated energy to solar energy.

Thus this chapter ends as it began in acknowledging that our future salvation, just as in our evolutionary past, lies with the sun. By harnessing a nanotherm of its immense power to keep ourselves in relative comfort, we give the planet a chance to adapt to our changing demands at a pace that it can accommodate. Prostrating ourselves before it and trusting in its bounty alone will not get us off the hook, however; political will on an international scale needs to be generated to make very significant changes to society's expectations and values if all those who inhabit the planet are to experience a real and lasting sense of well-being. Nonetheless, architects have a critical role to play. As leaders in the construction process, and providers of a central link between it and those who commission buildings, they are in a prime position to influence, cajole and to demonstrate, through their designs, the path to sustainability in architecture.

The Birth of
Bioclimatic Architecture

01>The Prairie House,
Norman, Oklahoma
(1961) by Herb Greene.

On 28 June 1979, with turmoil in Iran after the fall of the Shah, the OPEC (petroleum-exporting) countries met at Geneva and raised oil prices by 15 per cent. This followed a rise of 14 per cent just two months earlier. Another oil crisis had arrived, with rationed petrol and queues outside fuel pumps in those countries dependent on Middle East suppliers.

This action finally brought home to governments and the public at large the fragility of the divide separating the affluent, energy-hungry nations from those of the deprived Third World. Energy consciousness at last took root in the public mind – not through an awareness of the environmental issues involved, but through the realization that limited energy supply would have a major impact on the way of life to which we had grown accustomed.

When in 1981 the crisis was finally overcome, and the OPEC countries were forced to reduce prices, Western governments took measures to try to ensure that they could not be 'held to ransom' in this manner again. One of these measures was to take alternative forms of renewable energy sources more seriously. With this in mind, the International Energy Agency (IEA), set up in 1974 after an earlier oil crisis by the countries of the Organization for Economic Cooperation and Development (OECD), introduced a series of 'tasks' to research, develop and promote alternative energy sources.

This was not the first time that Western countries had been alarmed by an actual or perceived threat to the supply of oil.

The Suez crisis in 1956 contributed to the initiation of an atomic energy programme in the UK and other European countries, and conflicts between Israel and Arab countries from time to time promoted further jitters. The 1979 crisis, however, coincided with society's growing concern over the effects of technological development and the consequences of exponential growth in energy demand on the Earth's ecology, and indeed on the survival of the planet itself.

Most commentators place the advent of a Green sensibility as a focused and adversarial issue, rather than the preoccupation of isolated individuals, with the publication of Rachel Carson's *The Silent Spring* in 1962. Carson, a biologist living in California, had come to the conclusion that man's inexorable expansion and development were having an irreversible impact on the natural environment. *Silent Spring* was probably the first instance where a trade-named product – DDT – was directly accused of having such an impact. This chemical, Carson claimed, was the cause of the alarming decline in numbers of robins and other songbirds visiting suburban backyards in the United States. It was as an indirect result of this accusation that DDT came to be banned almost everywhere by 1980 (India being the most notable exception) and that heavy curbs were introduced for other damaging chemicals. Carson's pronouncement kindled other areas of disenchantment. The massive technological input into Vietnam, for example, seemed to many not only to reinforce the immorality of the US presence there, but to heighten a sense of science

and technology being the harbingers of doom and destruction.

This negative feeling towards technology was, to some extent, countered by the launch of Apollo 8 in 1968 and its pictures of Earth transmitted from space. These images were to transform our perception of the planet; it was indeed 'spaceship earth' and, from a distance, its blues, whites, greens and yellows showed it to be entrancingly beautiful. The consequences of Vietnam and the exploration of space combined with a general disenchantment with the status quo helped to fuel the alternative culture of the sixties and seventies. Against the backdrop of flower power and 'dropping out', a number of scientists, anthropologists and sociologists began to question the values of conventional society. Thinkers such as Claude Levi-Strauss, E. F. Schumacher, Ivan Illich, Fritjof Capra and James Lovelock challenged assumptions about environmental systems and ever greater technology-fuelled production.

In the summer of 1969 half a million young people made the pilgrimage to Max Yazgur's farm at Woodstock, New York State, set up camp, laid back and submitted themselves to tidal waves of folk and rock. It was the apogee of the flower power era. Vietnam, drugs, new technologies and a growing acquaintance with ancient forms of spirituality helped to shift large sections of the younger generation away from the pursuit of property and commodity, to the pursuit of experience. In architecture, the result was a weird combination of the homespun and 'spinning home'.

^
02

In the United States, where the spirit of coexistence between settler and the wilderness lived on – at least in the nation's collective subconscious – the children of Woodstock followed in the steps of their pioneering forefathers and set up alternative communities in semi-desert and forest areas eschewed by 'civilized' society. The pattern book made a reappearance, helping those with limited skills and limited property needs. Printed on rough recycled paper, publications such as *The Dome Book* (1971) became the technical manuals for many self-help communities. They offered a fusion of the sophisticated technology of Buckminster Fuller with the primitive techniques of the tepee and the yurt. Traditional materials such as earth, canvas and timber were promoted along with urethane foam, metal sheeting and components salvaged from abandoned cars. There were also early signs of corporations aligning themselves with the counter-culture. Heineken, for example, produced the WOBOL (World Bottle), square beer bottles that could be cemented together and used as building bricks, once the contents had been consumed. (This was in the days before greater value could be found in recycling the bottle glass.)

In one or two cases these alternative communities developed more ambitious plans for their settlements. The Italian-born architect and visionary Paolo Soleri set up a workshop and home in the Arizona desert to make cast iron wind chimes; he ended up designing and (with volunteer help) partially constructing a multi-tiered, organically conceived desert city, reminiscent of those of Chaco Canyon described in Chapter One.

The idea of radical new urban morphologies, however, was more prevalent in those parts of the world where population densities were intense. In the architectural schools of Europe and the ateliers of Japan quite different urban archetypes were being invented. In these schemes new technology was not used to rehabilitate an arcadian dream of harmonious communities living self-sufficiently in the wilderness, but became the *raison d'être* of ambitious and visionary proposals prepared by cliques of architectural students and teachers. They saw that rapid technological developments in such areas as the aerospace and automotive industries, cybernetics and the media were throwing up an awesome menu of innovative products and concepts that could readily be applied to urban society. For example, repetitive and inflexible mass-production methods were challenged by the introduction of more adaptable, computer-programmed production line machinery. Instead of relying on existing demand and future projections to determine the performance, appearance and cost of mass-produced components, a manufacturer could now (in certain industries) offer the customer bespoke products at competitive prices.

For those with the prescience to observe what was happening in leading-edge industries and for those who wished to break away from the socially accountable and architecturally constrained attitudes of the post-war period, these emerging technologies and mind-expanding concepts had an overwhelming appeal. One new vision was of a building that would be intelligent – robotic, even. Le Corbusier's aphorism of the modern house

as a 'machine for living in' was given a literal interpretation by groups such as Archigram, based at the Architectural Association in London. Archigram's Walking City (1964) proposed a series of giant, self-contained living pods, their forms derived from a combination of insect and machine, which would roam the cities. They would be autonomous, but potentially parasitic in that they could 'plug in' to way stations to exchange occupants or review their energy resources. In this view, the stable city of subtle, continuous and multi-layered connections and interactions was dead. It would be replaced by moving conveyances in which occupants lived in sensory-heightened, highly serviced confinement. In concept these 'spinning homes' were not too far removed from today's executive car.

In Japan, where overcrowding was becoming an even greater problem than in Europe, similarly radical urban schemes were being proposed. Unlike the polemical fantasies of Archigram, however, these schemes were offered as real, practical solutions. The Metabolists proposed 'mega-cities' such as Ocean City by Kiyonori Kikutake. The city's composition was expressed in terms of two elements: permanent infrastructure and temporary, interchangeable occupied space with associated servicing. Space City by Arata Isozaki (1960) and the Helicoids project for the Guiza area of Tokyo by Kisho Kurokawa (1961) also created visions of a high density, high consumption and high speed future. These visions were never realized. They only survive as archived documents in architectural libraries and

02> Arcosanti, a 'city' in the Arizona desert, USA (1970–) by Paolo Soleri.

03> The Walking City (1964) by the Archigram Group.

^
03

as gewgaws at World Fair sites, serving as reminders of what might have been. Even the rash of new capital cities in emerging nations around the world – Abuja, Canberra, Brasilia, Dacca – rejected the transient and dynamic for the grandiose and static.

While it is clear how the settlements and aspirations of the drop-out communities of the sixties can be placed in a historical context of nature and built form, it is harder to see any symbolic connection between the mega-city and nature. Indeed, quite the reverse would appear to be true. Clearly the mega-city holds no regard for resource depletion, for global effects or for the subtle potentiality of place on form. Conceptually, these neo-futurists shared many 'Green' sensibilities. They passionately believed in freedom of the individual and freedom of the mind, providing a refreshing break from the pipe-gripping, trilby-hatted paternalism of 1950s home insurance advertisements. This sense of freedom flowed both from the younger generation's new affluence and confidence, and the influence of literary radicals in the United States such as Allen Ginsberg, Jack Kerouac, William Burroughs and James Baldwin; style-of-life radicals such as R.D. Laing and Timothy Leary; and rock culture in general. However, this ability to open the mind and re-think, while important in helping people to understand and respond to the assaults of internationalization, industrialization and commercialization on the globe, was misconceived in creating urban models which, if realized, would have exacerbated the impact of these assaults.

Modernism's Green Legacy

Chapter One traced the relationship between architecture and nature through history. We noted the relationship in respect to climate, resource and culture and concluded by looking at the work of four masters of the Modern Movement – Le Corbusier, Alvar Aalto, Frank Lloyd Wright and Richard Buckminster Fuller – who we took to represent the span of Modernist sensibility towards nature and the environment. We contended that, far from being extinguished, the dialogue between architecture and nature flourished during the Modern period. Indeed in many respects it was then at its richest and most rewarding.

This reciprocity only failed under the impact of the worldwide building boom that followed the astringencies of the immediate post-war period. It was at this time that, through a combination of values embracing expediency, convenience and self-image, a new 'International' style came to rule.

International Style was not completely dominant, however. Having already noted the two autonomously inspired manifestations of alternative living (the arcadian settlement and the mega-city), it is possible to continue tracing a seam of sensitivity towards nature through the post-war period to its resurgence in the seventies and eighties. In doing so, it is convenient briefly to trace the legacy of the Modernist pioneers previously referred to.

Following the precedent of Chandigarh and the Carpenter Center for the Visual Arts at Harvard (1961–4), Le Corbusier's mythic

and gut-felt response to nature lived on, but in the work of his followers it became increasingly the province of grandiloquent nationalism and the cultural ghetto. Many notable architects took up his flame, including Paul Rudolph, Oscar Niemeyer and Eero Saarinen; but, of that era, it was the American architect (of Baltic descent) Louis Kahn (1901–74), who most insistently pursued the mythopoeic: those elemental attributes of architecture which Le Corbusier so convincingly expressed.

Kahn did not come to public prominence until relatively late in his career. During the first 25 years of his professional life he was known more as a thinker than as a practitioner. Then, at the age of 52, he collaborated on the extension to the Yale Art Gallery in New Haven which was notable for its accomplished handling of space. He went on to design the Richards Medical Research Building in Philadelphia (1957–61) which, with its radical ordering of function and form, was quickly recognized as a major contribution to modern architecture.

At the heart of Kahn's work lay a deeply felt (if somewhat cryptic) philosophy. He saw architecture as the meeting of the measurable and the unmeasurable. He used the word 'silence' for the unmeasurable, for that which is not yet; and the word 'light' for the measurable, for that which is. Kahn saw architecture as existing on the threshold between silence and light (for further discussion see John Lobell, *Silence and Light*, 1979). He felt that a great building begins with the realization of the unmeasurable.

49

04

Measurable means are then used to build it, and when it is built, it gives a view back to the original realization of the unmeasurable.

Kahn said: 'All material in nature, the mountains and the streams and the air and we, are made of Light which has been spent, and this crumpled mass called material casts a shadow, and the shadow belongs to Light. So Light is really the source of all being ....' In appropriating elemental metaphors to explain his approach to building, he echoes a sensibility expressed by architects throughout history, but which in our current era has – at least until recently – been suppressed for fear of derision.

Kahn lived at a time of uncertainty, change and loss of spirit. Perhaps partly as a consequence, he turned to the eternal, to that which transcends the circumstances of the given moment. There he found the order, form and quiescence which allowed him to create buildings and settings with a palpable sense of place – the *genius loci* – that holy grail of Modernist architects which was so neglected by those designing to the tune of Mammon. It is extraordinary that a poet, a man who was uncompromisingly other-worldly, could not only survive in a land ruled by the dollar and the delivery deadline, but also build a handful of unquestionable masterpieces.

Like Le Corbusier, Kahn designed a city for the Indian subcontinent; in his case Sher-E-Banglanagar, the government centre of Dacca, Bangladesh (Le Corbusier having turned down the commission on the grounds of being too busy and Alvar Aalto on the grounds of ill

health). Kahn's approach to the master plan was not based on regional archetypes and physical manipulation of the ground plane. It was, he said, inspired by thoughts about the transcendent nature of the building's use (where 'men came to assemble to touch the spirit of the community') and the relative position of the temporal (the Assembly) and the spiritual (the Mosque). In this way he included the community – its hierarchy and its symbolic role – as a component of the natural world. He was able to use this sensibility as a potent form provider for the buildings of the new city. His plan consisted of the centrally placed Assembly and Supreme Court, flanked on either side by hostels, dining halls and the diplomatic enclave. To the north he located a lake, and beyond that a small town.

Several important aspects of Kahn's designs were a direct response to the harsh sub-tropical climate, with its scorching sun and seasonal monsoons. The designs included vast and elaborate screen walls ('glare walls') perforated with large geometrically shaped openings (squares, circles and triangles) to shelter the interior space from the elements. He described the concept thus: 'The architectural approach to the Assembly Building, as for all the buildings, is to find a design which protects both enclosed and outdoor spaces from sun, heat, rain and glare by the use of overhangs, deep verandahs and protecting walls to accompany the directly usable spaces ' (*Louis I. Kahn: In the Realms of Architecture*, David B. Brownlee and David G. De Long 1992). (None of the buildings, to this day, are air conditioned.) The massive shading elements fuse a response to climate

with Kahn's preoccupations with shape and form.

At Sher-E-Banglanagar, there is none of the physical reference to traditional architecture of the region that can be seen in Lutyens's New Delhi or the railway stations, museums and government buildings of other colonial architects. These may have referred to local architectural styles but they paid scant attention to the local climate. Kahn's sources of inspiration were European: the Roman Baths of Caracalla for the Assembly Building and the Great Mosque at Cordoba for the undercrofts of the government complex.

Indeed, the construction site must have been reminiscent of the raising of a Roman monument. At its peak, over 2,000 labourers swarmed over wooden scaffolding and formwork to cast the concrete (five feet at a time) and lay the red bricks. The construction kept many employed for a number of years (it was completed in 1983) using local materials and without recourse to sophisticated imported technology and components.

Like the Classical architects of the eighteenth century, Kahn wished to imbue both nature and building with order, and develop an orchestrated dialogue between the two. His architecture undoubtedly has a presence but, unlike Classical architecture, it is not dressed up; it is spare and primordial. He wished to express the innate quality and potential of the materials he used. It is this combination of Classical order and truth to materials that gives his architecture the grandeur, symbolic power and timelessness of ancient monuments.

Architecture of this quality can only be realized when a generous budget and relaxed timescale are combined with an architect of conviction and insight, commissioned by an enlightened patron. These conditions, perhaps surprisingly, can still be found today. The legacy of Le Corbusier and Kahn survives in the patronage of city mayors, national governments and corporate foundations and is mostly confined to expressions of cultural prestige, national standing and self-aggrandizement. Examples include the Staatsgalerie at Stuttgart (1977–84) by Stirling and Wilford, the National Gallery of Art in Washington (1971–8) by I. M. Pei, the Sydney Opera House (1956–73) by Jorn Utzon and the Getty Center in Los Angeles (1984–96) by Richard Meier. However, it is the work executed over the last two or three decades by Japanese architects, working on their home soil, that consistently and often rewardingly continues this line. This work comprises not only large-scale projects by the likes of Arata Isozaki and Kisho Kurokawa, but also exquisite small-scale homes and local museums by architects such as Tadao Ando and Naito Architect & Associates. Some of these are illustrated in the next chapter.

The second modern master we looked at was Alvar Aalto, whose legacy lives on and whose modest lyricism and regional sensibility have been a particular influence on today's bioclimatic architecture. In northern Europe, in the years immediately following World War II, the certainties and simplicities of Modernist tenets lost their hold on the architectural profession. The pioneering spirit had evaporated and a pragmatic attitude

prevailed. Early Modernism's white buildings with their flat roofs and minimalist detailing were not suited to the northern climate of snow, wind and rain, becoming stained and dilapidated.

Aalto's earlier initiative was widely seen as indicating a way forward. His reputation was international, but the direct influence of his work was largely confined to northern Europe and in particular to social democrat Sweden where, as in Britain, there already existed an Arts and Crafts tradition. Key to this tradition was the work of the painter Carl Larsson who in the 1880s was given by his father-in-law a summer house at Sundborn in central Sweden. With a succession of decorative rooms added to an existing simple timber cottage, this building, like the Red House in England, has had a seminal influence on subsequent domestic architecture. It was reinterpreted in an organic Modernist mode throughout suburban Sweden in the late 1940s and 1950s, from whence it quickly spread to surrounding countries. The Scandinavian brand of relaxed regional Modernism had a particularly strong influence on post-war British architecture. The Festival of Britain in 1951 provided a showcase for the 'New Empiricist' architecture that combined European Modernism, the unaffected pragmatism of Sweden and the engineering skills of the UK.

Despite the fanfare of the Festival of Britain, this Scandinavian-influenced architecture was bound closely to the recognition of social needs and the community; and, following the destructiveness of World War II, these needs

were pressing. Before the war, purist Modern architecture was regarded by most as artful and alien. Afterwards, in its new, more accommodating form it became, without significant dissent, the mode of modern democratic socialism.

Architects of British new towns, and those responsible for the new universities, schools, housing and factories across Europe, saw themselves as social engineers as much as designers in form and space. Many issues that are part of today's bioclimatic credo – designing for good health, the beneficial effects of daylight and sunlight, the need for green space, the notion of mutually supportive communities – were incipient in this pragmatic architecture. Indeed, the tendency within today's bioclimatic architecture movement that is most uncompromising in its espousal of sustainability and the radical social change needed to bring it about, can be directly traced to the socially conscious architecture arising from the aspirations of the post-war years.

Meanwhile, in quite another part of the world, one man was leading a crusade that closely paralleled this concern for providing practical accommodation for the community. In 1969, the Ministry of Culture in Cairo published a book entitled *Architecture for the Poor* by the Egyptian architect Hassan Fathy. The book described his unconventional approach to rural mass housing in his own country, an approach which he believed could raise the standard of living and culture among the world's desperately poor.

^
05

^
06

In Fathy's radical vision the poor of the earth, many of whom had lost their traditional building skills, would be best housed using the materials immediately to hand: mud brick in the Middle East, wood in south-east Asia and so on. With an appropriate and attractive architectural style, and with someone to help the people in each country re-learn their native skills, even the poorest could have affordable housing in which they could take pride. According to Fathy this would both serve their indigenous needs and be socially and aesthetically satisfying.

Between 1945 and 1946 Fathy carried out an experiment based on his theory, designing a new village for a group of Egyptian peasants at Gourna near Luxor. Fathy worked with each family to incorporate their individual needs into the design for their particular dwelling. He planned a brickyard to make the mud bricks for the structures, and revived the long-lost skill of creating brick-built domes and vaults without falsework. He also designed buildings for the manufacture and sale of local products, laid out a marketplace, and built a mosque, theatre and schools.

Although ultimately unsuccessful (due to a combination of bureaucratic red tape and the pressures of mass tourism which undermined its simple, self-sustaining communal objectives), this and other later projects of Fathy's had an enormous influence in the 1960s on those looking for an alternative to technology-based mega-cities and the ubiquitous exportation of International Style. To those beginning to formulate the precepts of the Green movement in architecture,

Gourna represented an ideal and an exemplar for rural self-sufficiency and cultural and social well-being.

The third modern master looked at in Chapter One was Frank Lloyd Wright. In terms of built form his influence was largely confined to the United States or at least to lands with wide open spaces and a burgeoning culture. In Europe, his expansive individualism and the settings of his buildings were too alien to invite much emulation.

Wright's concept of an 'organic' architecture, however, has had a strong influence on today's bioclimatic practitioners. As we have seen, for Wright this notion combined a number of aspects: fluidity of planning, plasticity of form, expressiveness in the use of materials and recognition of change wrought by passing time. Subsequent development acknowledges these ideas, but moves towards more literal manifestations. Organic architecture became less an attitude to abstractions derived from nature, and more an expression of nature itself – not so much organic as an organism.

Of Wright's immediate successors, Bruce Goff (1904–82) is the architect most closely associated with this aspect of the architect's work. Throughout his long career, Goff continually explored and experimented with materials. Like Wright, he nurtured and celebrated an individuality of expression and his work has a particular feel for the dimension of time – an important aspect of organic architecture. This is not a 'timelessness' expressed by the Classical architect, but a sense of architectural space

responding to and reflecting the passage of time. Goff described his most celebrated building as follows: 'The past is gone, the future is not here, but the present is continuous. The Bavinger House, earthbound as it is, is a primitive example of the continuity of space for living ... it is not a "back-to-nature" concept of living space. It is a living with nature, today and everyday, continuous space again as part of a continuous present' (*Forty-Four Realizations,* 1970). The spiralling roof of the Bavinger House, designed in 1950, clearly derives its form directly from nature. The form is also imbued with mystic significance, symbolizing both passage of time and ascent to enlightenment. The materials used to construct the house are a combination of the raw and the processed: the spiral copper-clad roof hangs from steel tension cables, which extend to support a suspension bridge linking the house to the bank of the shallow ravine within which it stands. Massive stone walls, constructed from sandstone boulders from the site, form the core of the spiral. It is supported at the centre by a mast which rises above the walls.

A direct descendant of this building is the Prairie House outside Norman, Oklahoma, designed by Herb Greene (b. 1929). The house was built in 1961. John Farmer, in his book *Green Shift* (1996), devotes a whole chapter to this building; he sees it as both central to the Wrightian organic tradition and seminal in its response to fears of nuclear apocalypse and concerns about the vanishing wilderness.

It is a tiny building, but charged with potent symbolism. The house is constructed from

52

05 > Gouache of the
'Turkish House' at Fayoum,
Egypt by Hassan Fathy.

06 > The Bavinger House,
Norman, Oklahoma
(1950) by Bruce Goff.

07 > The Prairie House,
Norman, Oklahoma
(1961) by Herb Greene.

53

timber, but in such a way as to suggest a fusion of American Indian tepee and colonial balloon-framed villa. Roof and walls merge in a cascade of heavy timber shingles and overlapping planks. Close up, the surface suggests featheriness, with the junctions between the planes of shingle and planking looking like the plumage of a rooster or the scales of an armadillo. Seen from a distance, however, the shingles merge, the surface texture flattens and the overall form prevails. The building becomes less chicken and more buffalo, one with a recognizably bowed and wounded head. It is this image of a slumped and dying prairie beast – one so central to American mythology – that conjures up connotations of loss and sacrifice (described and elucidated in Farmer's book). Individually crafted and inspired by its site, the Prairie House epitomizes the healthy-living dream house of the stressed-out city denizen. And, since this is America, the dream is often realized. Tucked away in ocean dunes, the folds of the prairie, the aspen and birches of the Rockies and the boulders of the desert, numerous middle-class homes unabashedly commune with nature. They are sensitive to setting, individual, and increasingly, designed according to sound bioclimatic principles. Nor is this domestic diaspora confined to the United States; the huttes of Norway, the dachas of Russia, the seaside cabins o f northern Europe, the villas of the Mediterranean and the chalets of the Alpine countries demonstrate a rekindled regard for the solace that the natural environment can bring. Seekers of such solace are but a step away from proactively protecting the conditions that provide it.

The overt anthropomorphism (or more properly, zoomorphism) noted in Greene's Prairie House is a characteristic that derives, in recent times, more from Gaudí than from Wright. Generally, however, architecture has been less affected in this respect than has furniture, ceramics, metalwork and other decorative arts. This may be due to architecture's more intransigent functional requirements and its less accommodating structural technologies. It may also be due to the rather more abstract aspirations arising from necessary constructional logic. A building may be required to reach for the sky for religious or hubristic reasons, but it is not often required to resemble an elephant, dog or tortoise.

The most renowned contemporary exponent of this expressive form of architecture is the Hungarian, Imre Makovecz (b. 1935). His buildings can be described as both regional and organic. Although they are all located in Hungary and are clearly influenced by the culture and tradition of that country, they also draw on international stimuli. Makovecz's work lies in a direct line from Wright, Goff and Greene and its anti-orthogonal, chromatic expression is strongly influenced by the anthroposophy of Rudolf Steiner. The son of a carpenter, Makovecz has an innate, sensuous feel for wood. He manipulates the material to suit his expressive purpose, whether it be the warping of planes, the joining of skeletal structures or the interlocking of grids. Many of his buildings (for example, the Cultural Centre at Sarospatak, completed in 1980) are embedded in the ground and seem to be emerging from it like some primitive animal.

By 'rooting' them in this way he also suggests a return to Mother Earth. With these half-buried buildings one senses that the motivation has more to do with primordial symbolism than the practicalities of energy conservation, a rationale usually claimed for most buried buildings constructed today.

For Makovecz, like his mentors, an 'organic' architecture is one that integrates a building closely with its site; it is based on fluid, biomorphic spaces and invariably promotes a response that starts with 'It looks like ...'. In contrast to those designed by other practitioners in this field, many of his buildings are basically symmetrical – as is the human body. However, like the body, when these buildings are studied in a little more detail one becomes aware of displacements and minor imbalances which derive from particular subsidiary functions. They are thus saved from predictability and given character and individuality.

And so the line of development flowing from Wright's organic architecture survives, albeit vested in the idiosyncratic work of a few individuals. Its influence on bioclimatic architecture is focused at the more 'fundamental' end of the Green movement – those who see Green architecture as being very much a product of its particular locality and community. Unfortunately, in this parochial milieu, the aspect of the pioneering organic architecture of, say, Goff and Makovecz that usually does not survive is that which attracts us to it in the first place: its individuality, its intrinsic and particular peculiarity.

The fourth strand important to bioclimatic architecture – that of a particular and an appropriate harnessing of technology – cannot exclusively be traced to our fourth master in the way that we have tended to follow a direct line of descent from the other three. Richard Buckminster Fuller was a pioneering and charismatic figure in developing and promoting a technological response to the social and environmental condition, and was central in pointing out the interdependency between communities and economies of the world. Technology, however, would have advanced without him, driven by stimuli that have always been present: armed conflict, economic growth and personal convenience. Others would have applied (and did) technological innovation to the building process and, in particular, towards using resources efficiently and effectively in construction. Nevertheless, Buckminster Fuller remains an important figure, particularly within the architectural fraternity, by representing the appropriate use of technology and developing a global consciousness. Indeed, he has become even more so now that some of those who were inspired by him when they were students have become, in their maturity, the high priests of 'high-tech' architecture.

For the proponents of bioclimatic architecture, therefore, the Buckminster Fuller legacy represents on the one hand the channelling of scientific research and technological invention towards reducing material resource (and thus leading to energy conservation) and, on the other, the mobilization of the global community away from environmentally destructive habits and towards more sustainable practice.

Unlike the aeronautical, nautical and automotive industries, for example, the building industry is not constituted to produce a limited range of products which then compete against other very similar products. In competitive markets survival is directly tied to technological development. Each company, therefore, invests heavily in technological resource and expertise so that advancement is continuous and productive, and is constantly pressing specialist suppliers to do likewise.

The building industry, despite a few courageous attempts in the public sector at producing a standardized product (as in housing, schools and hospitals), remains largely in the bespoke market, although the procedures for delivering buildings may have a standardized basis. Those who commission buildings normally require them to be tailored to their particular requirements and to be sufficiently distinctive in appearance and character to be identified as being uniquely theirs (or, in many cases, uniquely their tenants'). It largely falls to the manufacturers of the components of buildings, therefore, to provide the technological development necessary to meet a particular demand, with architects doing their best to put them together to form an integrated entity. On the whole, these companies trail in the wake of the theoretical thinking and innovation provided by planners and designers, whereas in consumer industries it is the manufacturers who are proactive.

Technological development in the building industry can be seen following two parallel but closely interconnected paths: that of physical development of materials and components, and that of providing the means for adaptation and change over time. Both are important aspects of bioclimatic architecture.

The physical development of materials and components is relatively straightforward, with most innovations occurring since the time of the industrial revolution (with marked acceleration, as in all technological development, since the 1930s). We therefore have James Bogardus and the steel skeletal frame in the 1850s; Elisha Graves Otis and the elevator in 1853; Auguste Perret and the first use of ferro concrete as a medium for architectural expression in 1903; Jean Prouvé and others in the development of prefabrication in the 1940s and 1950s, followed by more recent development in the fields of seals and sealants, insulation materials, glass, plastics, air treatment, fibre optics, composites, computer-based control systems, and so on.

These developments were driven by a wide range of stimuli, including demographic migration, land prices, physical challenges of the terrain, demand for comfort and the need to communicate. None of the companies involved had a particular regard for the impact that the products might have on climate, ecology or the environment of the senses, whether aural, visual or olfactory. Nor were they unduly concerned with the wider social implications of their

08 > The Roman Catholic church at Paks, Hungary (1987).

09 > Main stadium roof, Munich Olympics (1972) by Günter Behnisch and Frei Otto.

09

inventions and discoveries, or even the health and welfare of those exposed to them. Pressure from environmentalists and their advocates in the building industry has brought about a significant change in this state of affairs, and legislation has curtailed the manufacture of products and systems with more extreme detrimental effects. Change, however, has been tentative, and like organic produce on a supermarket shelf, the wares have been overpriced, erratic in availability and limited in range.

Of a number of architects with an engineering and technological bent, the German architect Frei Otto (b. 1925) is probably the most obvious figure to link Buckminster Fuller's inventiveness with the architects of today's technology-expressive buildings. He has devoted his career to developing structures that use materials sparingly but with great elegance and assurance. Otto's ideal, he has said, would be 'to develop the actual structure out of existence altogether, so as to get more space and energy for what should be done inside our buildings, for the people for whom we are building' (*Frei Otto: Structures*, Conrad Roland, 1972).

For him, therefore, the structure is not an end in itself or a pretext for producing interesting sculptured shapes, but an integrated element which must be as technically efficient as possible. The question that has governed Otto's development as a structural designer is that of how to solve a structural problem with minimum expenditure of constructional energy.

The result has been an extraordinary succession of nature-inspired structures employing cables, membranes and panels. Despite the architect's stated disassociation with aesthetic considerations, these buildings with their sumptuous curves and taut tendons appear to float over the landscape with sensuous and ephemeral grace. To some extent this appearance is illusory. In many cases, these forms and shapes are only possible if their high tensile loads are countered by massive concrete bases hidden in the ground; furthermore, the materials he uses are often highly refined and sophisticated. Nevertheless, the manifest demonstration of doing 'more with less', and doing it with such elegance, has contributed significantly to reducing building technology to its essentials – a 'honing down' process that brings it closer to the glider technology with which Frei Otto started his career.

Science and technology, aside from offering the means to improve existing building materials and components and develop new ones, also allow buildings to respond to social and cultural change. We have noted how in the 1960s the Archigram group and the Metabolists trailblazed ideas for futuristic, technology-dependent communities. These schemes caused a stir in architectural circles at the time, but it was the graphic techniques used to depict them that were enthusiastically adopted rather than their physical reality. The notion that had real impact and a lasting influence was that of mobility, change and indeterminacy in architecture. Ironically, Archigram members Peter Cook, Ron Herron, Warren Chalk, Michael Webb and the others

had hit upon an aspect of modern society – its mobility – that, at least in its physical sense, had always been an important province of vernacular architecture. In many parts of the world tribes and communities were and are (but increasingly less so) nomadic or semi-nomadic, moving from season to season or when food and water in the vicinity are exhausted.

The sense that architecture had an ephemeral aspect, that it could be a transitory, indeterminate presence just as well as it could be an edifice of bricks and mortar, was pursued most notably in the UK by the critic Reyner Banham and the architect Cedric Price. The latter posited (designed would not be quite the right word) two memorable projects: a Fun Palace located in the East End of London (with the director/impresario Joan Littlewood), and the Potteries Thinkbelt, a 'travelling university' located in an area of industrial decline. In both of these projects, the sociological and technological underpinning were more important than the physical realization. Price, very much in the vanguard of 1960s social iconoclasm, picked up on two of the period's more notable attributes – the broadening and loosening of tertiary education and the pursuit of fun – and propounded highly cerebral proposals to meet and respond to these freedoms. Both schemes proposed structures that would be off-the-shelf, transient or temporary, but at the same time highly and flexibly serviced. In these projects the ancillary and support spaces and systems were very much seen as functions having their own innate expressive qualities. (The distinction between serviced and served

55

10 > The Malaparte
House, Capri (1938)
by Adalberto Libera.

11 > The Autarkic
House, Cambridge, UK
(1971 – 79) by
Alexander Pike.

∧
10

space in buildings had also been made, albeit
in very different expressive form, in Louis
Kahn's service towers of the Alfred Newton
Richards Medical Research Building at the
University of Pennsylvania.) The Potteries
Thinkbelt was particularly radical; its 'non-
architectural' university was designed (at least
in part) to shuttle on railway tracks between
the pottery producing towns of England's
Midlands. A further aspect of these projects
was that they would build on structures and
infrastructure that, in essence, already existed
– in contrast to the new city capitals arising
around the world at that time, and the British
New Towns which were spreading over the
countryside.

The ideas embodied in these projects are all
central to bioclimatic thinking: the notion of
buildings, structures and services having
differing lifespans; the view that buildings
which have become redundant in respect
of their original use can be regenerated
for another; and an awareness of how
misconceived is the common architectural
practice of designing a building as an
immutable object that, once handed over, will
somehow remain the same for the rest of its
life. These ideas are all of a practical nature,
relating to how buildings actually work and
the way they are treated by their owners and
occupiers. They lend themselves accordingly
to fruitful consideration of of energy
conservation and resource economy.

These notions also became the bedrock of
the high-tech architecture practised by
Richard Rogers, Norman Foster, Nicholas
Grimshaw and others. As developed by these

practitioners, however, the ideas of mobility
and impermanence were mined as much for
their expressive and symbolic content as for
any intrinsic social radicalism or sensitive
humanism. The critic Charles Jencks, for one,
has carefully dissected the characteristics of
this movement, declaring it a 'style' in the
same way that he has classified the various
other stylistic schools that have emerged
following the Modernist era. The extraction
of potent architectural expression from
underlying social theory and technical
innovation is the stuff of architecture and
is, as we have already noted, a characteristic
of mature bioclimatic architecture. In this
instance, however, a cross-fertilization has
taken place. While it is clear that technical
innovation is celebrated in much bioclimatic
architecture, it is also apparent that the
high-tech school has, over the last few years,
espoused and appropriated both the Green
manifesto and its inherent architectural
vocabulary.

The strand of thinking emanating from
Buckminster Fuller (and many others in the
post-war period) which led to the notion of
'globalization', is beyond the scope of this
book. This issue is a fundamental one for the
Green movement in general, however, and
does have some repercussions for architects.
There is a rural community in Zimbabwe
whose life is preoccupied with the cultivation
of mange-tout peas, and mange-tout of a very
particular size and shape. One-third of the
crop is discarded because it does not conform
to the specified size and shape. The farm
labourers believe there is a country to the
north with a name which is in fact that of

a leading British supermarket, representatives
of which visit the community annually to press
for greater productivity and greater precision
in the size and shape of the pods. When one
learns that the income and well-being of the
community is totally dependent on this
supermarket, and understands the resources
needed to ensure pristine peas for European
dinner tables, then clearly one begins to
question the priorities that have brought
about this situation. And once this is
challenged, there are many more such follies
to denounce.

There are clear connections between the effects
of globalization and architectural practice.
There is a direct link between the destruction
of the rainforests and how we build and with
which materials; and the erosion of the ozone
layer has led to a reassessment of how energy
is used in buildings. Architects, however, are
dependent on other bodies for the gathering
and assessment of data, for the analysis of
causes of degradation and for proposals for
its reversal. These bodies come in various
forms: international agencies, national
ministries, research institutes, pressure groups,
independent consultancies and individuals.
The individuals tend to be in the vanguard,
with such figures as the environmental activist
Amory Lovins in the USA, and the author and
literary editor Edward Goldsmith in the UK
rattling the doors of the establishment. It is
left to the architects to make sense of it all
in the context of a building where energy and
environment may be seen as important issues,
but where there are other equally important
requirements (particularly in the eyes of the
client) and where at the end of the day the

^
11

building must be a complete architectural statement. So far, there are relatively few buildings that manage to assimilate good environmental practice with real creativity and flare. Notable examples of these are included in Chapter Four.

The Contemporary Scene

The buildings illustrated in Chapter Four are grouped into six sections. These sections relate to architectural form: towers, pavilions, mansions, campuses and so forth. Another grouping might have been the use to which the buildings are put, such as housing, offices, cultural buildings or laboratories. Such a categorization would show a marked difference between the sectors in the extent to which a bioclimatic approach has been developed. The most energy- and environmentally-conscious buildings tend to be in the fields of housing, education and offices. The reason for this is not difficult to see. These sectors have fixed design parameters and a procurement framework which is well established and fairly standardized. This allows building research institutes to target designers, funding agents, clients and their facilities managers more easily and effectively, and to prepare guidance specifically focused on their particular sector.

Information about and guidance to the whole field of low-energy design is now widely disseminated. There now exists (at least in more developed countries) a considerable range of recommendations, standards, codes of practice and, to some extent, legislation directed towards the types of building noted above. The route taken to reach this position is interesting and instructive, and throws light on the new generation of low-energy designs that some of the buildings we will look at represent. Housing, schools and offices have the clearest evolutionary process, and houses, perhaps more than any other building type, illustrate the polarization of architectural approach between the poetic and the intellectual.

In 1938, Adalberto Libera designed and constructed an extraordinary house in Capri. Sitting on top of a rocky peninsula jutting out into the Mediterranean, the Malaparte House stands as a mysterious catalyst between space, light and time. Its austere masonry walls merge with the craggy cliffs which rise from the sea. The walls support a rectangular platform, the landward end of which returns to the natural rock in a single giant flight of steps. There is no baluster or parapet; the only architectural feature is a curved wall facing the setting sun. It evokes the sacrificial platform of a Mayan temple. The house is without style, almost without identifiable elevations, and completely timeless. Although noted by architects when it was built, it only entered into the wider public's consciousness in 1963 when it served as a location in Jean-Luc Godard's film *Le Mépris* (Contempt).

A decade later, in the 1970s, Alex Pike and a group of architectural students from Cambridge University designed an experimental residence named the Autarkic House. Prompted by the first major oil crisis, this group took note of the earliest experiments in solar design in the Modernist era by such pioneers as Professor Felix Trombe in France and Steve Baer, Donald Watson, David Wright and Doug Kelbaugh in the USA. They developed a design which combined sophisticated technology with locally available resources. It was also one of the first house designs (it was only ever built at one-tenth of its intended size) to tackle the challenge of self-sufficiency. It included solar collectors for heat and to provide distilled drinking water. Full height glazing on three sides assisted winter space heating. Electric power was provided by the wind from a rotor on the roof, while methane generated from sewage disposal was used for cooking. The masonry north wall provided a thermal store and acted as a vertical internal garden, designed to provide both food and oxygen from the plants.

These two houses – the Malaparte and the Autarkic – encapsulate opposite extremes in an architectural response to nature. The first is intuitive and holistic; the second science-based, rational and pragmatic.

The low-energy aspects of the Autarkic House influenced a line of housing projects, many of them government-sponsored. These are characterized by south-facing conservatories which mediate between conditions outside and inside; by well insulated and leak-free structures of high mass, and by maximized use of daylight. In direct line of descent from the Autarkic House is the recent house in Nottingham, UK, designed by Brenda and Robert Vale. Employing current technologies such as photovoltaics and Krypton-filled double glazing, the house aims at 'zero' energy consumption and adopts the full

12

13

gamut of measures in support of global sustainability, such as locally sourced building materials of low-embodied energy. The descendants of the Autarkic House have so far either been built as one-off demonstration projects or in small collective groups. However, there are now indications that this approach may soon be adopted on a larger scale. The Linz-Pichling solar city project in Austria jointly by Thomas Herzog, Foster Associates and Richard Rogers Partnership, and the Parc BIT solar village in Majorca by Richard Rogers Partnership alone, are two carefully conceived 'ideal' low-energy, environmentally sensitive developments pitched at a scale where real advances could be made.

The ultimate realization of Autarkic self-sufficiency took place in the New Mexico desert in the early 1990s with the construction of an enormous, mechanically ventilated greenhouse known as Biosphere 2. Seven different ecological habitats representing the ocean reefs, the coastal desert, the tropical rainforest and so forth were installed inside, and eight volunteers, together with a selection of animals and insects, were incarcerated within it for a period of two years. The technology and resource needed to support this community could only be assembled by the likes of a visionary multi-millionaire from Texas, in this case Edward Parry Bass. However, the ultimate goal here was the colonization of Mars, not sustainability on planet Earth.

The Malaparte House is one of the first in a long line of projects which strike a particular

symbiosis between dwelling, nature and location. This felicitous quality is perhaps best exemplified in contemporary architecture by the work of the Australian architect, Glenn Murcutt (b. 1936). He is of particular interest since his strongest early influence was Mies van der Rohe – the first houses that he designed followed all the Miesian disciplines of spartan and abstract Internationalism. In successive projects ranging across the Australian outback, however, Murcutt has developed an architectural approach and language that is recognizably his own. His work defines a contemporary rural vernacular whilst remaining truthful to its Modernist heritage – a singular feat.

In researching residential projects to include in this book, it has been difficult to find ones that effectively and creatively combine the attributes of technology-led energy conservation with an intuitive response to nature. It is difficult to believe it cannot be done, but it requires an architect whose brain is equally developed on both left and right sides; a rarity it seems.

Schools and colleges based on low-energy principles followed a similar path to housing. Perhaps the most notable pioneering school in this respect was Emslie Morgan's extension to St Georges School, Wallasey, near Liverpool in the UK, constructed in 1961. This building exploits three fundamental principles of passive solar design: a highly insulated building envelope; the thermal storage potential of concrete and masonry construction; and the 'greenhouse' properties of south-facing glass. In order to successfully

achieve the last, Morgan developed a remarkably sophisticated solar wall comprising two layers of glass 600mm (2 feet) apart. The inner layer consists largely of obscure glass to shed diffuse light into the classrooms. In some areas, the inner layer is formed of reversible opaque panels – reflective on one side to reject solar gain in summer and painted black on the other to absorb heat in winter. The school was not conceived as a demonstration building. The measures incorporated arose as a practical and economical way of providing comfort in classrooms which are characterized by widely varying intensity of use.

School design involves clients and architects who are likely to be predisposed to issues of energy and the environment, at least in their practical aspects. Successive programmes of school design around the world, including the Rudolph Steiner and Hampshire County Council schools in the UK, are testimony to this understanding.

The development of the low-energy office appears to be a largely British initiative. At the same time that Norman Foster and Richard Rogers were preparing landmark designs for, respectively, the Hong Kong and Shanghai Bank and Lloyds of London, two other British practices were preparing office schemes that would set the future direction for environmentally sound office design. The first, by Arup Associates, was prepared for the paper manufacturers Wiggins Teape at Basingstoke and is now known as Gateway Two. Begun in 1981, this was the first large office building to incorporate a central

<14

^
15

12> Nicholas House, Mount Irvine, New South Wales, Australia (1977–80) by Glenn Murcutt.

13> The atrium of Gateway Two, Basingstoke, UK (1983) by Arup Associates.

14> ING-Bank headquarters, Amsterdam, The Netherlands (1987) by Ton Alberts and M. van Huut.

15> National Farmers Union Mutual and Avon Insurance head office, Stratford-upon-Avon, UK (1984) by Robert Matthew, Johnson-Marshall and Partners (RMJM).

'free running' atrium – one allowing air to pass through the surrounding offices and out through its roof, thus mediating between internal and external conditions. As the designs progressed, the atrium became a key element in maintaining comfort in the building. It also provided a space right at the building's heart which was neither external, like a courtyard (and therefore limited in its use) nor standard internal office space. It played havoc with the development agents' gross to net lettable space calculations, but it did have particular qualities aside from its low-energy functions that appealed to the occupier and which partly account for the central atrium having become the *sine qua non* of contemporary bioclimatic office buildings. It provided a central, building-height volume on which the surrounding office space could focus. Here it was possible to locate in a dramatic way many of the functions needed to support the work space: the reception, meeting areas, main circulation spaces (including lifts), restaurant and so on. It also provided a corporate focus, transforming the stratified arrangement of stacked and tenuously connected floors into an arena where the occupants were aware of every part of the building and could see people coming and going in the atrium.

Gateway Two was one of the first buildings to break with the concept of the 'deep plan floor plate'. In the 1960s and early 1970s the concept of Bureaulandschaft (office landscape) prevailed: deep space which ostensibly allowed a more egalitarian regime and greater flexibility of layout. It also required the space to be air-conditioned which in turn meant that the windows had to be sealed. Arup questioned this approach on social, operational and environmental grounds.

The other seminal UK office building of the period was the head office for the National Farmers Union Mutual and Avon Insurance (NFUM+AI) at Stratford-upon-Avon, designed by Robert Matthew, Johnson-Marshall and Partners (RMJM) and completed in 1984. The plan of this building was set out in 'ladder' form with office space of limited depth (14 metres/50 feet) enclosing a series of open courtyards with a single atrium space at the centre. It incorporated a range of measures that are now commonplace in the design of bioclimatic offices: cross-ventilation, externally fixed solar control, generous floor to ceiling heights, good daylight levels, high insulation, exposure of the building mass to even out temperature peaks, night-time ventilation, sensitive controls and knowledgeable building management. What is more, this was achieved within a singular architectural aesthetic. There was nothing of the ungainliness of most prototype buildings. Whereas Gateway Two's architectural vocabulary was neutral Modernism, the NFUM+AI building, entirely constructed of limestone, presented itself uncompromisingly in the clothes of stripped-down humanist Classicism, redolent of the aristocratic country seats so liberally located in the surrounding shires. The NFUM+AI headquarters and Gateway Two had an enormous influence on the subsequent development of bioclimatic office designs.

Individual buildings in Europe were also influential – Hertzberger's Centraal Beheer building at Apeldoorn took reaction to deep plan to an extreme, dividing the floor plate into cruciforms with the building fabric defining to a considerable extent the organization's work groups. In the late 1980s Niels Torp's SAS building near Stockholm, which introduced the idea of the atrium 'street', and Ton Albert's NMB (now ING) Bank headquarters in Amsterdam, which picked up on the precepts of Rudolf Steiner's anthroposophy – further developed, in more idiosyncratic ways, approaches to sustainable design in offices. Taken together, these five buildings encapsulated a strategy for energy conservation and environmental awareness in office design. They also established an approach to healthier and more stimulating work practice.

This chapter has pursued the historical relationship between architecture and nature, viewing this within the context of our current energy and environmental predicament. It has traced the recent evolution of this relationship through intuitive, organic, pragmatic and technological perspectives, and examined the bioclimatic evolution of the house, the school and the office. It is now time to take a detailed look at some contemporary buildings which have a distinctive and harmonious relationship with nature.

59

CHAPTER 04

Contemporary Buildings

60

Every effort was made to obtain full technical data for the projects included in the following pages, but in some cases information was not available. The following abbreviations are used in the data boxes:

N/S > information not supplied
N/A > not applicable

This section illustrates 44 recently completed buildings from around the world which have, as a central creative impulse, a clear and considered response to the natural environment. Buildings having a relationship with nature might be expected to be set within some sort of tranquil arcadia. The buildings illustrated in the following pages, however, are located in every type of setting: cities, suburbs and the countryside.

The selection is catholic. It covers both the didactic and the poetic, the rational and the romantic. Demonstrable energy efficiency and overt environmental credentials were not the overriding criteria for inclusion. The critical attribute was a positive and inspirational response to local setting and global welfare. Included, therefore, are buildings based on a clear environmental agenda, some of which have literally accumulated points against a list of measures incorporated within government-sponsored environmental rating systems. There are others whose response to the environment is essentially intuitive; designed by architects who could not design any other way, and who do not feel the need of energy targets, computer modelling, building energy management systems and performance monitoring. And there are also many buildings whose approach to nature and the environment falls somewhere between the two.

Viewed objectively, the various ecosystems that sustain life on Earth function independently of human agencies, just as they did before the ascendancy of *Homo sapiens*. The corollary to this is that all such natural systems have, for better or worse, been substantially modified by human culture. This process has been taking place since man first became settled. Until very recently the evolution of raw nature into landscape had been essentially benign and, to our civilized eye, often picturesque. Man's mythologizing – the river of life, the sacred mountain and the primeval forest – has had as much effect on our cultural perception of nature as have the transformations brought about by elemental forces, marauding animals and the ravages of blight and insect infestation on its appearance. It is this universally modified world that is all the nature we have.

Buildings, therefore, whether located in the countryside or the city, are in settings that are equally artificial – or un-natural – the difference between the two being that cities are dominated by buildings, whereas the countryside is dominated by vegetation. Wherever it is located, an inspirationally designed building will generate a charge between its setting and itself, and, in so doing, illuminate both its physical presence and its wider, cultural context. It is this physical and cultural anchoring that allows an urban building, just as much as a rural building, to have a relationship with nature.

The collection of buildings in the following pages illustrates the point made in Chapter One about the stylistic heterogeneity of bioclimatic buildings. An environmentally aware building brief does not, in itself, seem to generate a common aesthetic or a singular architectural language. The Japanese museums featured, for example, have a very

01 > Tokyo Gas 'Earth Port'
Yokohama, Japan (see page 66).

02 > Museum of Wood
Mikata-gun, Hyogo, Japan (see page 174).

direct sense of dealing with nature, but this may emanate as much from their programmatic content – the elucidation and display of sea-folk life, of ice and snow or of wood – as from any measures they might incorporate in their design to mitigate environmental depredation. On the other hand, the designs for many of the office buildings, which do not generally have the diversity of use and operation to allow for much modulation of form or expressive variety, proudly flaunt the accoutrements of energy conservation in the form of external solar shading, wind towers, glazed atria and the like. More complex buildings are designed on the basis of an extremely rigorous energy strategy, though nothing in their appearance hints at this approach. The Elizabeth Fry Building at the University of East Anglia, for example, presents itself as a well-mannered exercise in manipulating the universal architectural verities of form, space and light, eschewing any expression of the measures adopted to make it one of the lowest energy users of its type.

For want of any other categorization, therefore, I have divided the buildings into six generic types which relate purely to size, form and layout. With the exception of Houses, the categories do not relate to the use to which the building is put; neither do they differentiate in any way between issues of style or expression. The categories are: Mansions (large and complex single buildings); Houses (individual residences set in their own grounds); Campuses (compositions of physically or visually linked buildings); Pavilions (isolated low buildings); Metropolis (building complexes set within a city and contributing to the quality of that city); and Towers (isolated buildings whose heights are considerably greater than their depths or widths).

The architects of each building were asked to supply a description, specific technical information, photographs and drawings. The workings of bioclimatic buildings are varied; they are sometimes visually suppressed and often complex. Because of this, we felt it important to back up the photographs with data and drawings where they were available. Sections through the buildings are usually particularly revealing.

The photographs of the buildings are, without exception, carefully composed abstractions showing them in their pristine, newly finished (and occasionally pre-finished) state. These shots are generally a record of the building, more or less as the architect conceived it, at the point of handover to the client. What the owner does next with it is out of the architect's control and what succeeding generations do, he is unlikely even to witness. A quick scan through albums in architectural libraries show the extent to which buildings do change. Successive generations repaint, alter, extend and demolish to suit their needs and, often, those of fashion. The way buildings are reinvented over time is very much a concern of bioclimatic architecture. What we are witnessing here is their birth. Perhaps, in time, their adolescence, their maturity and their old age will also be witnessed and an assessment made of their qualities of endurance.

'The Gods in peace their golden Mansions fill
Rang'd in bright Order on th'Olympian Hill'

(Alexander Pope, *Iliad*, IX.103)

Complex societies demand complicated buildings. All over the world, settings have been created for the complexities of ceremony and religion. Some are well documented: the Temple in Jerusalem and the Great Palace in Constantinople, for instance. But it is the more functional public buildings of Ancient Rome, the huge markets, baths and theatres, in the city itself and scattered across its empire, that have most relevance today. Contemporary mansions – government offices, arts centres, company headquarters – raise the same challenges of ensuring architectural coherence and operational efficacy.

Ruins of the Baths of
Caracalla, Rome
(AD212–16).

NAME OF BUILDING
Tokyo Gas 'Earth Port'

Client/owner
Tokyo Gas Urban
Development Co. Ltd

Occupier
Tokyo Gas Co. Ltd

Location
Yokohama, Japan

Architect
Nikken Sekkei

Date completed
May 1996

Gross area
5,634m²

Construction cost
£9 million

Climatic zone
Temperate

BUILDING ENERGY FEATURES

Orientation of main façades
North and south

Natural ventilation: Approx. percentage of gross floor naturally ventilated
58%

Night-time ventilation provision
Natural

Thermal transmission of building envelope
0.33 W/m²°C

Utilization of building mass thermal storage as part of energy strategy?
No

Solar control systems
Fixed external and internal blinds

Daylighting Approx. percentage of net floor area needing artificial lighting during daylight hours
58%

Energy-saving controls for artificial lighting?
Yes

Other
–

HVAC SYSTEMS

Fuel/approx. % use
Natural gas 100%

Boiler type
Gas absorption type chiller and boiler

Heating system
All air (VAV)

Mechanical ventilation
–

Air conditioning type
All air (VAV)

Heat recovery
–

ENERGY PERFORMANCE

Total
19kW/h/m² (July)

Artificial lighting
2kW/h/m² (July)

Refrigeration cooling
14kW/h/m² (July)

Mechanical ventilation
3kW/h/m² (July)

Heating
–

Total estimated carbon dioxide output
N/S

ENVIRONMENTAL/HEALTH FEATURES

Materials/components selection strategy to reduce embodied and transport energy?
No

Use of recycled materials
Recycled concrete block, paper and brick

Use of timbers from managed sources
–

Special water conserving installation
Waste water and rainwater treatment system

Natural organic sewage treatment
No

Measures to encourage use of public transport
No

Tokyo Gas 'Earth Port'
Yokohama, Japan

The headquarters of Tokyo Gas Co. Ltd was designed to demonstrate the principles of energy efficiency and the company's commitment to the protection of the environment. The office space is located on three 15-metre (49-foot) deep floors. The site is restricted, so supporting facilities and car parking are accommodated in a two-level semi-sunken plinth to the building. Key to the energy strategy is the concept of an 'ecological core' incorporating a north-facing atrium along the building's length. This is used for primary circulation and for display of the company's products.

The office space is ventilated by exploiting the stack effect caused by warm air rising in the atrium. The atrium draws air from outside into its base and thence through the office floors which open on to it. (The offices themselves are separated from the atrium by a walkway and a three-quarter height semi-translucent glazed screen.) Air is expelled via wind towers located at roof level and via high-level louvres. Support space, such as conference facilities, in the plinth are air conditioned.

Daylight reaches the office space either via the atrium or from the ribbon glazing on the south side. External horizontal sun breakers also act as daylight shelves; these are located about 1.25 metres (4 feet) from the head of the window. The opening lights are situated above the sun breakers and incorporate diffuse glazing to reduce the effects of glare.

The upper light of the window is partially protected from solar gains by extending the

floor slab about 600mm (24 inches) beyond the façade. This projection is also used for window cleaning. The ceilings of the offices slope slightly towards the centre of the office space to maximize the effect of the daylight.

The atrium glazing is supported by giant curved laminated timber beams. The glazing comprises fixed sealed units with a low-emissivity outer skin. No solar control has been provided since, unusually for this type of building, it faces north.

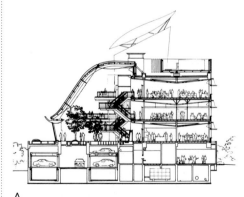

01

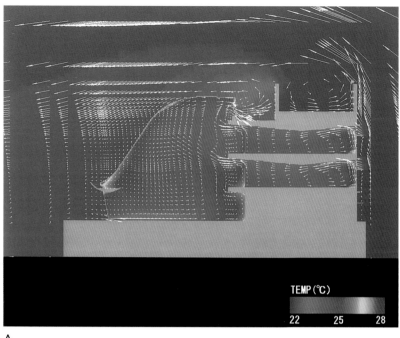

01> Section showing the three floors of office space, the contiguous atrium and the car parking and support facilities in the building plinth.

02> A computational fluid dynamic (CFD) plot through the building section showing predicted temperatures and air flow.

03> A view of the north façade. The atrium of this building is unusually placed to the north side. This mitigates the problems of heat gain, but reduces its ability to benefit from warmth provided by winter sunshine.

TEMP (℃)

22   25   28

^
03

Mansions / Tokyo Gas 'Earth Port'

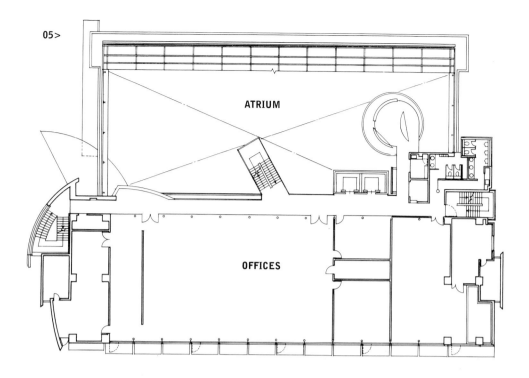

ATRIUM

OFFICES

04> The atrium has a laminated timber support structure. It is used as a circulation and display space.

05> First-floor plan. A glazed screen is located between the offices and the atrium, but air is allowed to flow above it.

06> The windows on the south façade are partially protected from the sun by projecting shelves. The upper windows provide cross-ventilation and are automated.

^06

NAME OF BUILDING
John Menzies Headquarters

Client/owner
John Menzies Wholesale

Occupier
John Menzies Wholesale

Location
Edinburgh, Scotland

Architect
Bennetts Associates

Date completed
1995

Gross area
4,800m²

Construction cost
N/S

Climatic zone
Temperate

BUILDING ENERGY FEATURES

Orientation of main façades
West, north-east, south-west

Natural ventilation: Approx. percentage of gross floor naturally ventilated
0%

Night-time ventilation provision
Forced

Thermal transmission of building envelope
Above standard

Utilization of building mass thermal storage as part of energy strategy?
Yes

Solar control systems
Mid-pane blinds

Daylighting Approx. percentage of net floor area needing artificial lighting during daylight hours
0%

Energy-saving controls for artificial lighting?
–

Other
–

HVAC SYSTEMS

Fuel/approx. % use
N/S

Boiler type
N/S

Heating system
Perimeter radiators

Mechanical ventilation
Deplacement

Air conditioning type
Fan coil units in cellular offices

Heat recovery
–

ENERGY PERFORMANCE

Total
N/S

Artificial lighting
N/S

Refrigeration cooling
N/S

Mechanical ventilation
N/S

Heating
N/S

Total estimated carbon dioxide output
N/S

ENVIRONMENTAL/HEALTH FEATURES

Materials/components selection strategy to reduce embodied and transport energy?
No

Use of recycled materials
No

Use of timbers from managed sources
No

Special water conserving installation
No

Natural organic sewage treatment
No

Measures to encourage use of public transport
No

John Menzies Headquarters
Edinburgh, Scotland

The John Menzies Headquarters houses the wholesale section of the Scottish retail and distribution company, which supplies magazines and newspapers to retailers throughout the UK. The building is located on the Edinburgh Park business estate, designed to a master plan by Richard Meier and landscaped by Ian White Associates. It is situated on the outskirts of Edinburgh, which has a cool temperate climate with cold winters – often with high wind speeds – and cool summers. Within Meier's rectangular grid the building faces east overlooking a lochan (small lake) and is separated from the main access road by car parking.

The headquarters reflects current thinking in the UK on low-energy office buildings, duly adapted for the northerly location. The design follows closely on from Bennetts Associates' influential head office for the electricity supply company, PowerGen. The building is arranged around four sides of an atrium, providing a mixture of cellular and open-plan office space on three sides. The east side, with meeting rooms and a restaurant overlooking the water, is shallow and transparent, allowing office occupants views of the landscape. Service cores are located to the west, giving a buffer against road noise. The office floor plate of 12 metres (40 feet), together with the partially glazed atrium, allows natural daylight to reach all spaces.

The structural system of a pre-cast elliptically coffered floor with exposed soffit, within an in-situ concrete frame, is fully integrated with the mechanical services. Together they provide cooling through exposed thermal mass and a mixed-mode system of ventilation, as well as recesses for light cabling and luminaires. Windows have low-emissivity double glazing and mid-pane blinds, and can be opened for additional comfort control in mid-summer. The Scottish climate and the high degree of cellularization required by the client preclude full reliance on natural ventilation. Thus in normal operating mode the windows are closed and a raised floor plenum supplies air through swirl grilles which exhaust air either through the atrium or, in the case of cellular offices, through service ducts in the ceiling by a process of displacement. Air conditioning is provided for the meeting rooms.

The façade comprises largely curtain-wall glazing on the east, with granite cladding panels elsewhere, as an externally insulated rain screen cladding system.

This building is a sleek addition to the growing numbers of low-energy atrium-focused office buildings in the UK.

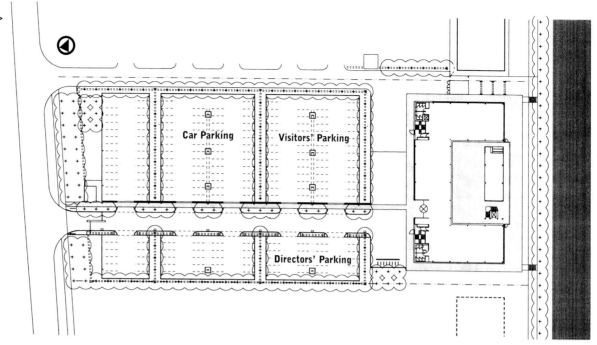

Car Parking

Visitors' Parking

Directors' Parking

01> Site plan showing the lochan to the north-east and the access road to the south-west.

02> The façade seen over the lochan.

^
02

Mansions / John Menzies Headquarters

03 > North-south section through the atrium.

04 > The south-facing meeting rooms seen from the atrium.

05 > The offices are open to the atrium. Supplementary fresh air ventilation is provided via a floor plenum to all areas, with extract in the atrium.

03 >

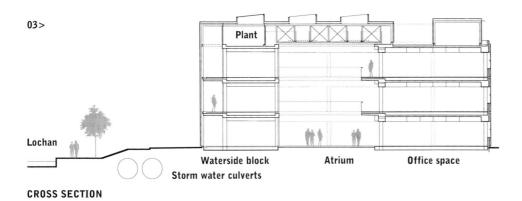

Plant

Lochan

Waterside block   Atrium   Office space

Storm water culverts

CROSS SECTION

< 04

Chapter Four / Architecture and the Environment

Mansions / John Menzies Headquarters

NAME OF BUILDING
J. Walter Thompson Headquarters

Client/owner
Michael Loulakis, Frankfurt

Occupier
J. Walter Thompson

Location
Frankfurt, Germany

Architect
Schneider & Schumacher

Date completed
November 1995

Gross area
5,915m²

Construction cost
£8 million

Climatic zone
Continental

BUILDING ENERGY FEATURES

Orientation of main façades
North and south

Natural ventilation: Approx. percentage of gross floor naturally ventilated
50%

Night-time ventilation provision
Forced

Thermal transmission of building envelope
Standard

Utilization of building mass thermal storage as part of energy strategy?
Yes

Solar control systems
Solar control glazing and external shading devices

Daylighting Approx. percentage of net floor area needing artificial lighting during daylight hours
N/S

Energy-saving controls for artificial lighting?
N/S

Other
–

HVAC SYSTEMS

Fuel/approx. % use
Mains electricity 66%; natural gas 34%

Boiler type
Modular natural gas-fired

Heating system
Central hot water system

Mechanical ventilation
Displacement ventilation

Air conditioning type
Small decentral system (conference room only)

Heat recovery
No

ENERGY PERFORMANCE

Total
N/S

Artificial lighting
N/S

Refrigeration cooling
N/S

Mechanical ventilation
N/S

Heating
N/S

Total estimated carbon dioxide output
N/S

ENVIRONMENTAL/HEALTH FEATURES

Materials/components selection strategy to reduce embodied and transport energy?
No

Use of recycled materials
No

Use of timbers from managed sources
No

Special water conserving installation
No

Natural organic sewage treatment
No

Measures to encourage use of public transport
No

J. Walter Thompson Headquarters
Frankfurt, Germany

This advertising agency headquarters is located at the northern end of a projected green belt in the east of Frankfurt. A busy main road runs parallel to the building on its north side, while to the south are docks. The building is entered through a small reception block containing an advertising museum, set at right-angles to the main building.

The north elevation is designed to resemble a giant shop window. A roof-hung glazed façade extending over all six storeys reveals the building's structure, its methods of access and the people working within. Behind the glass wall runs a six-storey staircase; two elevators are also visible. This clarity and openness has in part been designed to counter the generally accepted notion that large corporations are opaque and lack a broader vision.

The north façade with its contained access space acts as both a thermal and acoustic buffer, shielding the interior from the noise of the road and minimizing energy loss. Being north-facing there is no danger of overheating, while the south façade employs heat-reflecting glass to counter this problem. Cantilevered balconies also help, and offer pleasant views over the nearby docks.

To conserve heat, exposed concrete ceilings have been used to act as heat stores, while controlled ventilation optimizes the energy balance. Fresh air is supplied to the office areas by means of a raised floor system, which also houses computer and telecommunications cables. As the used air is sucked upwards out of the room, heat is transferred to incoming fresh air. The cellular offices on the quieter south side can be ventilated by the use of windows.

At present the building is gas-powered, but the design allows for the future integration of solar energy. Roof terraces, conference rooms and a cafeteria are located on the roof, whose trapezoid shape reflects its load-bearing function.

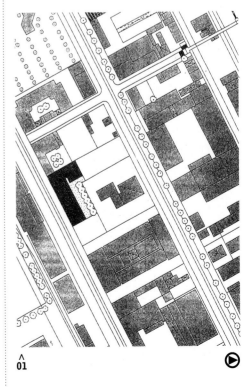

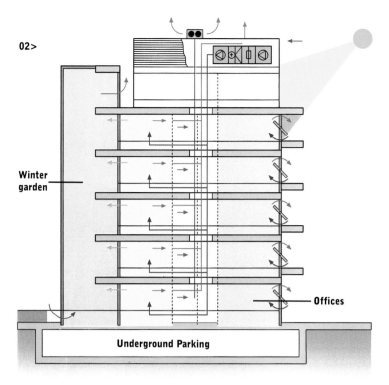

02>

Winter garden

Offices

Underground Parking

01> Site plan. The office block is located in the old dockland area on the east of the city, facing the busy Hanauer Landstrasse.

02> Section. The winter garden on the north side (left), behind a roof-hung façade of insulating glass, acts as a thermal and acoustic buffer. A small air-conditioning plant is provided for the central conference area, but the offices on either side are naturally ventilated.

03> The south façade is also glazed, but with windows that can be opened to provide natural ventilation for the offices behind. Long balconies on every storey offer views across the old docks.

^
03

Mansions / J. Walter Thompson Headquarters

^
04

05
v

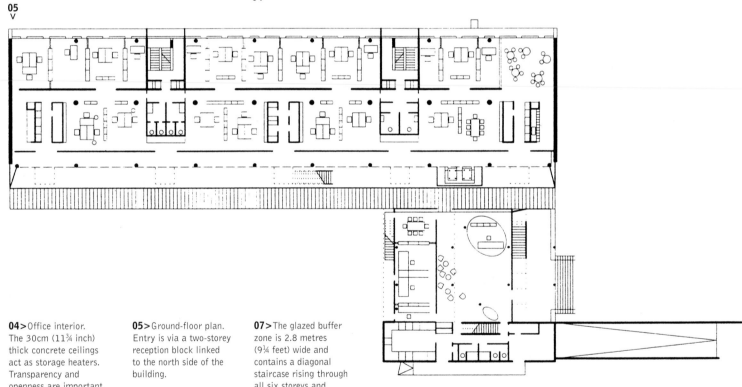

04> Office interior. The 30cm (11¾ inch) thick concrete ceilings act as storage heaters. Transparency and openness are important features of the building. Each floor has balconies projecting into the winter garden and on to the open south façade.

05> Ground-floor plan. Entry is via a two-storey reception block linked to the north side of the building.

06> View from the south-east. The tall glass front, made up of panels measuring 3.4 by 1.8 metres (11 by 6 feet) suspended on steel cables, serves not only to insulate the building behind, but also as a symbolic transparent 'shop window' appropriate for the offices of an advertising agency.

07> The glazed buffer zone is 2.8 metres (9¼ feet) wide and contains a diagonal staircase rising through all six storeys and running the whole width of the building. It is spanned by horizontal members tying the glass front to the reinforced concrete structure behind.

NAME OF BUILDING
Ionica

Client/owner
St John's College Cambridge

Occupier
Ionica

Location
Cambridge, UK

Architect
RH Partnership

Date completed
September 1994

Gross area
4,500m²

Construction cost
£6 million

Climatic zone
Temperate

BUILDING ENERGY FEATURES

Orientation of main façades
North and south

Natural ventilation: Approx. percentage of gross floor naturally ventilated
70%

Night-time ventilation provision
Natural; forced

Thermal transmission of building envelope
Above standard

Utilization of building mass thermal storage as part of energy strategy?
Yes

Solar control systems
Fixed external; internal blinds/louvres

**Daylighting
Approx. percentage of net floor area needing artificial lighting during daylight hours**
N/S

Energy-saving controls for artificial lighting?
Yes

Other
–

HVAC SYSTEMS

Fuel/approx. % use
Mains electricity 100%

Boiler type
–

Heating system
Electric

Mechanical ventilation
Displacement ventilation system

Air conditioning type
Displacement ventilation system

Heat recovery
Yes

ENERGY PERFORMANCE

Total
127kW/h/m²/y

Artificial lighting
15kW/h/m²/y

Refrigeration cooling
N/A

Mechanical ventilation
18kW/h/m²/y

Heating
35kW/h/m²/y

Total estimated carbon dioxide output
95kg/m²/y

ENVIRONMENTAL/HEALTH FEATURES

Materials/components selection strategy to reduce embodied and transport energy?
–

Use of recycled materials
No

Use of timbers from managed sources
Yes

Special water conserving installation
Standard

Natural organic sewage treatment
No

Measures to encourage use of public transport
No

Ionica
Cambridge, UK

This building provides head-office facilities for a telecommunications company. It is on three floors and symmetrical in plan, incorporating at its centre a small atrium or, more accurately, a large lightwell. It relies on a 'mixed mode' strategy for creating energy-efficient comfort, combining natural ventilation with a mechanical, peak-lopping system.

Natural ventilation is driven by the stack effect of the atrium and is assisted by six wind towers located in a line immediately above it. The mechanical system comprises displacement ventilation delivered through the floor slab. Apart from a limited area of bulkheads, no suspended ceilings have been installed, allowing good connection between the air in the office space and the mass of the floor slabs. This provision, together with that of passing air through the slab by mechanical means, enables the structure to be used as a thermal flywheel, taking up heat during the day and releasing it when it is cooler at night. Acoustic panels are integrated into the light fittings to compensate for the lack of suspended ceilings. Outside air is used when temperatures are suitable but, at other times, the air is artificially cooled or heated as required. A heat-reclaim plant has also been installed adjacent to wind towers. This allows heat to be transferred from hot, stale air to incoming fresh air.

The south-facing windows are heavily shaded with horizontal external louvres, giving this façade a horizontal emphasis and a distinctly nautical feel. The convex north façade, which faces a motorway, is more austere being composed of hole-in-the-wall brickwork.

This is one of a series of recent British office developments that provide humane and responsive interiors through the agency of energy-conservation measures, and are based on a profound reaction against the socially debilitating and operationally questionable deep-plan, air-conditioned offices of the 1960s and 1970s.

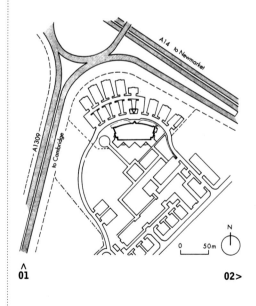

^
01

02>

01> Site plan. The short axis of the building is orientated north/south so as to minimize the need for windows facing east and west which are more vulnerable to low morning and evening sun.

02> The heavily screened south façade with its overhanging cornice element.

Key

1 Raised planting bed
2 Meeting room
3 Plant
4 Entrance hall
5 Office
6 Open-plan office

03>

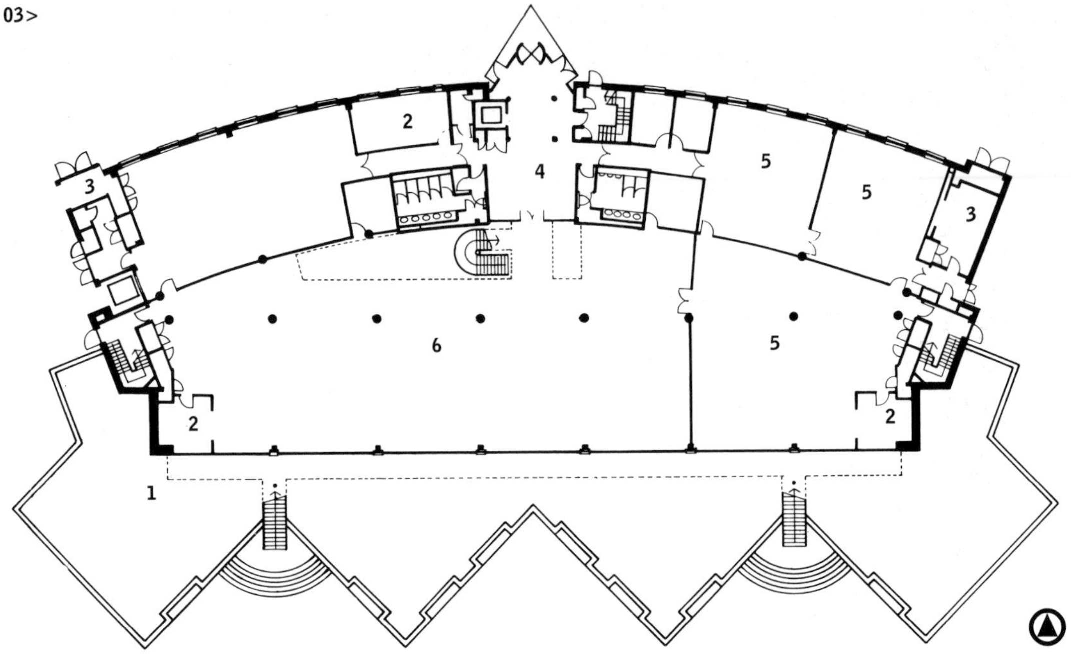

^
04

<05

03> Ground-floor plan. The central main entrance is on the north façade, with terracing to the south. The relatively small atrium is marked with a dotted line.

04> View from the south-east showing the six wind towers.

05> The atrium seen from the open office space.

06> Cutaway isometric of the roof and one of the wind towers through which warm air is expelled in summer. Considerable care was taken in its design to ensure that it would operate effectively in all wind conditions.

06>

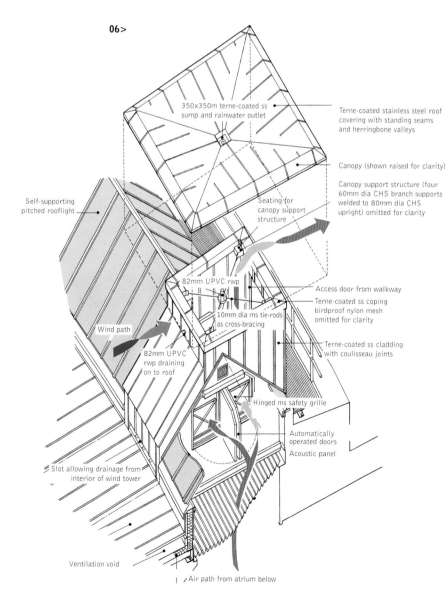

350x350m terne-coated ss sump and rainwater outlet

Terne-coated stainless steel roof covering with standing seams and herringbone valleys

Canopy (shown raised for clarity)

Canopy support structure (four 60mm dia CHS branch supports welded to 80mm dia CHS upright) omitted for clarity

Self-supporting pitched rooflight

Seating for canopy support structure

82mm UPVC rwp

Access door from walkway

Terne-coated ss coping birdproof nylon mesh omitted for clarity

10mm dia ms tie-rods as cross-bracing

Wind path

Terne-coated ss cladding with coulisseau joints

82mm UPVC rwp draining on to roof

Hinged ms safety grille

Automatically operated doors

Acoustic panel

Slot allowing drainage from interior of wind tower

Ventilation void

Air path from atrium below

Mansions / Ionica

NAME OF BUILDING
Advanced Photovoltaic Systems (APS) Manufacturing Facility

Client/owner
EJC Inc.

Date completed
1993

Occupier
BP Solar Inc.

Gross area
6,500m²

Location
Fairfield, California, USA

Construction cost
£8.5 million

Architect
Kiss and Cathcart

Climatic zone
Mediterranean

BUILDING ENERGY FEATURES

Orientation of main façades
North and south

Utilization of building mass thermal storage as part of energy strategy?
No

Natural ventilation: Approx. percentage of gross floor naturally ventilated
0% (convective ventilation of the PV curtain wall cavity)

Solar control systems
Fixed external; internal blinds/louvres

Daylighting Approx. percentage of net floor area needing artificial lighting during daylight hours
N/S

Night-time ventilation provision
Forced

Thermal transmission of building envelope
Standard

Energy-saving controls for artificial lighting?
No

Other
–

HVAC SYSTEMS

Fuel/approx. % use
Mains electricity

Mechanical ventilation
–

Boiler type
Gas-fired

Air conditioning type
Chilled water loop and fan coil units

Heating system
Gas-fired hot water

Heat recovery
–

ENERGY PERFORMANCE

Total
120.6kW/h/m² per year

Heating
N/S

Artificial lighting
15.8kW/h/m² per year

Total estimated carbon dioxide output
N/S

Refrigeration cooling
83.4kW/h/m² per year

Mechanical ventilation
21.4kW/h/m² per year

ENVIRONMENTAL/HEALTH FEATURES

Materials/components selection strategy to reduce embodied and transport energy?
No

Special water conserving installation
No

Use of recycled materials
No

Natural organic sewage treatment
No

Use of timbers from managed sources
No

Measures to encourage use of public transport
No

Advanced Photovoltaic Systems (APS) Manufacturing Facility
Fairfield, California, USA

The APS Manufacturing Facility in Fairfield, California houses a facility for the production of the first of a new generation of solar-electric modules. The building was designed not only to produce photovoltaic modules but also as a prototype for the integration of photovoltaic systems into building construction. Above the main entrance is a 'solar cube' housing production control and visitors' facilities. Embedded in the concrete and stainless steel structure of the production hall, the cube is self-sufficient in energy: photovoltaic modules incorporated in its curtain wall and skylight, and in the awning running along the south façade, produce sufficient power for all of the cube's cooling and lighting loads.

The production hall houses a flow line process, utilizing advanced robotics to produce 186,000 square metres (610,000 square feet) of thin-film PV modules each year. While the main structure makes little concession to energy and environmental issues, the building services employ energy-conserving measures where possible. One approach has been to provide systems flexibility on a zone-by-zone basis. Energy is saved by placing ducts, diffusers and vents along a central spine which can then condition individual areas as required. Jet diffusers can be adjusted to direct cooling air to occupied areas on the floor, while unoccupied areas and the hall's upper spaces are allowed to rise in temperature. Roof vents located above the tin oxide and silicon deposition ovens allow convective heat to escape in the summer, reducing the load of the chillers and, thus, conserving energy.

The dry climate of Fairfield is ideal for energy-saving and pollution-free evaporative cooling. The cooling system uses APS's cooling towers as the source of process cooling, minimizing the use of chillers and, thereby, making further energy savings.

^
01

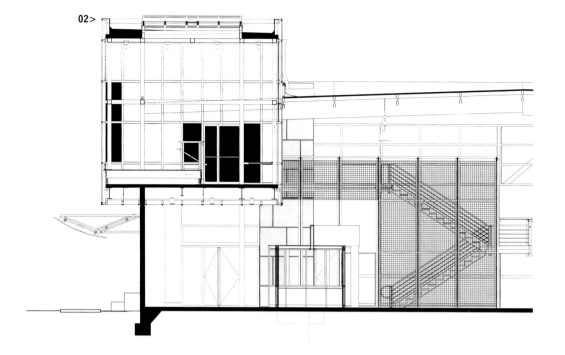

01> The 'solar cube' is adjacent to the main entrance. Photovoltaic modules are incorporated in the curtain walling and in the canopy (also on the roof).

02> Section through the 'solar cube'.

03> The entrance door with the staircase that gives access to the 'solar cube'.

^
03

NAME OF BUILDING
Library and Cultural Centre

Client/owner Town of Herten	**Date completed** September 1994
Occupier N/S	**Gross area** 4,610m²
Location Herten, Germany	**Construction cost** £9.8 million
Architect LOG ID, Dieter Schempp	**Climatic zone** Temperate

BUILDING ENERGY FEATURES

Orientation of main façades
South-east

Natural ventilation: Approx. percentage of gross floor naturally ventilated
100%

Night-time ventilation provision
Natural

Thermal transmission of building envelope
Walls: 0.35 W/m²°C;
glazing: 1.3 W/m²°C;
roof: 0.30 W/m²°C;
floor: 0.21 W/m²°C

Utilization of building mass thermal storage as part of energy strategy?
Yes

Solar control systems
Shading by plants

Daylighting Approx. percentage of net floor area needing artificial lighting during daylight hours
Library 50%;
glasshouse 0%

Energy-saving controls for artificial lighting?
None

Other
–

HVAC SYSTEMS

Fuel/approx. % use
Indirect solar 40%

Boiler type
N/A

Heating system
Air heating by absorber roof and district heating from power station

Mechanical ventilation
Yes (in library)

Air conditioning type
None

Heat recovery
Yes

ENERGY PERFORMANCE

Total
N/S

Artificial lighting
N/S

Refrigeration cooling
N/S

Mechanical ventilation
N/S

Heating
N/S

Total estimated carbon dioxide output
N/S

ENVIRONMENTAL/HEALTH FEATURES

Materials/components selection strategy to reduce embodied and transport energy?
Use of natural materials

Use of recycled materials
N/S

Use of timbers from managed sources
N/S

Special water conserving installation
N/S

Natural organic sewage treatment
N/S

Measures to encourage use of public transport
Situated in pedestrian zone

Library and Cultural Centre
Herten, Germany

This public building comprises two interconnected elements: a four-storey public library, and a cultural centre in the form of a glazed rotunda rising through four storeys. Library and cultural centre share the same entrance foyer on the building's north-west side. Balconies open from the library into the cultural centre rotunda and can be used by the audience when performances are held there. On the west side of the rotunda is a café facing a small circular public space, with glass walls that can be opened up in summer.

This project, situated in the built-up centre of a small Ruhr town, called for new solutions from its architects. The innovative architectural practice behind it specializes in exploiting the potential of passive solar energy and green vegetation.

To make optimal use of sunlight a large zig-zag glass roof spans the entire building. Beneath it are solar collectors for heating domestic hot water and air. The heated air is used to warm the library and glass rotunda. This can then be supplemented by district heating (waste heat from a power station) when exterior temperatures are too low. The concrete mass of the walls and ceilings of the library absorbs heat and keeps the interior at an even temperature. The roof of the cultural centre can be opened on hot days, creating a thermal chimney to cool the space below.

Subtropical plants are planted on the balconies and in the rotunda to boost oxygen levels, as well as to provide some acoustic absorption and shade on sunny days.

∧
01

01> The north-west façade with the main entrance. The projecting elements are parts of the unusual glass roof, the building's most striking feature.

02> Sections through the building show the cylindrical glazed drum and the four-storey library. Beneath the zig-zag roof are solar collectors which heat water and air, a low-tech feature characteristic of LOG ID's buildings.

03> View from the north across the circular Jakobsplatz which echoes the cylindrical tower at the corner of the library and the glass drum of the arts centre. The massive concrete structure of the library (left) conserves heat, and contrasts with the glass and steel drum sheltering beneath the same zig-zag roof.

02>

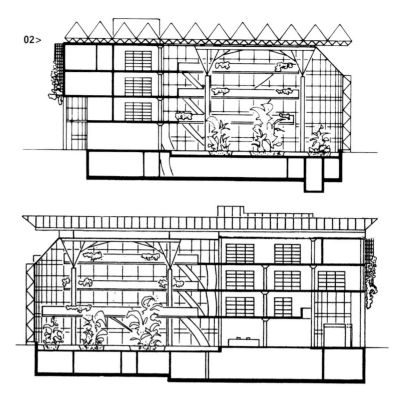

^
03

<04

04> View up the side of the glass drum to the overhanging glass roof. The glass of the drum walls has a high insulation value. The roof of the drum can be opened on hot days, creating a thermal chimney to draw out the warm air and cool the building.

05> Ground-floor plan. At first sight, the complex building, located in a built-up town centre, is not an ideal vehicle for LOG ID's solar architecture, but they have remained true to their strategies.

Key

1 Staircase
2 Reception
3 Issue desk
4 Café
5 Rotunda

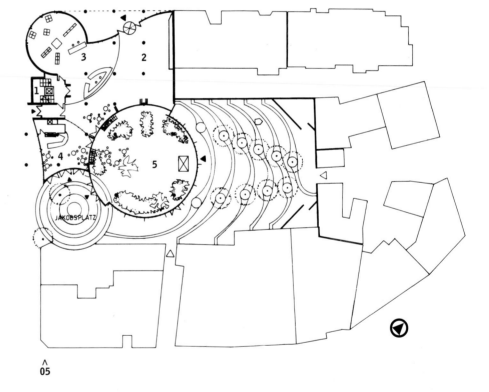

^
05

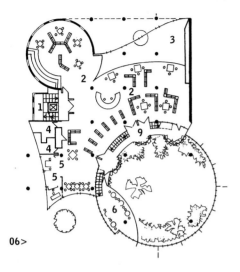
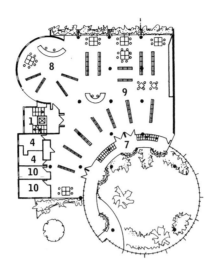
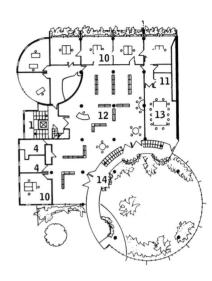

06>

07

06> Plans of the upper floors.

Key

1 Staircase
2 Children's library
3 Air space
4 WC
5 Work room
6 Gallery café
7 Library balcony
8 Audio-visual media
9 Non-fiction
10 Office
11 Kitchen
12 Fiction
13 Conference room
14 Gallery

07> The second-floor balcony overlooking the flexible space within the glass drum, which resembles a giant conservatory. Plants are an important element, not only for their appearance, but because they provide shade and raise oxygen levels in the building.

87

NAME OF BUILDING
NREL Solar Energy Research Facility

Client/owner
US Dept. of Energy

Date completed
October 1993

Occupier National Renewable
Energy Laboratory

Gross area
10,683m²

Location
Golden, Colorado, USA

Construction cost
£12 million

Architect Anderson
DeBartolo Pan, Inc. Lead
designer: Jack DeBartolo Jr

Climatic zone
Continental

BUILDING ENERGY FEATURES

**Orientation of main
façades**
South

**Natural ventilation:
Approx. percentage
of gross floor naturally
ventilated**
None

**Night-time ventilation
provision**
None

**Thermal transmission
of building envelope**
Standard

**Utilization of building
mass thermal storage as
part of energy strategy?**
Yes. Use of trombe wall.

Solar control systems
Fixed external;
motorized/variable external
(for east and west façades);
solar control glazing (south
façades)

**Daylighting
Approx. percentage
of net floor area needing
artificial lighting during
daylight hours**
50%

**Energy-saving controls
for artificial lighting?**
Yes

Other
–

HVAC SYSTEMS

Fuel/approx. % use
Mains electricity 100%;
renewable (photovoltaics)
12kW (grid connected test
installation)

Boiler type
Electric

Heating system
Exhaust air heat recovery

Air conditioning type
Offices: single duct vav,
terminal reheat system with
economizers and direct
evaporative cooling.
Laboratories: conditioned
make-up air supply,
distribution system and
constant volume terminal
control with reheat

ENERGY PERFORMANCE

Total
N/S

Heating
N/S

Artificial lighting
N/S

**Total estimated carbon
dioxide output**
N/S

Refrigeration cooling
N/S

Mechanical ventilation
N/S

ENVIRONMENTAL/HEALTH FEATURES

**Materials/components
selection strategy to
reduce embodied and
transport energy?**
No

Use of recycled materials
No

**Use of timbers from
managed sources**
No

**Special water conserving
installation**
No

**Natural organic sewage
treatment**
No

**Measures to encourage
use of public transport**
No

NREL Solar Energy Research Facility
Golden, Colorado, USA

The Solar Energy Research Facility (SERF) is a 15,000 square foot (1,394 square metre) laboratory office building for the US Department of Energy's National Renewable Energy Laoratory. Located on South Table Mountain, a high, semi-arid area in Colorado, it provides a state-of-the-art, modular and flexible facility for conducting research in photovoltaics, basic science, materials science superconductivity and photoconversion. The facility is composed of three contiguous stair-stepped modules, each containing an office pod at the front and a laboratory pod at the back. The east-west office modules reflect each other, each leaning back against its laboratory pod. The central module contains the lobby, solarium with adjoining terrace, auditorium and meeting rooms.

The office space is located across a corridor allowing close proximity between laboratories and workstations. Most of the office space is at ground level. Each office has a view to the outside and is day-lit by stepped clerestory windows which allow light to penetrate 90 feet (27.4 metres) into the space, thereby reducing lighting energy consumption on both office levels.

Laboratories are equipped with adjustable environmental controls, waffle-slab, vibration-free flooring and state-of-the-art safety features in air management, utility efficiency and materials handling. Movable walls and a flexible utility network allow laboratories to be expanded, reduced or relocated as research needs change.

A range of energy-conserving technologies are utilized in the facility, which it is estimated will save nearly $200,000 a year in operating expenses. These include a 'trombe' wall to radiate heat into the building, photo-sensitive window shades that are automatically raised or lowered according to the intensity of the sun, and an exhaust heat recovery system that extracts heat from outgoing air and uses it to preheat incoming air.

Energy savings in buildings derive in part from their day-to-day management, and in part from concern for the environment of the occupants and their understanding of the operation of the energy measures provided. The management and staff of an Energy Research Facility will clearly be particularly sensitive to these issues. Their concern to run the building efficiently, and their knowledge of how to achieve this aim, is likely to have had a significant influence on the energy savings made.

<01

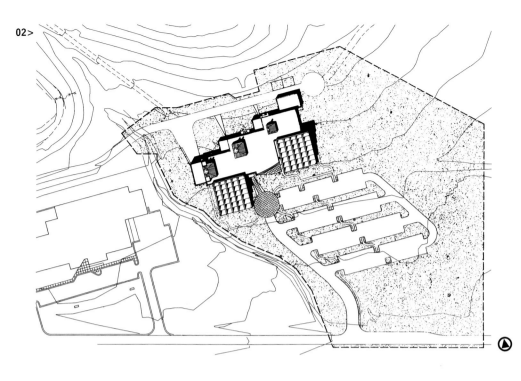

01> The double-height solarium with adjoining terrace is located between the two south-facing laboratory 'pods' and provides a pleasant meeting place for staff and visitors.

02> Site plan. The building lies along the contours of the sloping mesa.

03> The solarium with one of the two stepped laboratory 'pods' to the right.

^
03

Mansions / NREL Solar Energy Research Facility

 04

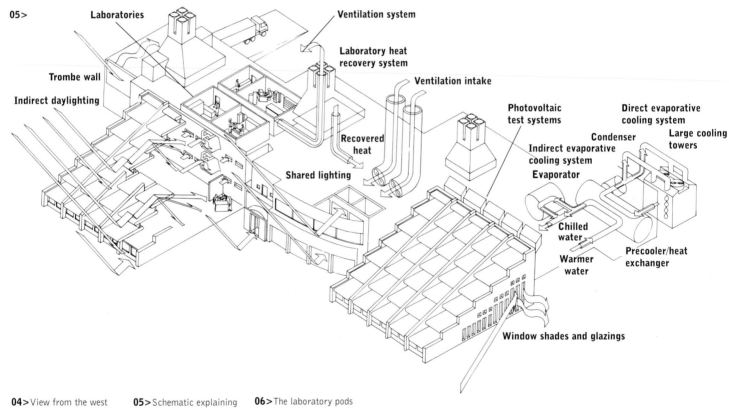

05>

Laboratories

Ventilation system

Trombe wall

Laboratory heat recovery system

Indirect daylighting

Ventilation intake

Recovered heat

Photovoltaic test systems

Direct evaporative cooling system

Condenser

Large cooling towers

Indirect evaporative cooling system

Shared lighting

Evaporator

Chilled water

Warmer water

Precooler/heat exchanger

Window shades and glazings

04> View from the west showing the fall of the land and the stepped east office pod. The laboratory building behind it is built into the hill to conserve energy.

05> Schematic explaining the energy strategy and systems for the building.

06> The laboratory pods have clerestory windows protected from direct sun by overhangs and the careful grading of the daylight. Air trees provide ventilation to each office cubicle.

NAME OF BUILDING
Matsushita Electronic

Client/owner	**Date completed**
Matsushita Electric Co. Ltd	June 1996
Occupier	**Gross area**
Matsushita Electric Co. Ltd	43,926m²
Location	**Construction cost**
Shinagawa, Japan	N/S
Architect	**Climatic zone**
Nikken Sekkei	Temperate

BUILDING ENERGY FEATURES

Orientation of main façades
East

Natural ventilation: Approx. percentage of gross floor naturally ventilated
100%

Night-time ventilation provision
Through the raised floor space and atrium

Thermal transmission of building envelope
Standard

Utilization of building mass thermal storage as part of energy strategy?
Yes

Solar control systems
Aluminium honeycomb sandwich glass in skylight windows

Daylighting Approx. percentage of net floor area needing artificial lighting during daylight hours
0% (net atrium floor area); Approx. 94% (net floor area)

Energy-saving controls for artificial lighting?
Daylight sensor controls

Other
–

HVAC SYSTEMS

Fuel/approx. % use
Mains electricity 81%; natural gas 19%

Boiler type
Steam boiler

Heating system
Underfloor air conditioning system

Mechanical ventilation
Air supply and air outlet

Air conditioning type
VAV, Floor supply, ceiling return

Heat recovery
–

ENERGY PERFORMANCE

Total
502kW/m²/y

Artificial lighting
N/S

Refrigeration cooling
N/S

Mechanical ventilation
N/S

Heating
N/S

Total estimated carbon dioxide output
200ppm

ENVIRONMENTAL/HEALTH FEATURES

Materials/components selection strategy to reduce embodied and transport energy?
Yes

Use of recycled materials
Foam insulation recycled glass panels for exterior walls

Use of timbers from managed sources
–

Special water conserving installation
Rainwater and other water using water-conserving toilet and cooling water

Natural organic sewage treatment
No

Measures to encourage use of public transport
City location

Matsushita Electronic
Shinagawa, Japan

This building is the information and communications centre for the giant Japanese corporation, Matsushita Electronic Company. Its design is based on two overriding conceptual objectives: an expressive realization of the Panasonic Matsushita credo of harmony between humanity and technology, and the creation of an efficient and versatile research centre.

Matsushita Electronic is located in a mixed industrial and residential area in Tokyo. The designers adopted a trapezoid form in order to minimize the effect of bulk, overshadowing and the acceleration of wind at ground level. The floor plates to the north and south were thus designed to step towards each other, forming an atrium of a similar trapezoid shape between them. The east end of the atrium is fully glazed, the west closed in by the lifts and core facilities. Reception spaces are located on the floor of the atrium together with an elaborate garden of sculpture and plants. The garden includes a waterfall designed both to have a soothing effect on the building's occupants and mask the noise of the ventilation.

The energy strategy is based on a mixture of natural ventilation and air conditioning and a finely tuned combination of artificial light and daylight. The design was comprehensively modelled and simulated, and the result is highly elaborate and sophisticated. Fresh air is drawn in under the windows and enters the floor via diffusers. It is extracted both through the light fittings and through the atrium. Floors can be either open to the atrium or fully or partially closed off by roller shutters.

Daylight enters the atrium through a relatively narrow space at roof level, where it passes through an arrangement of prisms and through the east façade. Reflecting mirrors are fixed along the north edge of the top light to introduce sunshine to the atrium floor in winter and to create a subdued effect of sun filtering through the foliage of the plants in summer. There are also 104 panels of circular mirrors to reflect artificial light down into the atrium. Daylight is reflected into the depth of the office space by utilizing reflectors. These are installed on deep, floor-level shelves located outside the office space created by the step-back of each floor. There is also space for planting on these shelves.

01> Ground-floor plan showing the atrium floor and the base of the two stepped office blocks that enclose it.

02> The fully glazed end wall incorporates the main entrance.

03> The stepped façade with its seismically engineered supporting structure.

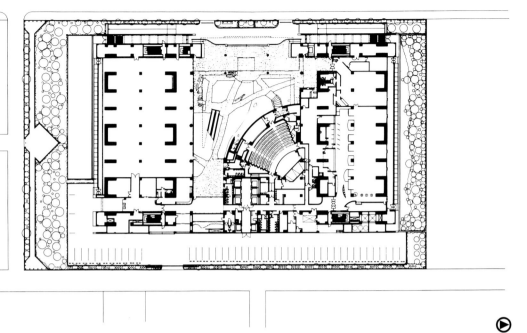

<03

Mansions / Matsushita Electronic

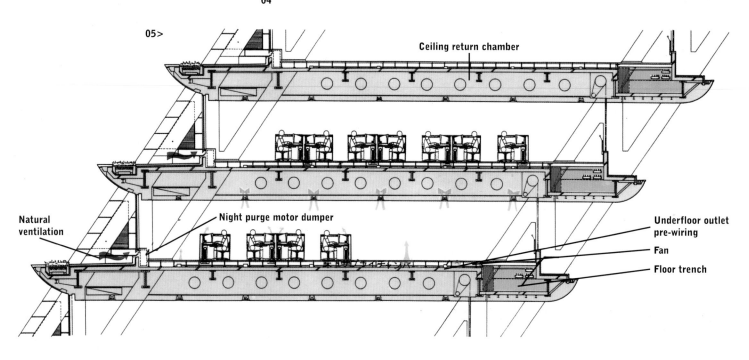

05>

Ceiling return chamber

Natural
ventilation

Night purge motor dumper

Underfloor outlet
pre-wiring

Fan

Floor trench

94

04> The atrium floor
has a striking, sculpted
quality.

05> Section through
an office floor explaining
the daylight and
ventilation strategy

06> On the inside, the
glazed atrium wall
combines solar-control
and catwalk elements.

Mansions / Matsushita Electronic

NAME OF BUILDING
Barclaycard Headquarters

Client/owner
Barclays Property Holdings Ltd; F.H.L Project Managers

Occupier
Barclaycard

Location
Northampton, UK

Architect
Fitzroy Robinson Limited

Date completed
December 1996

Gross area
37,500m²

Construction cost
£37 million (plus £5 million fit-out)

Climatic zone
Temperate

BUILDING ENERGY FEATURES

Orientation of main façades
North and south

Natural ventilation: Approx. percentage of gross floor naturally ventilated
95% (in mid-season mode)

Night-time ventilation provision
Forced

Thermal transmission of building envelope
Above standard

Utilization of building mass thermal storage as part of energy strategy?
Yes

Solar control systems
Fixed external

Daylighting Approx. percentage of net floor area needing artificial lighting during daylight hours
0%

Energy-saving controls for artificial lighting?
Yes

Other
High-frequency ballast fluorescent lighting

HVAC SYSTEMS

Fuel/approx. % use
Mains electricity; natural gas

Boiler type
Gas

Heating system
Perimeter radiators

Mechanical ventilation
Through floor troughs

Air conditioning type
Chilled beam cooled by lake water

Heat recovery
No

ENERGY PERFORMANCE

Total
N/S

Artificial lighting
N/S

Refrigeration cooling
N/S

Mechanical ventilation
N/S

Heating
N/S

Total estimated carbon dioxide output
N/S

ENVIRONMENTAL/HEALTH FEATURES

Materials/components selection strategy to reduce embodied and transport energy?
No

Use of recycled materials
Demolition materials used in hard core

Use of timbers from managed sources
Yes

Special water conserving installation
6-litre flush WC

Natural organic sewage treatment
No

Measures to encourage use of public transport
Local buses routed by site

Barclaycard Headquarters
Northampton, UK

The Barclaycard Headquarters is a leading example of contemporary British low-energy mixed-mode office building. It achieved an 'excellent' rating under the UK Building Research Establishment Environmental Analysis Method (BREEAM) which sets energy and environmental standards for new offices. The building was commissioned initially to house Barclaycard's UK staff of 2,300 (requiring a typical headquarters building with high internal heat loads from extensive use of computers), but with the additional requirement that it could subsequently be let to another occupier in three separate sections. The Headquarters is located on a business park on the outskirts of Northampton in the British Midlands, which enjoys a temperate climate with mild summers and cold winters.

The plan comprises double-banked, 15-metre (50-foot) wide open-plan office blocks, allowing natural light and ventilation, astride a 9-metre (30-foot) wide linear glazed atrium or 'street'. A large artificial lake has been constructed as a balancing pond to the north. The main façade, which looks north over the lake, is extensively glazed; the south façade comprises deeply chiselled masonry (of in-situ concrete and stone cladding) with deep window reveals and light shelves. The concrete frame, with hollow troughs for services, has exposed concrete soffits and high ceilings to allow natural cooling through the building's own thermal mass.

The building is designed to operate in three seasonal modes. In intermediate seasons, openable windows provide natural ventilation across the 15-metre (50-foot) deep office floors into the atrium. In summer, a mechanical air supply is provided via the floor void incorporating night-time purging. Further cooling is provided by chilled beams in the ceiling which are cooled by lake water. In winter, heating is provided by perimeter radiators from a gas boiler.

As well as good daylight to all areas from windows and the atrium, the artificial lighting consists of high-frequency ballasts with occupant operation and photosensors. Timber is selected from sustainable sources, and materials and surfaces selected to avoid hazardous volatile organic chemicals. Low-flush 6-litre WCs are provided. The site lies on a bus route and also provides facilities for cyclists.

This is one of a number of office buildings influenced by the headquarters for the National Farmers Union Mutual and Avon Insurance at Stratford-upon-Avon, UK, designed by RMJM in the late 1970s. They are characterized by a limited depth plan with in-board courtyards, atria or 'streets', generous floor-to-ceiling heights, high mass construction, good daylight and 'mixed-mode' energy strategy (see Chapter Three).

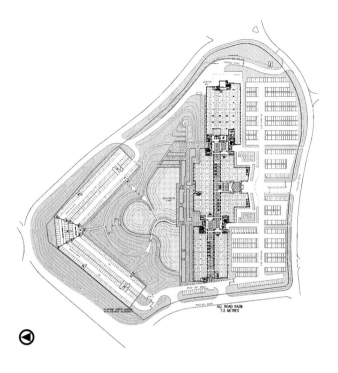

01> Site plan.

02> The south façade showing the linear and stepped layout and the hole-in-the-wall treatment of its masonry elevations.

^
02

03> The main entrance.

04> Typical cross-section showing the mixed-mode energy strategy.

05> A framed drum defines the entrance hall.

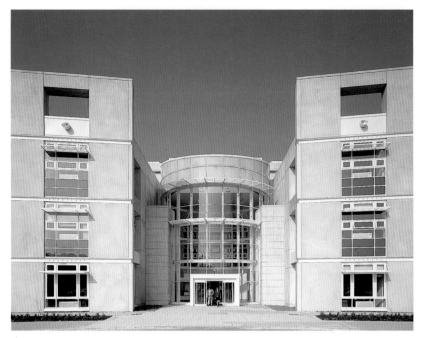

^
03

04>

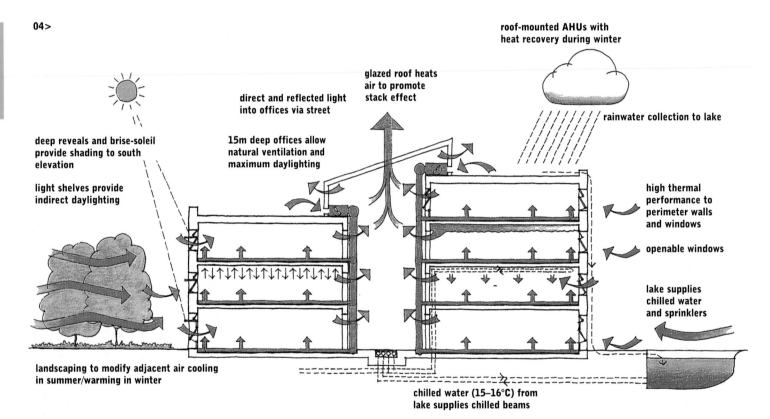

roof-mounted AHUs with heat recovery during winter

glazed roof heats air to promote stack effect

direct and reflected light into offices via street

rainwater collection to lake

deep reveals and brise-soleil provide shading to south elevation

15m deep offices allow natural ventilation and maximum daylighting

high thermal performance to perimeter walls and windows

light shelves provide indirect daylighting

openable windows

lake supplies chilled water and sprinklers

landscaping to modify adjacent air cooling in summer/warming in winter

chilled water (15–16°C) from lake supplies chilled beams

^
05

Mansions / Barclaycard Headquarters

NAME OF BUILDING
Science Park Gelsenkirchen

Client/owner
Land Nordrhein-Westfalen

Occupier
Wissenschaftspark und
Technologiezentrum
Rheinelbe Gelsenkirchen
Vermögensgesellschaft mbH

Location
Gelsenkirchen, Germany

Architect
Kiessler + Partner

Date completed 1995

Gross area 27,200m²

Construction cost
£28.6 million

Climatic zone
Temperate

BUILDING ENERGY FEATURES

Orientation of main façades
West

Natural ventilation: Approx. percentage of gross floor naturally ventilated
90%

Night-time ventilation provision
Natural

Thermal transmission of building envelope
0.81W/m²K (average)

Utilization of building mass thermal storage as part of energy strategy?
Concrete floor slabs

Solar control systems
External shading

Daylighting Approx. percentage of net floor area needing artificial lighting during daylight hours
5%

Energy-saving controls for artificial lighting?
Instabus

Other
Roof-mounted PV installation

HVAC SYSTEMS

Fuel/approx. % use
N/S

Boiler type
N/A

Heating system
District: underfloor (arcade); radiators (offices, laboratories)

Mechanical ventilation
–

Air conditioning type
'Kühldecke'

Heat recovery
No

ENERGY PERFORMANCE

Total
N/S

Artificial lighting
N/S

Refrigeration cooling
N/S

Mechanical ventilation
N/S

Heating
N/S

Total estimated carbon dioxide output
N/S

ENVIRONMENTAL/HEALTH FEATURES

Materials/components selection strategy to reduce embodied and transport energy?
No

Use of recycled materials
No

Use of timbers from managed sources
Yes

Special water conserving installation
Lake used as rainwater reservoir

Natural organic sewage treatment
No

Measures to encourage use of public transport
No

Science Park
Gelsenkirchen, Germany

This building is one of many imaginative projects initiated by the Emscher Park Internationale Bauausstellung (IBA), a ten-year programme of environmental improvements set up in 1989 by the Länder government of North-Rhine Westphalia. It forms the axis of the Rheinelbe Science Park, a centre for technological innovation established on the site of a redundant steelworks. The land has been decontaminated and landscaped with a lake, which also serves as a rainwater reservoir.

Along the east side of the building are nine pavilions for research institutes, together with access to an underground car park. On the west side is a 300-metre (980-foot) 'arcade', a public space which is planned to contain shops and cafés. The arcade occupies the three storeys of the building immediately behind a sloping glass façade, and overlooks the lake.

Efficient energy management on a tight budget was central to the development of the design. Inspiration for the arcade came from nineteenth-century garden architecture and the big spaces of industrial buildings. The 10-metre (33-foot) wide internal boulevard acts as a buffer to the building behind. The façade is glazed with Thermoplus heat-insulating glass and can be adapted to seasonal changes. In the winter the lower panels are closed, but in summer they slide upwards, like large sash windows, for ventilation and access to the lake. In summer the underfloor heating system is used to cool the interior, and use is made of the water that is warmed in the process. There is also an external awning to protect the floor of the arcade from overheating in summer.

The façades of the pavilions are constructed of simple wood and aluminium elements with heat-insulating glass and French windows. They incorporate ventilation panels for night cooling the concrete floor slabs which, accordingly, act as a thermal flywheel. The façades are fitted with automatically controlled external fabric blinds.

On the roof a huge solar energy plant – claimed to be the biggest building-integrated photovoltaic generator in the world – produces 200,000 kW annually. The building's performance is controlled by its energy management system. Lighting is automatically adjusted in accordance with external light levels, and heating switches off when the ventilation panels are opened.

These offices were built speculatively. Developers, when building for unknown occupants, will normally wish to provide for a 'fallback' air-conditioned option. In this case the developers have shown a strong commitment to green tenets by providing no such alternative.

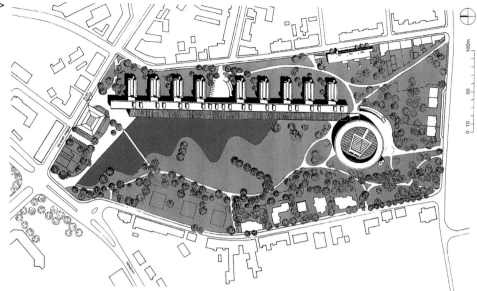

Plan of the science park laid out on the site of a redundant steelworks. The long glazed arcade, with research pavilions attached to the rear, forms the backbone of the park.

02> The winter garden arcade runs along the west front of the block and overlooks a lake. At its northern end the old courthouse will be open to the public with shops and restaurants.

Mansions / Science Park

03 > Evening view from the north-west. The roof incorporates an extensive array of photovoltaic panels.

04 > Schematic showing the ventilation strategy. The arcade acts as a thermal buffer, and the glass front can be adjusted for optimal energy conservation in different climatic conditions.

05 > The galleries overlooking the arcade are reached from the research offices in the attached pavilions.

06 > On summer days awnings are raised and blinds are drawn to reduce the solar gain through the large sloping glass façade. The lower panels are raised like sash windows to allow access to the lakeside.

Key

1 Heat-insulating glass
2 Buffer zone
3 Solar heat gain
4 Underfloor heating
5 Solar power station
6 Radiator
7 External sun protection
8 Spent air
9 Air intake
10 Arcade
11 Office

∧
03

< 04

Winter day

Summer day

Summer night

NAME OF BUILDING
Vice Chancellor's Office, Académie des Antilles et de la Guyane

Client/owner Ministère de l'Education Nationale

Occupier
University administration

Location Martinique, French West Indies

Architect
Christian Hauvette & Jérôme Nouel

Date completed
1994

Gross area
8,251m²

Construction cost
£10 million

Climatic zone
Tropical

BUILDING ENERGY FEATURES

Orientation of main façades
North and south

Natural ventilation: Approx. percentage of gross floor naturally ventilated
95%

Night-time ventilation provision
Natural

Thermal transmission of building envelope
Standard

Utilization of building mass thermal storage as part of energy strategy?
No

Solar control systems
Fixed external

Daylighting Approx. percentage of net floor area needing artificial lighting during daylight hours
10%

Energy-saving controls for artificial lighting?
No

Other
–

HVAC SYSTEMS

Fuel/approx. % use
Electricity 100%

Boiler type
None

Heating system
None

Mechanical ventilation
None

Air conditioning type
Meeting rooms and information centre only

Heat recovery
No

ENERGY PERFORMANCE

Total
62,000kW/h/month

Artificial lighting
33,000kW/h/month

Refrigeration cooling
29,000kW/h/month

Mechanical ventilation
N/A

Heating
N/A

Total estimated carbon dioxide output
N/S

ENVIRONMENTAL/HEALTH FEATURES

Materials/components selection strategy to reduce embodied and transport energy?
–

Use of recycled materials
–

Use of timbers from managed sources
–

Special water conserving installation
No

Natural organic sewage treatment
No

Measures to encourage use of public transport
–

Vice Chancellor's Office, Académie des Antilles et de la Guyane
Martinique, French West Indies

The administration of the University of the West Indies and Guyana is accommodated in a new building located between Martinique's west coast and its capital, Fort-de-France. The site is a plateau whose altitude provides some relief from the hot, humid climate but is subject to stronger winds than elsewhere on the island. The building is a fascinating experiment in how to use prevailing winds as ventilation. The 'wind machine' aims to provide an office environment that is comfortable for the occupants, but without the cross-ventilation being irritatingly draughty or causing papers to be blown around.

Fundamental to the main building's design is the plan form which is flat on the north side and bowed on the south: the prevailing wind hits the south of the building at an angle of 15 degrees, creating an area of low pressure along the south side. This helps to draw air through an internal 'street', the corridors and offices. Five internal patios, rising through three floors, provide a stack effect, further assisting the same passage of air.

Two smaller buildings have been arranged in front of the main building's north elevation. The purpose of these is to channel air through high openings in the middle of the main façade. Large, vertical louvres are moved automatically, according to the current wind speed, to control the amount of air entering the four-storey internal street. Movement of the air inside the building is dependent on the positions of horizontal and vertical louvres, which also make up the entire wall of the

building. In order to achieve satisfactory internal conditions, it is important that the volume of moving air is large, but slow in velocity. This necessitates constant adjustment of the louvres to suit external conditions. A consequence of this arrangement is that there is little aural privacy. Meeting rooms, therefore, have had to be air conditioned. Moreover, windless days do occur and unusual wind directions and strengths can, at times, run contrary to the intended air flows.

The overall budget of the facility was similar to a conventionally air-conditioned environment, but running costs are substantially reduced.

<01

02>

Expelled air

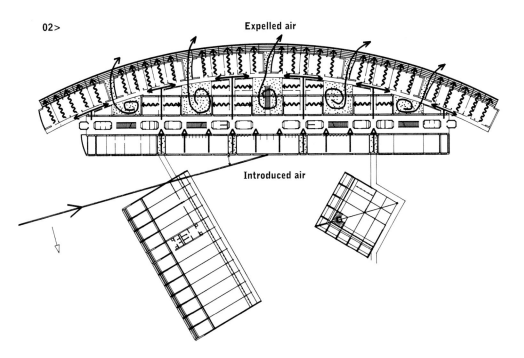

Introduced air

01> Aluminium sun-screens curve around the south façade of the building, presenting the minimum impediment to air movement through it.

02> Block plan showing the main building in relation to the prevailing wind direction and the internal street. The five internal patios or lightwells are also shown.

03> The principal façade and main entrance, with the examinations building to the left and the restaurant to the right.

^
03

Mansions / Vice Chancellor's Office

04 > Cross-section through the building. The prevailing wind enters through the principal façade on the right.

05 > Meeting room.

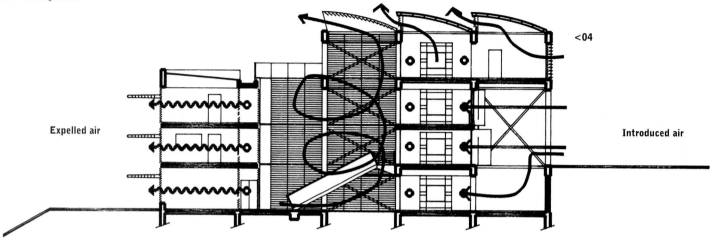

Expelled air

Introduced air

< 04

∧
05

'It is a most miserable thing to feel ashamed of home.'

(Charles Dickens, *Great Expectations*, Chapter 8)

'...damp, cracked and leaky "architecture" must give way to houses as efficient as a bicycle.'

(W.R. Lethaby, *Architecture*, 1911)

4.2
Houses

'Munstead Wood',
Godalming, Surrey, UK
(1896) by Sir Edwin
Lutyens.

A dwelling has always had two aspects, practical and emotional: 'house' and 'home'. The practical takes precedence: the house should provide shelter for its occupants and keep pace with ever-rising expectations of comfort and convenience. As a home, the dwelling is the focus of belonging and a vehicle for self-expression, a status symbol and a place of refuge. The sentimental Victorian cult of the home and of domesticity has left a powerful legacy.

NAME OF BUILDING
Akira Kusumi's Guest House

Client/owner	**Date completed**
Akira Kusumi	March 1995
Occupier	**Gross area**
Akira Kusumi	61.9m²
Location	**Construction cost**
Awaji Island, Hyogo, Japan	£5,000
Architect	**Climatic zone**
Kota Kawasaki	Temperate

BUILDING ENERGY FEATURES

Orientation of main façades	**Solar control systems**
North	No
Natural ventilation: Approx. percentage of gross floor naturally ventilated	**Daylighting Approx. percentage of net floor area needing artificial lighting during daylight hours**
100%	0%
Night-time ventilation provision	**Energy-saving controls for artificial lighting?**
Natural	No
Thermal transmission of building envelope	**Other**
High	—
Utilization of building mass thermal storage as part of energy strategy?	
No	

HVAC SYSTEMS

Fuel/approx. % use	**Mechanical ventilation**
Mains electricity 100%	None
Boiler type	**Air conditioning type**
None	None
Heating system	**Heat recovery**
None	No

ENERGY PERFORMANCE

Total	**Heating**
N/S	N/A
Artificial lighting	**Total estimated carbon dioxide output**
N/S	N/S
Refrigeration cooling	
N/A	
Mechanical ventilation	
N/A	

ENVIRONMENTAL/HEALTH FEATURES

Materials/components selection strategy to reduce embodied and transport energy?	**Special water conserving installation**
Yes	No
Use of recycled materials	**Natural organic sewage treatment**
Logs for scaffolding	No
Use of timbers from managed sources	**Measures to encourage use of public transport**
Yes	No

Akira Kusumi's Guest House
Awaji Island, Hyogo, Japan

This is a guest house for Akira Kusumi who is a famous plaster craftsman in Japan. His skills range from traditional Japanese to Western plasterwork (he has taught Western plasterwork), and he has also invented innovative plaster techniques. This project was designed by students from Waseda University workshop and built with the Hanasaka-dan, a group of plaster craftsmen who are promoted by Kusumi. The main concept behind this project was to create a beautiful space without using expensive or special materials.

The structure uses Ashiba-maruta, an inexpensive log usually used for scaffolding. One of the themes of this project was how best to exploit the character of timber. 'Mitsumata structure' was therefore employed, whereby the ends of three timber members are bundled together with wire and the other ends are opened like a tripod. The resulting structure is simple, stable and flexible.

The Mitsumata structure forms the basis of the house which is the shape of a comma. In one unit, two logs make one face of the wall and the last log projects from it. The wall has been formed by connecting these structural units. Moreover, by changing the distance between one unit and another and changing the inclination of the wall, in plan, any curvature can be shaped. The wall is formed by boards fixed to the logs, followed by applying mortar and soil as a finishing surface. Straw, sand and glue have been mixed in the mortar to make the wall stronger and to stop it cracking. Corrugated translucent plastic has been used for the roof, making it very light.

Awaji Island was very close to the seismic centre of the disastrous earthquake which occurred in Kansai in 1994. Many of the surrounding houses were completely destroyed, but the guest house survived intact, a testimony to its strong, pliable structure.

01> Section showing the timber scaffold pole construction.

02> View of the house from the south.

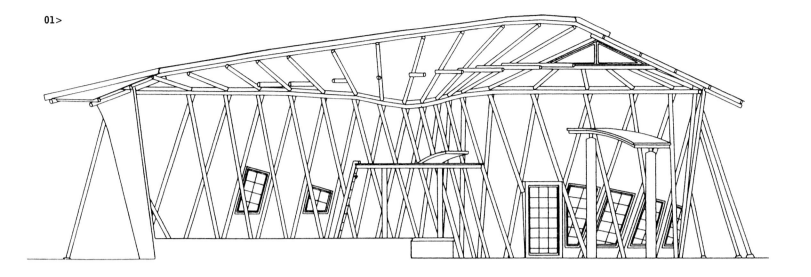

Houses / Akira Kusumi's Guest House

03 > View of the interior showing the range of levels and the suspended timber bridge and platform.

04 > The organic plan form of the house is a radical departure from the traditional orthogonal house plan and is based on the tatami mat module.

05 > View from the north.

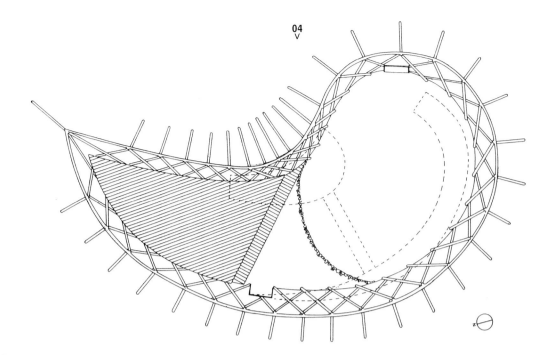

Houses / Akira Kusumi's Guest House

NAME OF BUILDING
Apartment Building

Client/owner Stettler AG	**Date completed** 1993
Occupier N/S	**Gross area** 1,305m²
Location Biel, Switzerland	**Construction cost** N/S
Architect LOG ID, Dieter Schempp	**Climatic zone** Continental

BUILDING ENERGY FEATURES

Orientation of main façades South-east	**Utilization of building mass thermal storage as part of energy strategy?** Yes
Natural ventilation: Approx. percentage of gross floor naturally ventilated 100%	**Solar control systems** Automatic window regulation
Night-time ventilation provision None	**Daylighting Approx. percentage of net floor area needing artificial lighting during daylight hours** None
Thermal transmission of building envelope Walls: 2.0 W/m²°C; glazing: 1.3 W/m²°C	**Energy-saving controls for artificial lighting?** No
	Other –

HVAC SYSTEMS

Fuel/approx. % use N/S	**Mechanical ventilation** None
Boiler type N/S	**Air conditioning type** None
Heating system Passive solar energy (30%)	**Heat recovery** No

ENERGY PERFORMANCE

Total N/S	**Heating** N/S
Artificial lighting N/S	**Total estimated carbon dioxide output** N/S
Refrigeration cooling N/A	
Mechanical ventilation N/A	

ENVIRONMENTAL/HEALTH FEATURES

Materials/components selection strategy to reduce embodied and transport energy? Use of natural materials	**Special water conserving installation** –
Use of recycled materials –	**Natural organic sewage treatment** –
Use of timbers from managed sources –	**Measures to encourage use of public transport** –

Apartment Building
Biel, Switzerland

This three-storey private residential scheme, on a suburban site with a fine view over a small town, comprises eight dwellings of different sizes. The lower floors contain two-storey maisonettes, the upper floor one-storey flats. On the roof area, which is intended for communal use, are children's play houses with pitched roofs that mirror the style of existing nearby buildings.

The south-east facing, steeply sloping site is ideally suited for LOG ID's concept of green solar architecture. Each residential unit has a balcony, but the most important feature is the glasshouse. Placed in front of each dwelling and integrated with it, these winter gardens are a simple but effective means of making the most of ambient energy from the sun. The glasshouses of the maisonettes rise through two storeys, while those of the upstairs flats rise above roof level.

In the summer the glasshouses are used as conservatories. In the winter they are not heated and act as a thermal buffer. On hot summer days the outer glazing can be opened, creating a thermal chimney which draws cool air from the back of the building through the dwellings, and on sunny winter days the inner glazing between the interior room and the glasshouse can be opened to warm the interior. The concrete mass of the building retains the heat collected in this way and warms the interiors at night. Overall, heating energy needs are reduced by 20 to 30 per cent.

The glasshouses are fitted with automatically watered plant beds for semi-tropical plants.

These plants are an important element of the design: they absorb carbon dioxide and produce oxygen, as well as reducing harmful substances in the air and, through transpiration, lowering the temperature in summer.

^
01

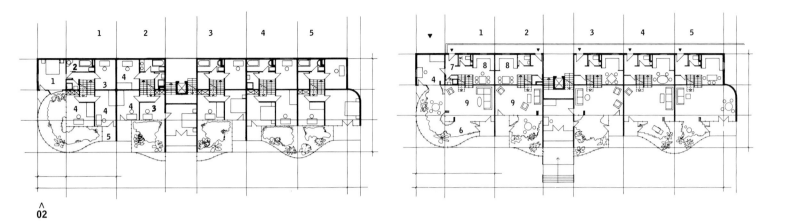

01> The south façade. Balconies and conservatories with greenery make the building appear more welcoming and are the key to the architect's ingenious but simple energy strategy.

02> Ground- and first-floor plans of the five maisonettes. The conservatories rise through two storeys and bring light into the whole of the interior.

03> The entrance to the block leads through to the maisonettes at the rear of the building which are set into the hillside. The gabled features on the roof are miniature houses which echo the forms of the surrounding buildings.

Key

1 Parents' room
2 Bathroom
3 Work room
4 Child's room
5 Balcony
6 Conservatory
7 Corridor
8 Kitchen
9 Living room

Chapter Four / Architecture and the Environment

<06

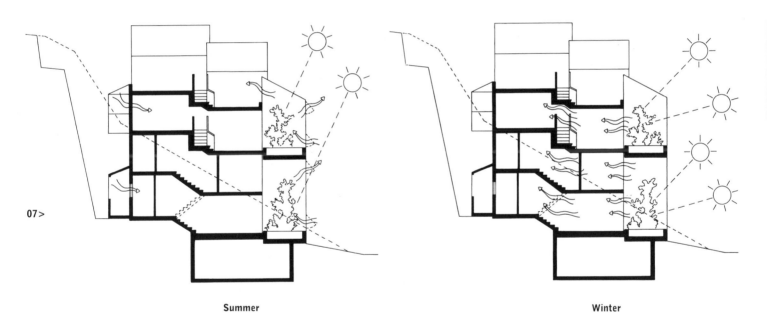

07>

Summer

Winter

04> The conservatory of one of the upper apartments. It rises above the roof level of the building to catch maximum sunlight and allow the introduction of large plants.

05> View from a maisonette living room. The south-facing conservatory is integrated into the interior, but in winter it can be closed off with glass panels to provide insulation.

06> The tall conservatories of the maisonettes give a spaciousness to the interiors. The plants bring natural greenery into the building and raise oxygen levels.

07> Section through the apartment block illustrating the energy strategy. On warm summer days (left) the glass wall dividing the conservatories from the interior of the apartments is closed. The large plants provide shade. At night the building is cooled by air drawn in from the north side of the block. On sunny winter days (right) the interior wall is opened and the warmed air is drawn into the apartments.

NAME OF BUILDING
Palmetto House

Client/owner
Jim Adamson (current);
Lescizek/Norma Watkins
(original clients)

Location
Miami, Florida, USA

Architect/builders
Jersey Devil (Steve
Badanes/Jim Adamson)

Date completed
1988

Gross area
167m² (shop); 111.5m²
(house)

Construction cost
N/S

Climatic zone
Tropical

BUILDING ENERGY FEATURES

**Orientation of main
façades**
East-west and north-south

**Natural ventilation:
Approx. percentage of
gross floor naturally
ventilated**
100%

**Night-time ventilation
provision**
Natural

**Thermal transmission
of building envelope**
Standard

**Utilization of building
mass thermal storage as
part of energy strategy?**
Yes

Solar control systems
Fixed external

**Daylighting
Approx. percentage of
net floor area needing
artificial lighting during
daylight hours**
0%

**Energy-saving controls
for artificial lighting?**
No

Other
–

HVAC SYSTEMS

Fuel/approx. % use
Electricity 100%

Boiler type
None

Heating system
None

Mechanical ventilation
Paddle fans (ten)

Air conditioning type
None

Heat recovery
No

ENERGY PERFORMANCE

Total
N/S

Artificial lighting
N/S

Refrigeration cooling
N/A

Mechanical ventilation
N/S

Heating
N/A

**Total estimated carbon
dioxide output**
N/S

ENVIRONMENTAL/HEALTH FEATURES

**Materials/components
selection strategy to
reduce embodied and
transport energy?**
Yes

Use of recycled materials
No

**Use of timbers from
managed sources**
Softwood

**Special water conserving
installation**
Graywater system; flow
control fixtures

**Natural organic sewage
treatment**
No

**Measures to encourage
use of public transport**
No

Palmetto House
Miami, Florida, USA

This building provides a combined house,
workshop and studio for the owners, who are
a writer and woodworker respectively. Located
south of Miami, on a site densely wooded
with palmettos, pines and pepper trees, the
house reflects its sub-tropical climate and
incorporates features of the local vernacular
'tin sheds' of area farmers.

The structure is of lightweight timber frame
over a ground floor of concrete post and
beam with concrete block infill. The building
has deep screened porches and eaves. The
plan is a cross: the lower level is orientated
north-south, while the main house above
runs east-west. The section is designed to
encourage cross-ventilation from south-east
breezes, and overhangs provide solar shading.
Living areas are located on the first floor
above the ground-floor woodwork shop.
The walls are of aluminium siding to reflect
the sun. In the roofs a 'radiant barrier' has
been installed; this comprises a layer of high-
emissivity metal foil in the airspace between
roof and attic to reflect infra-red light.
Continuous soffit and ridge vents allow
ventilation under the roof, so as to avoid heat
build-up. A high-level Plexiglas diffuser above
the sleeping loft houses fluorescent lighting.
Windows are single glazed. To increase air
movement, paddle fans have been used
together with metal grating between the
first and the loft floor.

Water is heated by solar panels on the south
face of the gable roof with built-in photovoltaic
panels for the pump. A supplementary
reverse-cycle heat pump supplies heating
and cooling in extreme conditions.

^
01

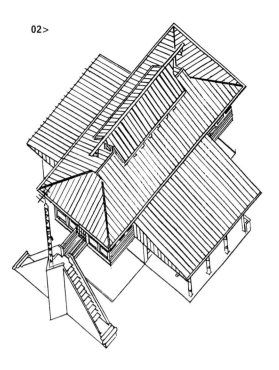

01> View down the length of the house on the first floor. The spiral stair leads to the loft bedroom.

02> Axonometric showing the cruciform composition of the house.

03> Overhangs provide solar shading. The walls are of aluminium siding to reflect the sun.

∧
03

Houses / Palmetto House

04 > Ground-floor plan.

Key

1 Shower/deck
2 Patio
3 Covered work area
4 Roof or building overhang above
5 Storage
6 Assembly/storage
7 Office
8 Woodworking shop

05 > View from the west.

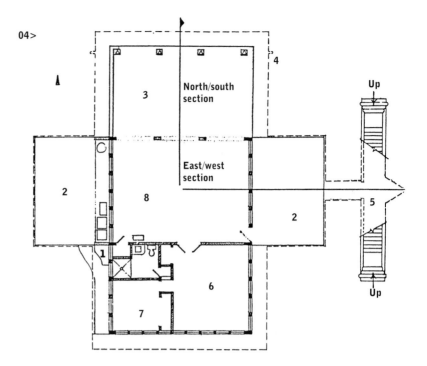

04 >

Chapter Four / Architecture and the Environment

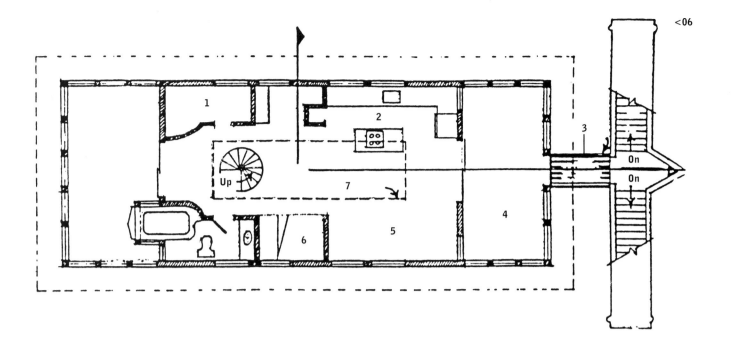

06> First-floor plan showing the main living spaces.

Key

1 Closet
2 Kitchen
3 Bridge
4 Entry porch
5 Living area
6 Sleeping alcove
7 Loft

07> The upper bedroom.

NAME OF BUILDING
Marika Alderton House

Client/owner
Marika Alderton

Date completed
1994

Occupier
Marika Alderton

Gross area
N/S

Location
Arnhem Land, Australia

Construction cost
N/S

Architect
Glenn Murcutt

Climatic zone
Subtropical

BUILDING ENERGY FEATURES

Orientation of main façades
North and south

Solar control systems
Motorized/variable external

Natural ventilation: Approx. percentage of gross floor naturally ventilated
100%

Daylighting Approx. percentage of net floor area needing artificial lighting during daylight hours
0%

Night-time ventilation provision
Natural

Energy-saving controls for artificial lighting?
No

Thermal transmission of building envelope
High

Other
–

Utilization of building mass thermal storage as part of energy strategy?
No

HVAC SYSTEMS

Fuel/approx. % use
Mains electricity 100%

Mechanical ventilation
None

Boiler type
None

Air conditioning type
None

Heating system
None

Heat recovery
–

ENERGY PERFORMANCE

Total
N/S

Heating
N/A

Artificial lighting
N/S

Total estimated carbon dioxide output
N/S

Refrigeration cooling
N/A

Mechanical ventilation
N/A

ENVIRONMENTAL/HEALTH FEATURES

Materials/components selection strategy to reduce embodied and transport energy?
Yes

Special water conserving installation
No

Use of recycled materials
No

Natural organic sewage treatment
No

Use of timbers from managed sources
Hardwood

Measures to encourage use of public transport
No

Marika Alderton House
Arnhem Land, Australia

Glenn Murcutt has been designing homes in the Australian countryside for over 25 years. His houses are airy, light, elegant and simple. They draw inspiration from the landscape – his simple planes and forms act in unison as a foil to the multiplicity of shape, detail and movement found in the surrounding vegetation and the wide skyscapes – and from the simple agricultural buildings that inhabit this landscape. They are built with economy of means, with materials that are readily available, and according to the Miesian dictum of fitness for purpose.

A recent building that admirably exemplifies this approach is the Marika Alderton House, designed for an Aboriginal artist and her family in the Yirrkala Community, Eastern Arnhem Land, Northern Territory. In this case, he had first to adapt to a tropical climate and then to submit his system of construction and detailing to the constraints of prefabrication imposed on him by the limited budget, the site's remote location and the lack of local construction skills. He also had to test whether his own spatial principles, partly formulated within the context of an Aboriginal way of life, measured up to the real thing. The house he designed takes the plan of an elegant and sturdy long hall which opens and closes on all sides, breathing like a plant.

The metal structure is designed to resist wind speeds of up to 227 kilometres (140 miles) per hour. The house is built entirely without glass. The façades are composed of broad plywood or slatted tallow – wood shutters with 8mm (¼-inch) gaps – according to

their orientation and the function of the rooms they enclose. During the daytime, these tilting panels are raised like awnings so the home becomes a sheltered platform, open on every side. At night the panels are closed. Natural cross-ventilation remains constant while the degree of privacy and intimacy can be adjusted at will. The roof oversails on all sides but to a slightly larger extent to the north, facing the sea, where there is also a terrace. Pivoting 'venturi' tubes along the ridge of the roof dispel any hot air caught beneath it.

Another of Murcutt's houses is the Simpson-Lee House, a sanctuary for retired couples located in the Blue Mountains in New South Wales. Backing on to the west and south-west winds, the house faces the views of the east and north-east. The residence's two pavilions (one residential, the other a studio) stand in a line on either side of a pond, and are connected by a walkway. The pavilions and the walkway are raised from the ground, which falls away as one advances towards the residential pavilion. The design is very spare, almost monastic in feel. Both this and the Marika Alderton House, like all of Murcutt's architecture, derive from a Modernist puritanism with roots clearly embedded in Mies van der Rohe's 'pavilion' structures. However, their architectural vocabulary quickly evolved in response to rural Australian conditions. They have accomplished this with such effect that it is difficult to discern to what extent they reflect or determine a distinct Australian regionalism.

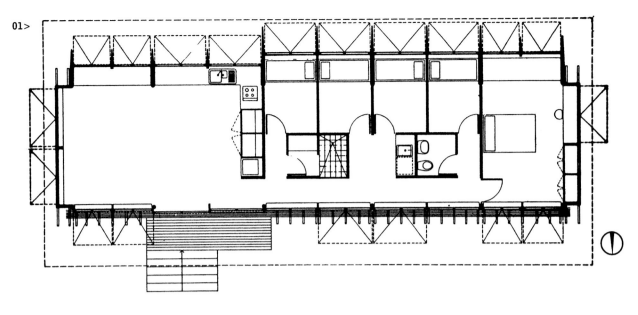

01> Plan showing the simple compartmentalization of the rectangular volume and the 'up-and-over' wall panels.

02> From the north, the thermal collector on the roof and the vents along the roof ridge are visible.

^
02

Houses / Marika Alderton House

04>

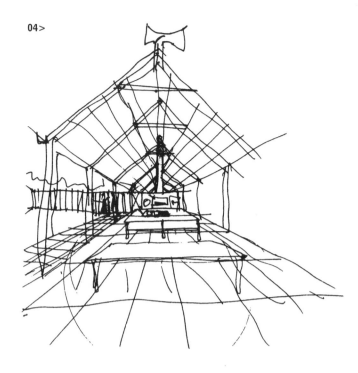

∧
03

∧
05

Chapter Four / Architecture and the Environment

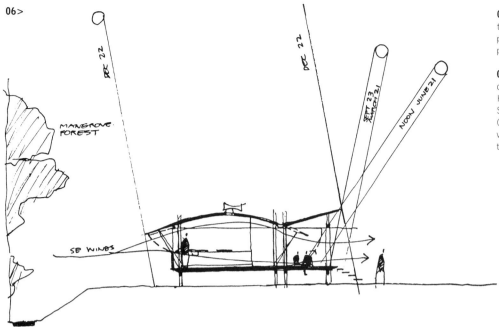

03 > The east end of the house, with the wall panels in their open position.

04+06 > Study sketches of Marika Alderton House (far left) and Simpson-Lee House (left) show structure and ventilation and response to climate.

05 > View from the east. The overhanging roof, vertical sunbreakers and 'up-and-over' walls provide plenty of shade around the house.

07 > The Simpson-Lee House. With the exception of the solid wood steps on the staircase and walkway, the house is constructed wholly of mineral elements: silver-plated steel and aluminium for the structure; metal casings and large sloping planes of the roof; pale grey polished concrete floors, and whitewashed brickwork and glass.

Houses / Marika Alderton House

NAME OF BUILDING
Temple of Time or Divided House

Client/owner
Fujie San, Arata Isozaki,
local authority architects

Location
Oshima, Toyama Valley,
Japan

Architect
Benson and Forsyth
Architects

Date completed
1993

Gross area
70m²

Construction cost
£256,500

Climatic zone
Continental

BUILDING ENERGY FEATURES

Orientation of main façades
Towards the Pole Star

Natural ventilation: Approx. percentage of gross floor naturally ventilated
100%

Night-time ventilation provision
Natural

Thermal transmission of building envelope
Standard

Utilization of building mass thermal storage as part of energy strategy?
Yes

Solar control systems
Fixed external

Daylighting Approx. percentage of net floor area needing artificial lighting during daylight hours
0%

Energy-saving controls for artificial lighting?
No

Other
–

HVAC SYSTEMS

Fuel/approx. % use
Mains electricity
100%

Boiler type
None

Heating system
None

Mechanical ventilation
None

Air conditioning type
None

Heat recovery
No

ENERGY PERFORMANCE

Total
N/A

Artificial lighting
N/A

Refrigeration cooling
N/A

Mechanical ventilation
N/A

Heating
N/A

Total estimated carbon dioxide output
N/A

ENVIRONMENTAL/HEALTH FEATURES

Materials/components selection strategy to reduce embodied and transport energy?
Use of untreated local materials

Use of recycled materials
Bamboo

Use of timbers from managed sources
Hardwood

Special water conserving installation
Rainwater for irrigation

Natural organic sewage treatment
No

Measures to encourage use of public transport
No

Temple of Time or Divided House
Oshima, Toyama Valley, Japan

Oshima today consists of a few factories and a scatter of suburban houses set in the featureless alluvial plain of the Toyama Valley. However, it is possible to decipher an older pattern of clusters of traditional dwellings, located on the higher ground surrounded by rice fields and frames for growing loofahs and drying rice grass.

The Divided House is not intended for permanent occupation. It is primarily a recondite investigation into a number of formal, social and environmental issues, and juxtaposes past and present. The two are separated by a double in situ concrete wall which houses a stairway pointing directly at the Pole Star. Over the whole floats a grid of steel squares which relate the building to its position in the geometry of the globe.

To the west of the wall, the Divided House reflects past tradition. It comprises a series of vertical timber ribs, carved and laminated to particular profiles, covered by a layer of bamboo poles that follow the ribs' contour, folding over each other at the changes of curvature. The narrow top section is covered with rice grass thatch, while the open roof allows views of the grid above. To the east of the wall a cylinder, within a raised fair-faced concrete cube, reflects the rational and the comtemporary.

Inside the western half, light falls through the gaps between the bamboo slots, gently illuminating the space. The plan arrangement allows the space to benefit from natural light throughout the day. During the winter months the low sun can penetrate between the bare bamboo slats at the base of the enclosure, thereby heating the space by means of passive solar gain. During the summer the interior is shaded from the high sun by the dense rice grass covering at the top. Although the bamboo slats along the western half provide no thermal protection, the building's geometry encourages snow to settle during the winter, allowing it to benefit from the snow's natural insulation properties.

The cube of the eastern half has a low ratio of volume to surface-area. The fair-faced concrete enclosure absorbs heat gradually, the depth of the concrete allowing the cylinder to remain cool throughout the day, whilst at night the concrete gradually releases the heat and warms the interior. The bamboo slats of the western half and the non-glazed window openings of the eastern half ensure natural ventilation at all times.

01> View of the house showing its distinctive polarized halves and the unifying metal grid. To the west, the building reflects the traditional and the past; to the east the present.

02> In winter the geometry of the western half of the house encourages snow to settle, allowing the benefits of its natural insulation.

Houses / Temple of Time or Divided House

03 > Development sketch.

04 > Interior of the
western half, showing the
timber ribs and bamboo
cladding.

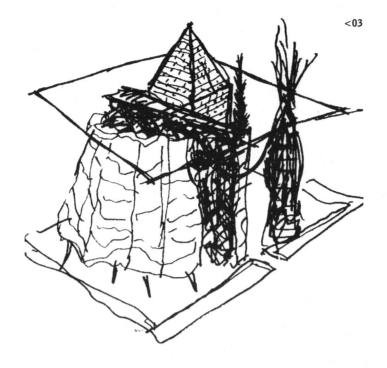

<03

^
04

Chapter Four / Architecture and the Environment

'Courts and camps are the only places
to learn the world in.'

(Philip Dormer Stanhope, Earl of Chesterfield,
Letter to his son, 2 October 1747)

'Love rules the camp, the court, the
grove – for love is heaven and heaven is love.'

(Lord Byron, *Don Juan*, CXII, xiii)

'The burrow and the camp abide,
the sunlight and the sword'

(Rudyard Kipling, *Sussex*)

4.3
Campuses

The cantonment, the campus, the shopping
centre, the laboratory complex, the prison
and the farmyard: all are assemblages of
interconnecting and interrelated buildings.
The interconnections and interrelationships
give a clue to those of the occupants and
reflect function, status, communication and
the passage of time. The buildings form
spaces and the spaces require enclosure.
Campuses can be read in positive or negative
terms – the spaces between the buildings,
like those of a city, are as crucial as those
contained within them.

The Alhambra, Granada,
Spain (built during the
13th and 14th centuries).

Campuses / Contemporary Buildings

NAME OF BUILDING
Women's Humane Society Animal Shelter

Client/owner	**Date completed**
Women's Humane Society	June 1994
Occupier	**Gross area**
Women's Humane Society	2,450m²
Location	**Construction cost**
Bensalem, Pennsylvania, USA	£1.9 million
Architect	**Climatic zone**
Susan Maxman Architects	Temperate

BUILDING ENERGY FEATURES

Orientation of main façades
East and west

Natural ventilation: Approx. percentage of gross floor naturally ventilated
60%

Night-time ventilation provision
Forced

Thermal transmission of building envelope
Above standard

Utilization of building mass thermal storage as part of energy strategy?
No

Solar control systems
Fixed external; solar control glazing; deciduous trees to east and west; heat mirror glazing to east and west

Daylighting Approx. percentage of net floor area needing artificial lighting during daylight hours
N/S

Energy-saving controls for artificial lighting?
Occupancy sensors

Other
–

HVAC SYSTEMS

Fuel/approx. % use
Natural gas 100%

Boiler type
Gas

Heating system
Underfloor in kennel areas, otherwise through AC system

Mechanical ventilation
Constant volume/variable air volume AC system

Air conditioning type
Gas absorption chiller; with condenser heat recovery

Heat recovery
–

ENERGY PERFORMANCE

Total (Clinic)
8.08kW/h/m²

Artificial lighting
1.17kW/h/m²

Refrigeration cooling
1.28kW/h/m²

Mechanical ventilation
4.60kW/h/m²

Heating
1.03kW/h/m²

Total estimated carbon dioxide output
N/S

ENVIRONMENTAL/HEALTH FEATURES

Materials/components selection strategy to reduce embodied and transport energy?
Yes

Use of recycled materials
Recycled used carpet, lightbulb glass, truck tyre linings and plastics

Use of timbers from managed sources
–

Special water conserving installation
Low flush WCs; on-site well water for cleaning kennels

Natural organic sewage treatment
No

Measures to encourage use of public transport
No

Women's Humane Society Animal Shelter
Bensalem, Pennsylvania, USA

The Women's Humane Society Animal Shelter in suburban Bensalem was commissioned to replace an inner-city facility whose catchment area had been experiencing a decline in pet ownership. The new building occupies a 4.5-hectare (12-acre) mixed designated wetland and wildflower meadow site, crossed by a main electricity power line. The building houses an animal shelter with veterinary clinic and treatment rooms, kennels, administrative offices, conference room and multipurpose community room.

The local climate is warm-temperate, humid summers and cold winters. Architect Susan Maxman's priority was therefore to orientate the building and glazing in a way that would avoid excessive solar gains in summer while permitting natural daylighting. The building is located around two open courtyards with the entry courtyard orientated to the east (towards the main access road and bus route). The main façades and kennel areas are orientated east and west, with limited glazing to the west and deciduous trees planted to the east and west.

Skylights in the kennel areas, and high-level clerestories with overhangs in the clinic, waiting rooms and corridors, are designed to avoid summer sun. High-efficiency, high-frequency ballast fluorescent lighting with photosensor controls is used to reduce lighting loads.

The shelter is constructed of double-skin cavity blockwork, fully filled with air crete cementitious foam insulation. Steel truss roofs have fibreglass batt or rigid polyisocyanurate insulation. Windows are clear double glazed with heat-mirror, low-emissivity glazing. West windows are shaded more extensively.

The HVAC system is arranged in zones to deal with the different functional areas. A central gas-fired boiler serves a hydronic (water-pipe) distribution system. The cooling is provided by a gas-fired absorption chiller, thus avoiding harmful CFCs and HCFCs in the air conditioning as well as reducing carbon dioxide emissions. The office areas are fully air conditioned with a variable volume AC system and terminal reheat. The clinical and animal holding areas require 100 per cent fresh air to avoid odours and have a heat recovery wheel reclaiming 80 per cent of heat from the exhaust air. The kennel areas which have heating only are mechanically ventilated with a desiccant coated heat recovery coil; this dries and warms incoming air in winter, and dries and cools incoming air in summer. Underfloor heating is supplied by heat recovered from the absorption chiller condenser.

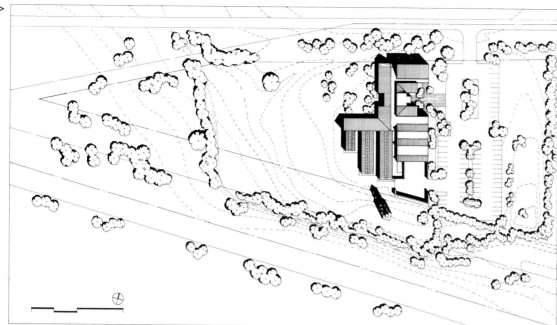

01>

01> Site plan showing the entry courtyard to the east.

02> Western elevation. The building has been organized in such a way as to avoid the power line and minimize disruption to the nature reserve that surrounds it.

129

^
02

<04

04> The façade of the kennels is clad in low-maintenance corrugated metal sidings.

05> Section through the surgery. Recycled materials are used in the WC partitions, for floor tiling and in the insulation (recycled polystyrene). Low-flush WCs are specified.

06> Section through the corridor and laboratory illustrating how the design of the clerestory and corridor downstand limits summer sun but admits winter sunlight.

07> The animal holding area with clerestory lighting.

05>

06>

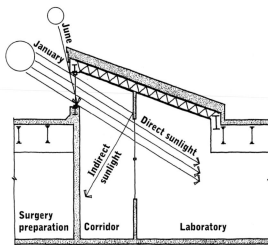

07>

NAME OF BUILDING
Ukichiro Nakaya Museum of Snow and Ice

Client/owner
Kaga City

Occupier
Museum of Snow and Ice

Location
Kaga, Ishikawa Prefecture, Japan

Architect
Arata Isozaki and Associates

Date completed
June 1994

Gross area
760m²

Construction cost
£8 million

Climatic zone
Temperate

BUILDING ENERGY FEATURES

Orientation of main façades
East and west

Natural ventilation: Approx. percentage of gross floor naturally ventilated
73%

Night-time ventilation provision
No

Thermal transmission of building envelope
Above standard

Utilization of building mass thermal storage as part of energy strategy?
Yes

Solar control systems
No

Daylighting Approx. percentage of net floor area needing artificial lighting during daylight hours
60%

Energy-saving controls for artificial lighting?
Yes

Other
–

HVAC SYSTEMS

Fuel/approx. % use
N/S

Boiler type
Cool and hot water generator

Heating system
Partially accumulated heating method; electric underfloor heating

Mechanical ventilation
Air outlet and inlet ventilation

Air conditioning type
VAV (exhibition space); fan coils (office space)

Heat recovery
No

ENERGY PERFORMANCE

Total
0.495kW/h/m²

Artificial lighting
0.057kW/h/m²

Refrigeration cooling
0.185kW/h/m²

Mechanical ventilation
0.009kW/h/m²

Heating
0.244kW/h/m²

Total estimated carbon dioxide output
N/S

ENVIRONMENTAL/HEALTH FEATURES

Materials/components selection strategy to reduce embodied and transport energy?
Yes, including composite seaweed and mud walls

Use of recycled materials
No

Use of timbers from managed sources
Yes

Special water conserving installation
No

Natural organic sewage treatment
No

Measures to encourage use of public transport
No

Ukichiro Nakaya Museum of Snow and Ice
Kaga, Ishikawa Prefecture, Japan

This museum was conceived as a memorial to Dr Ukichiro Nakaya, a physicist with a worldwide reputation as an expert on snow. Famous for his exclamation 'snow crystal is a hieroglyph from heaven', he was the first person to create snow crystals by artificial means. Located in a park in Nakaya's native town, the museum is dedicated to collecting, preserving and displaying his work and references, as well as gathering and disseminating information about snow. The project was designed three times before the museum and the park authorities felt that a satisfactory relationship between building and setting had been achieved.

In the siting of the building, careful consideration was given to the magnificent vista of Lake Shibayamagata and the sacred Mount Haku-san beyond. The circulation plan was developed gradually orientating the visitors towards the shore. Approaching the museum from the gently sloping arrival court, the visitor first sees a row of three hexagons topped with faceted roofs. On approaching further the full height of the towers is revealed. The bases of the towers are finished in mud, using diatomaceous earth brought in from the nearby Noto Peninsula. Natural materials inherited from traditional Japanese culture – such as woods, grasses and stones – are used extensively to harmonize with the natural setting. A 'fog sculpture' created by Nakaya's daughter, Fujiko, is a feature of the composition.

The bioclimatic attributes of this museum, as with some other buildings featured in this section, are largely sensual and emotive.

It gives the visitor – most likely arriving from one or other of the teeming Japanese cities – an opportunity for repose and communion with nature.

^
01

01> The fog sculpture.

02> Site plan showing the sloped and tapering entrance courtyard, the bridge, the three towers and the fog sculpture on the exhibition plinth, and the relationship of the building to the lake.

03> View over the fog sculpture across Lake Shibayamagata and towards the sacred Mount Haku-san.

∧
03

Campuses / Ukichiro Nakaya Museum of Snow and Ice

04>

Chapter Four / Architecture and the Environment

04> Upper level of the exhibition space with the three towers.

05> View from the forecourt towards the towers and the lake beyond.

06> Plans at terrace (bottom) and exhibition floor levels.

^
05

06>

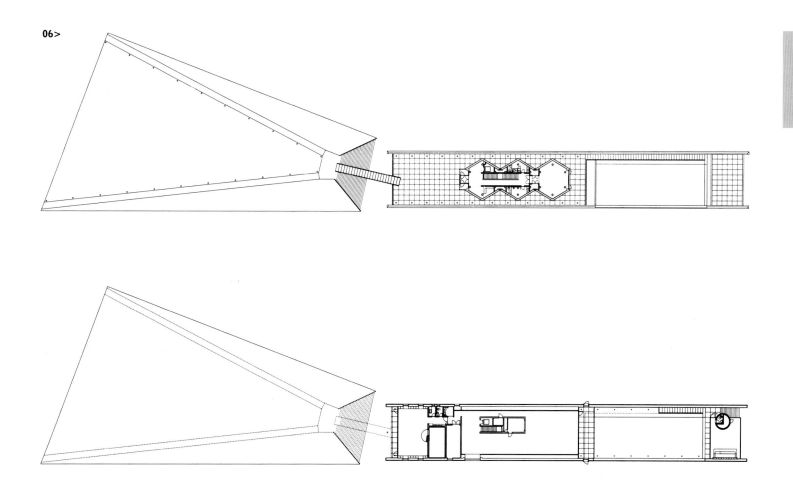

135

NAME OF BUILDING
Hostel for Youth Educational Institute

Client/owner/occupier
Prämonstratenser-Abtei
Windberg

Location
Windberg, Germany

Architect
Thomas Herzog,
Peter Bonfig (collaborator)

Date completed
1991

Gross area
1,720m² (heated area)

Construction cost
£1.6 million

Climatic zone
Temperate

BUILDING ENERGY FEATURES

Orientation of main façades
North and south

Natural ventilation: Approx. percentage of gross floor naturally ventilated
100%

Night-time ventilation provision
Natural

Thermal transmission of building envelope
Standard

Utilization of building mass thermal storage as part of energy strategy?
Yes

Solar control systems
Fixed external (roof overhang); solar control glazing (insulated glazing)

Daylighting Approx. percentage of net floor area needing artificial lighting during daylight hours
85%

Energy-saving controls for artificial lighting?
No

Other
–

HVAC SYSTEMS

Fuel/approx. % use
Mains electricity
40%; natural gas 60%

Boiler type
Gas

Heating system
Ducted hot air

Mechanical ventilation
None

Air conditioning type
None

Heat recovery
Yes

ENERGY PERFORMANCE

Total
N/S

Artificial lighting
N/S

Refrigeration cooling
N/A

Mechanical ventilation
N/A

Heating
45kW/h/m²/y

Total estimated carbon dioxide output
N/S

ENVIRONMENTAL/HEALTH FEATURES

Materials/components selection strategy to reduce embodied and transport energy?
Yes

Use of recycled materials
No

Use of timbers from managed sources
Softwood

Special water conserving installation
No

Natural organic sewage treatment
No

Measures to encourage use of public transport
Bus service

Hostel for Youth Educational Institute
Windberg, Germany

Windberg is a small community on the southern slopes of the Bavarian forest. At the heart of the village is a monastery complex comprising a number of buildings for the religious order and an educational centre for young people. The centre provides for about a hundred people, who typically stay for one to two weeks at a time intermittently during the year.

To conserve energy, account was taken of the temperature requirements of each of the spaces, and the length of time that they would be used. Thus, those used for several hours at a time were separated from those used for only a short period. They were also built with different materials.

The southern part of the building contains the rooms in use for longer periods. Its external wall is clad on the outside with a layer of translucent thermal insulation to work as a sun-trap and heating device, as well as to counteract heat loss in the heating period. During the summer months, a deep roof projection and external blinds protect the rooms against overheating. The northern part of the building houses sanitary facilities, storage and circulation areas. These spaces are used only briefly at certain times of the day. Hot water is supplied by tubular collectors in the south-facing roof slope, and there is a fast-action warm-air heating system. To minimize heat losses due to ventilation, a heat-recovery plant was installed in the roof space.

^
01

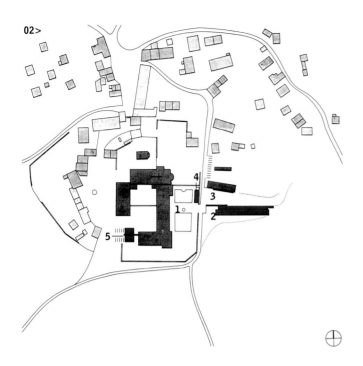

01> Elevational treatment of the service block facing north. The walls are clad in timber planks, the roof in sheet metal.

02> Site plan. The hostel is located to the east of the main complex.

03> The entrance and covered walkway.

Key

1 Monastery
2 New hostel building
3 Old building
4 Outbuilding
5 Covered car parking

^
03

Chapter Four / Architecture and the Environment

05>

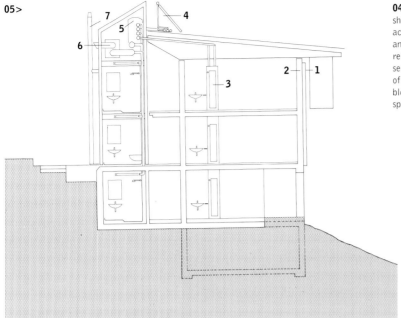

04> The east façade showing the south-facing accommodation block and its back-to-back relationship with the service block. The corner of the accommodation block contains communal spaces.

05> Cross-section.

Key

1 Translucent heat insulation and sun protection
2 Ventilation above window
3 Low-temperature radiator
4 Solar thermal collectors
5 Hot water tank
6 Mechanical ventilators
7 Flue

06> The south elevation has a projecting roof with thermal collectors above it. The lower ground floor is set back and colonnaded.

^
06

NAME OF BUILDING
The Center for Regenerative Studies

Client/owner
California State University

Occupier
Center for Regenerative Studies

Location
Pomona, California, USA

Architect
Dougherty + Dougherty

Date completed
1994 (Phase I); 1996

Gross area
1,667m²

Construction cost
£2.3 million

Climatic zone
Mediterranean

BUILDING ENERGY FEATURES

Orientation of main façades
South

Natural ventilation: Approx. percentage of gross floor naturally ventilated
100%

Night-time ventilation provision
Natural

Thermal transmission of building envelope
Above standard

Utilization of building mass thermal storage as part of energy strategy?
Yes (passive storage)

Solar control systems
Fixed external; pergolas with vines

Daylighting Approx. percentage of net floor area needing artificial lighting during daylight hours
Less than 10%

Energy-saving controls for artificial lighting?
Timers

Other
Compact fluorescent and metal-halide lamps

HVAC SYSTEMS

Fuel/approx. % use
Mains electricity 5%; photovoltaics 10%; indirect solar 75%; biomass 10%

Boiler type
N/A

Heating system
Electric (Phase I); fan coils with solar hot water (Phase II)

Mechanical ventilation
Circulating fans

Air conditioning type
None

Heat recovery
No

ENERGY PERFORMANCE

Total
N/S

Artificial lighting
N/S

Refrigeration cooling
N/S

Mechanical ventilation
N/S

Heating
N/S

Total estimated carbon dioxide output
N/S

ENVIRONMENTAL/HEALTH FEATURES

Materials/components selection strategy to reduce embodied and transport energy?
Yes

Use of recycled materials
Rockwool from steel manufacture

Use of timbers from managed sources
Softwood

Special water conserving installation
Recycled water used in WC and irrigation

Natural organic sewage treatment
Yes

Measures to encourage use of public transport
Shuttle to campus, and bicycles

The Center for Regenerative Studies
Pomona, California, USA

The Center for Regenerative Studies at Cal Poly by Dougherty + Dougherty houses a resident community of students of interdisciplinary environmental and sustainability studies in a cluster of buildings which itself acts as a demonstration ecological community. The design optimizes the efficient use of energy, materials and water in response to the southern Californian climate of hot dry summers and mild winters. The 6.5-hectare (16-acre) site is located adjacent to the Cal Poly campus on an east-west orientated valley with an almost treeless hillside (formerly used as grazing land).

A group of aquaculture ponds, which will eventually link up to a complete sewage treatment and irrigation system, are lined along the Riverfront building. This lightweight timber-frame building on concrete piles hovers over the water. Clad in cedar and Douglas fir, with wide balconies, timber pergolas and copper roofs, the buildings are reminiscent of the Greene & Greene shingle style. The upper buildings nestle into the hillside and house staff accommodation, lecture rooms, and dining and common rooms. Constructed of mass-concrete retaining walls with earth berms at the base, these are clad with cedar on upper storeys. Internal floors are bare concrete or quarry tile.

All of the buildings are designed to promote cross-ventilation, with high- and low-level openable windows. Ceiling fans are used for cooling in summer and mixing stratified air in winter. Passive stack-ventilation towers are located on the north side above roof level. Insulation surpasses the levels set by local building regulations. Compact electrical space heaters in Phase I will eventually be powered by on-site renewable energy generation. Space heating in Phase II utilizes solar hot water in localized fan coil units. Lighting is by high-efficiency compact fluorescent and metal-halide lamps. Internal finishes have been selected for low toxicity and durability and to avoid products which use petrochemicals. Solar collectors are used for hot water. Low-flush WCs and low water-use showers are used.

The site includes a solar park with focusing solar collectors and photovoltaics, and a wind generator. In a later phase an existing methane-powered co-generation plant, built by the County of Los Angeles, will be deeded to the University with the adjacent landfill property.

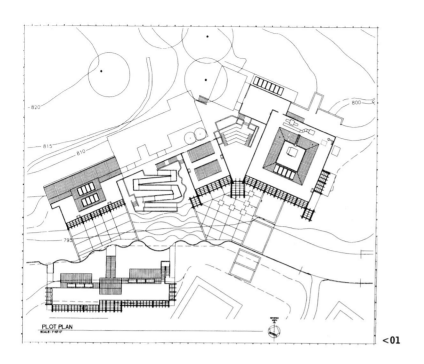

02> View of the buildings from the northern hillside above the development. The Centre is located 40 miles south of Los Angeles in a semi-arid valley lying between California State Polytechnic and a county landfill.

Campuses / The Center for Regenerative Studies.

03> The cedar-clad lecture and seminar building seen from the scissors ramp.

04> Ground-floor plan of the buildings on the southern terrace.

05> View north-west towards the 'Sunspace' building which contains faculty housing. The trellises will carry plants and vines to help shade the buildings.

∧
03

Key

1 Faculty housing
2 Scissors ramp
3 Academic facility
4 Lecture/seminar
5 Amphitheatre
6 Commons
7 Lecture building
8 Public toilets

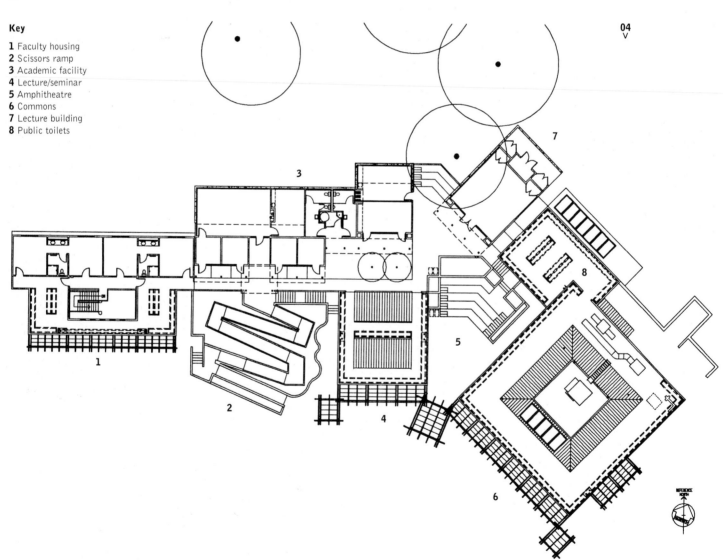

04
∨

NAME OF BUILDING
Center for Japanese Studies, University of Indonesia

Client/owner
University of Indonesia

Occupier
University of Indonesia

Location
West Jawa, Indonesia

Architect
Akihiko Takeuchi

Date completed
March 1995

Gross area
6,269m²

Construction cost
£6.2 million

Climatic zone
Rainforest/tropical

BUILDING ENERGY FEATURES

Orientation of main façades
South and north

Natural ventilation: Approx. percentage of gross floor naturally ventilated
78%

Night-time ventilation provision
Natural

Thermal transmission of building envelope
Standard

Utilization of building mass thermal storage as part of energy strategy?
No

Solar control systems
Deep eaves

Daylighting Approx. percentage of net floor area needing artificial lighting during daylight hours
5%

Energy-saving controls for artificial lighting?
No

Other
–

HVAC SYSTEMS

Fuel/approx. % use
N/S

Boiler type
N/S

Heating system
N/A

Mechanical ventilation
Exhaust window fan

Air conditioning type
Fan coil/heat pump package with air cooling type

Heat recovery
–

ENERGY PERFORMANCE

Total
0.066kW/h/m²

Artificial lighting
0.048kW/h/m²

Refrigeration cooling
0.018kW/h/m²

Mechanical ventilation
N/S

Heating
N/A

Total estimated carbon dioxide output
N/S

ENVIRONMENTAL/HEALTH FEATURES

Materials/components selection strategy to reduce embodied and transport energy?
No

Use of recycled materials
No

Use of timbers from managed sources
No

Special water conserving installation
No

Natural organic sewage treatment
Yes

Measures to encourage use of public transport
No

Center for Japanese Studies University of Indonesia
West Jawa, Indonesia

The University of Indonesia is one of the largest in the country. This campus brings together facilities that were previously located in three different parts of Jakarta. The contemporary vernacular of the city, as with most other Pacific Rim cities, is air conditioned high rise. This campus takes quite a different approach. It is low rise, dispersed in layout and humane in character. Without borrowing specifically from any tradition, the design reflects both the multiracial diversity of Indonesia and the serenity of traditional Japanese architecture. Each faculty reflects some aspect of traditional Indonesian architecture. The unifying element is the 45° pitch clay tiled roofs and the white supporting structure.

The buildings are organized on the site in a traditionally Japanese manner: an arrangement of relaxed order with the seminar hall as the focus. The landscape is characterized by undulating grassed slopes, shaded by trees retained from the site's previous wooded existence.

Jakarta has a tropical climate with high rainfall. The architect's response was to employ natural ventilation where possible, air condition the deeper and more heavily used spaces, provide generous shading in the form of the overhanging eaves, and ensure that all the walkways between the buildings were open but adequately protected from rain.

The larger internal spaces rise upwards to include the generous volume created at high level by the deeply pitched roofs, giving them a pleasant grandeur and airiness. Daylight, introduced at roof level, further enhances these spaces.

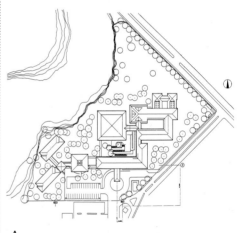

∧
01

01> Site plan. Campus buildings are deployed around the central seminar building.

02> Section through one of the major halls.

03> The clay-tiled roofs of the campus buildings dominate the carefully contrived informal landscape.

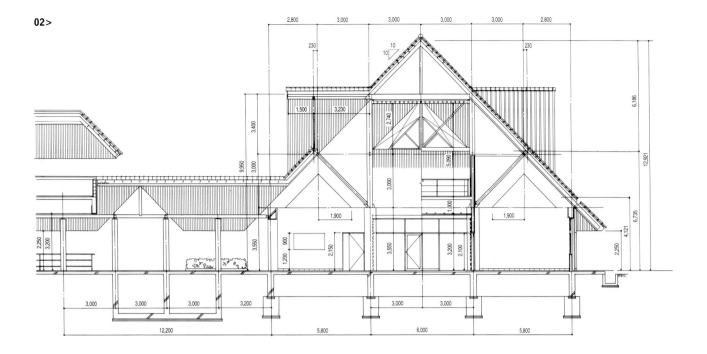

145

Chapter Four / Architecture and the Environment

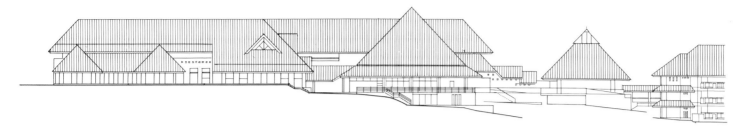

04> Elevation showing the simple and consistent use of a limited palette of materials.

05> A covered link between buildings.

06> Elevation.

07> Internal courtyard.

Client/owner/occupier
Mufifjulu Community
and Parks Australia –
Environment Australia

Location
Northern Territory,
Australia

Architect
Gregory Burgess Architects

Date completed
October 1995

Gross area
1,500m^2

Construction cost
£1.9 million

Climatic zone
Desert

BUILDING ENERGY FEATURES

**Orientation of main
façades**
Multiple

**Natural ventilation:
Approx. percentage of
gross floor naturally
ventilated**
100%

**Night-time ventilation
provision**
Natural

**Thermal transmission
of building envelope**
Standard

**Utilization of building
mass thermal storage as
part of energy strategy?**
Yes

Solar control systems
Fixed external; perforated
sand-brick walls; shingles

**Daylighting
Approx. percentage of
net floor area needing
artificial lighting during
daylight hours**
15%

**Energy-saving controls
for artificial lighting?**
No

Other
–

HVAC SYSTEMS

Fuel/approx. % use
Diesel generator 100%

Boiler type
Condensing gas

Heating system
None. Gas spot heating

Mechanical ventilation
In WCs and kitchen

Air conditioning type
–

Heat recovery
–

ENERGY PERFORMANCE

Total
N/S

Artificial lighting
N/S

Refrigeration cooling
N/S

Mechanical ventilation
N/S

Heating
N/S

**Total estimated carbon
dioxide output**
N/S

ENVIRONMENTAL/HEALTH FEATURES

**Materials/components
selection strategy to
reduce embodied and
transport energy?**
Yes

Use of recycled materials
No

**Use of timbers from
managed sources**
Hardwood

**Special water conserving
installation**
Roof collection for drinking

**Natural organic sewage
treatment**
Diston 'clearwater' sewage
system

**Measures to encourage
use of public transport**
N/A

Uluru-Kata Tjuta National Park Cultural Centre
Northern Territory, Australia

This building lies in the shadow of the massive Uluru (Ayers Rock). This famous rock is the focus of the Uluru-Kata Tjuta National Park, and both physically and symbolically lies at the epicentre of the Australian outback. The Cultural Centre sets out to explain to tourists the culture of the Anangu, the Aboriginal people of the region, and their relationship with this sacred place.

Before commencing the design, the architects spent over a month on the site evolving the concept through collaboration with the local community. They wanted to get an understanding of the site and its surroundings, and how best to convey the essence of the place and its spiritual importance. A brief was evolved and preliminary ideas sketched out in the sand. An important conclusion was that the building should be located at the point where the sand dunes of the desert meet the Uluru-created landscape of umbrella bush, bloodwood trees and bearded grass. It was also imperative to ensure the least possible disturbance to the site. It was decided that an ancient desert oak should form the focus of the complex.

The building evokes the shifting dunes of the desert but, as with this landscape, there are pockets that form places of repose. It comprises two parts: the southern building contains the entrance and main display galleries; the northern building houses the shop, café and a rounded multipurpose hall. The two are linked by enclosures and shaded verandahs which contain outdoor exhibition areas and a dance space. These two spaces will, in time, be shaded by traditional Wiltja structures and bush trees. To the local people, the two serpentine buildings have come to represent mythic snakes poised between separation and engagement.

The construction offers lessons for understanding the place. Some materials have been drawn from the site itself: the walls are bricks, formed from desert sand, and in combination with floors of stabilized sand provide thermal mass. The timbers are largely radial-sawn plantation hardwoods and natural poles. The building utilizes natural ventilation for comfort; of the little rain that falls on the roof, some is conserved for drinking water.

The building successfully captures the spirit and poetry of Uluru, without descending to the realm of kitsch which so often characterizes tourist facilities.

<01

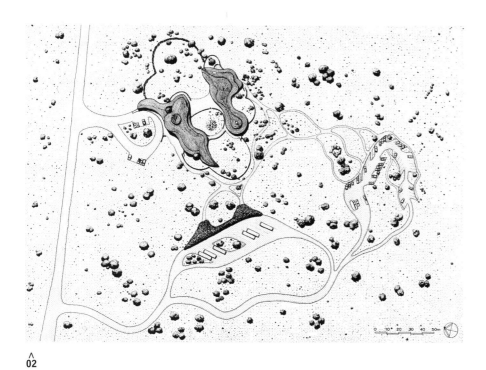

01 > The building in its setting beneath Ayers Rock.

02 > Site plan showing the two serpentine buildings facing each other in the desert setting.

03 > The ancient oak forms the focus of the complex.

^
02

^
03

Campuses / Uluru-Kata Tjuta National Park Cultural Centre

04 > Interior of the display space with a central, tree-like column allowing carefully controlled daylight to filter through its branches.

05 > View of the south building showing the very generous overhangs.

06 > Sections through the north and south buildings.

$\overset{\wedge}{05}$

06 >

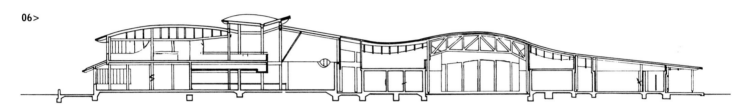

NORTH BUILDING

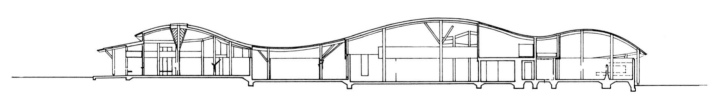

SOUTH BUILDING

< 04

NAME OF BUILDING
Elizabeth Fry Building, University of East Anglia

Client/owner
University of East Anglia

Occupier
University of East Anglia

Location
Norwich, Norfolk, UK

Architect
John Miller & Partners

Date completed
January 1996

Gross area
3,250m²

Construction cost
£2.9 million

Climatic zone
Temperate

BUILDING ENERGY FEATURES

Orientation of main façades
North and south

Natural ventilation: Approx. percentage of gross floor naturally ventilated
100%

Night-time ventilation provision
Forced

Thermal transmission of building envelope
Above standard

Utilization of building mass thermal storage as part of energy strategy?
Yes

Solar control systems
Fixed external; internal blinds/louvres

Daylighting Approx. percentage of net floor area needing artificial lighting during daylight hours
20%

Energy-saving controls for artificial lighting?
No

Other
–

HVAC SYSTEMS

Fuel/approx. % use
Mains electricity 40%; natural gas 60%

Boiler type
Condensing gas (60kW total)

Heating system
No distributed heating system

Mechanical ventilation
Tempered supply

Air conditioning type
–

Heat recovery
Recuperative heat recovery

ENERGY PERFORMANCE

Total
71kW/h/m² per annum

Artificial lighting
15kW/h/m²

Refrigeration cooling
N/A

Mechanical ventilation
16kW/h/m²

Heating
40kW/h/m²

Total estimated carbon dioxide output
N/S

ENVIRONMENTAL/HEALTH FEATURES

Materials/components selection strategy to reduce embodied and transport energy?
Yes

Use of recycled materials
No

Use of timbers from managed sources
Yes

Special water conserving installation
Rainwater for irrigation

Natural organic sewage treatment
No

Measures to encourage use of public transport
Bus service

Elizabeth Fry Building University of East Anglia
Norwich, Norfolk, UK

This new teaching building forms part of a concentrated development of recent teaching and student accommodation at the western end of the University of East Anglia campus. The accommodation comprises lecture theatres for general undergraduate use at lower ground level; and at upper ground level, suites of lecture rooms, seminar and tutorial spaces arranged for flexible use by external short course training, together with dining facilities and finishing kitchen. On the upper floors the accommodation consists of offices, tutorial and administration functions, common rooms, resource space and postgraduate rooms.

To achieve low-energy comfort within the building, ambient conditions are maximized by using the building structure as an energy store, combined with low-pressure mechanical ventilation, a system of heat recovery and windows that can be opened. Total fresh-air ventilation is delivered by utilizing hollow cores in the structural floor units; these allow air to be distributed through the building. To assist low energy consumption, the building envelope is super-insulated using 200mm (8-inch) thick mineral wool, a heavyweight concrete block inner leaf and triple glazing. Special measures, such as double seals and mechanical junctions between window and wall, were employed to ensure minimal leakage of air. There is no thermal bridging of the fabric, while summertime solar gains are minimized by screening. The result is a building with total heat demand from boilers of 24kW and no mechanical cooling, serving a building of 3,000 square metres (32,000 square feet) with a potential occupancy of 780 people.

This highly energy-efficient building achieves its aims with little overt display of means. Its architectural expression relies on the universal values of form, space and light, employing them to excellent effect.

01> Site plan with the Elizabeth Fry building located to the north-east of the university complex.

02> The central bay of the north façade forms the entrance to the building.

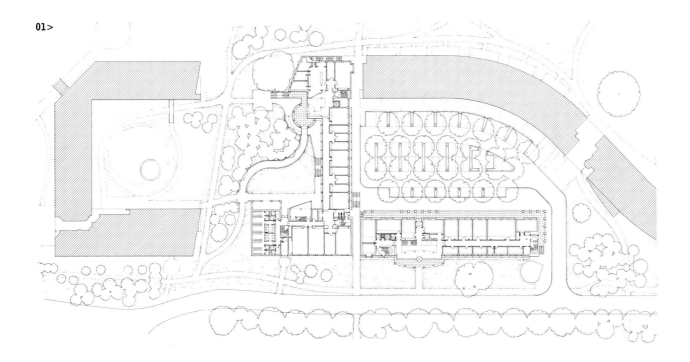

Campuses / Elizabeth Fry Building, University of East Anglia

Chapter Four / Architecture and the Environment

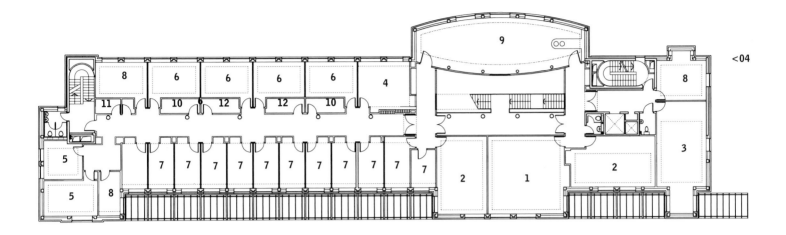

03> Daylight floods into the central staircase from the rooflight above.

04> First-floor plan.

Key

1 Lecture room
2 Seminar room
3 Research desk room
4 Department administration reception office
5 Professor's/course director's office
6 Faculty office (double)
7 Faculty office (single)
8 Secretary's office
9 Common room
10 Files/monograph store
11 Storage
12 Photocopying room

05> Screened balconies on the south façade.

^
05

06> Section through the building showing the heavy insulation – particularly of the roof – and the 'Termodeck' pre-cast floor panels through which air is channelled.

07> The main meeting space on the third floor has north-facing ribbon windows.

06>

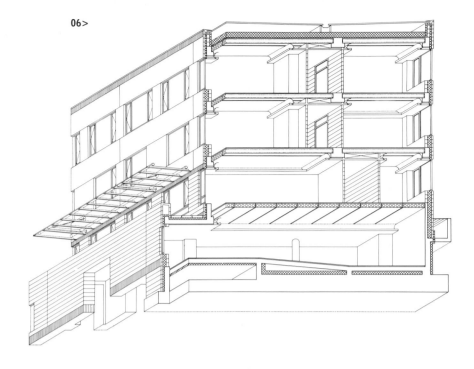

Chapter Four / Architecture and the Environment

**'And midst of all, clustered with bay
And myrtle, and just gleaming to the day
Lurked a pavilion – a delicious sight
– Small, marble, well-proportioned, mellowy white....'**

(Leigh Hunt, *The Story of Rimini*, Canto III)

4.4
Pavilions

Small-scale buildings are not always shackled by the operational requirements of larger ones; they can be playful. When designing pavilions, pleasure houses and follies on their estates, architects and their patrons knew that the stage was set for architectural conceit and experiment. While grander mansions demand solutions to complex requirements, pavilions are often occasional pieces – bagatelles. This is not to say that they are trivial, however: new departures in architecture often began with such apparently minor buildings.

Reconstructed German Pavilion built for the 1929 International Exposition, Barcelona, Spain by Mies Van der Rohe.

NAME OF BUILDING
Spring Lake Park Visitors Center

Client/owner
Sonoma County Water Agency

Occupier
Sonoma County Parks
and Recreation

Location
Santa Rosa, California, USA

Architect
Obie G. Bowman

Date completed
1992

Gross area
186m²

Construction cost
£250,000

Climatic zone
Mediterranean

BUILDING ENERGY FEATURES

Orientation of main façades
North, south, east, west
(solar collector to
south-east)

**Natural ventilation:
Approx. percentage of
gross floor naturally
ventilated**
100%

**Night-time ventilation
provision**
N/A

**Thermal transmission
of building envelope**
Standard

**Utilization of building
mass thermal storage as
part of energy strategy?**
Yes

Solar control systems
Fixed external

**Daylighting
Approx. percentage of
net floor area needing
artificial lighting during
daylight hours**
0%

**Energy-saving controls
for artificial lighting?**
No

Other
Dimmers

HVAC SYSTEMS

Fuel/approx. % use
Indirect solar 95%;
wood 5%

Boiler type
Wood-burning stove

Heating system
Air solar collector and
blower

Mechanical ventilation
Air pipes and vents; fan

Air conditioning type
None

Heat recovery
No

ENERGY PERFORMANCE

Total
N/S

Artificial lighting
N/S

Refrigeration cooling
N/S

Mechanical ventilation
N/S

Heating
N/S

**Total estimated carbon
dioxide output**
N/S

ENVIRONMENTAL/HEALTH FEATURES

**Materials/components
selection strategy to
reduce embodied and
transport energy?**
Yes

Use of recycled materials
No

**Use of timbers from
managed sources**
Softwood

**Special water conserving
installation**
N/A

**Natural organic sewage
treatment**
N/A

**Measures to encourage
use of public transport**
–

Spring Lake Park Visitors Center
Santa Rosa, California, USA

Spring Lake Park Visitors Center is a timber and glass square pyramid set into a deeply wooded hillside overlooking Spring Lake in northern California. The surrounding oak and buckeye trees are particularly fragile due to the volcanic soil. The building and its landscaping delicately carve into the hillside a sequence of open and enclosed spaces intended for viewing, nature study and talks. A meandering path leads uphill from the car park to an entry circle and further on to an enclosed outdoor 'storytelling' cavern, 2.5 metres (8 feet) in diameter, formed by boulders and tree trunks removed during construction. An outdoor amphitheatre is carved into the hillside on the south-east side behind the centre and there is an observation deck to the west. The building houses interactive displays and a pit for children's activities; the latter is enclosed with a fabric tent suspended from the ceiling and tensioned by great boulders at its base.

The Visitors Center pyramid is situated on a north-west-facing site. Its double glazed walls, set on a concrete base, are supported by a rigid steel frame and topped by a fir-clad attic. An external system of redwood louvres is tiered upwards, from wide to thin, in order to shield the glass walls, whilst allowing full views of the valley below. The south-east face is a large solar panel which collects warm air at the attic. Blowers vent this air through exposed ductwork into the single-space room below. In cold weather, heating is supplemented by a wood-burning stove which has a catalytic converter. In summer, air is drawn in from the cool north façade through vents in the base via a system of cooling pipes located below ground. Exhaust air is emitted through opening vents in the attic eaves, via a ceiling fan.

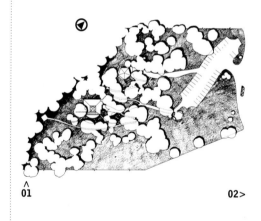

^
01

02>

01> Site plan showing
the Visitors Center and
car park set in the
woods.

02> Seen from the
north, the building
is integrated perfectly
with its setting. Impact
on the woodland was
minimized by reusing
existing parking and
allowing only pedestrian
access.

Key

1 Wood-burning stove with
catalytic combuster
2 Solar air heating collector
3 Supply manifold
with blowers
4 Intake manifold with
filtered openings

Key

1 Intake via underground
cooling tubes
2 Ceiling fan discharges
hot air through eave vents
3 Automatic louvres vent
collector via roof vents

03>

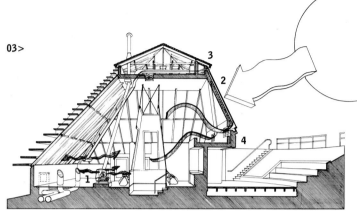

Heating section

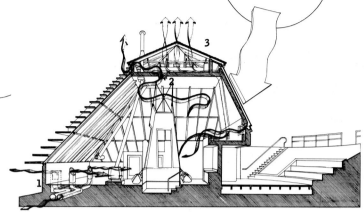

Cooling section

^
04

03> North-south section through the pavilion showing the winter mode of operation with south-facing air collector (left) and the winter mode with a reflective insulating panel covering the air collector, and attic vents open to release hot air (right).

04> The pavilion with its glazed wall and timber louvres. The fabric story-telling tent is on the left.

05> The south façade of the pavilion with the outdoor amphitheatre below and the air solar collectors above.

06> The north-west corner of the building. The louvres allow daylighting and views into the woodland but shade the interior from direct sunlight.

161

^
06

Pavilions / Spring Lake Park Visitors Center

NAME OF BUILDING
Sea Folk Museum

Client/owner
The Foundation of Tokai Suisan Kagaku Kyoukai

Location
Toba-City, Mie Prefecture, Japan

Architect
Naito Architect & Associates

Date completed
June 1992

Gross area
18,058m²

Construction cost
£1.6 million

Climatic zone
Temperate

BUILDING ENERGY FEATURES

Orientation of main façades
Multiple

Natural ventilation: Approx. percentage of gross floor naturally ventilated
None

Night-time ventilation provision
None

Thermal transmission of building envelope
Standard

Utilization of building mass thermal storage as part of energy strategy?
Yes

Solar control systems
Building fabric

Daylighting Approx. percentage of net floor area needing artificial lighting during daylight hours
N/A

Energy-saving controls for artificial lighting?
N/A

Other
–

HVAC SYSTEMS

Fuel/approx. % use
Mains electricity 100%

Boiler type
None

Heating system
Air-cooling heat pump

Mechanical ventilation
Duct fan (exhibition hall); industrial ventilator (repository)

Air conditioning type
Air-cooling heat pump

Heat recovery
No

ENERGY PERFORMANCE

Total
N/S

Artificial lighting
N/S

Refrigeration cooling
N/S

Mechanical ventilation
N/S

Heating
N/S

Total estimated carbon dioxide output
N/S

ENVIRONMENTAL/HEALTH FEATURES

Materials/components selection strategy to reduce embodied and transport energy?
N/S

Use of recycled materials
N/S

Use of timbers from managed sources
N/S

Special water conserving installation
Pond circulating pump

Natural organic sewage treatment
No

Measures to encourage use of public transport
Bus service

Sea Folk Museum
Toba-City, Mie Prefecture, Japan

This is a museum concerned with fishermen, their equipment and culture. Exhibits are mainly collected from the local area, the Shima region of Mie Prefecture. The region has a beautiful coastline and the Sea Folk Museum is located on a hill by the coast. A major concern of this project was how to solve the problems caused by the salt erosion, strong winds and heavy rain that are features of the area. The solution was to follow the precedent of the local vernacular.

A metal roof could not be used because of the salt problem from the sea, so a traditional Japanese tiled roof was adopted instead. Tiling, however, is vulnerable to high winds and it was necessary to compensate for this by planting trees as windbreaks and by carrying out earth works to the periphery of the site. Visual harmony between the museum and its surroundings is provided by the simple gable roofs.

The museum is divided primarily between exhibition hall and repository. The latter required a high level of humidity in order to preserve the fishing boats and nets; accordingly, a concrete structure was adopted. Pre-cast concrete was used because of the tight budget. Transportation by trailer restricted the modules to a width of 2.25 metres (7½ feet), with a span composed of five units post-tensioned together. The wall was protected by spraying resin directly on to the pre-cast concrete external surfaces.

A timber structure was adopted for the exhibition hall, being more in keeping with the nature of the museum's contents. Here the external walls comprise wooden panels treated with a tar-based coating. This resembles the finish of the local houses which traditionally use a coating of whale oil. In the interior, large-span wood beams are assembled structurally to suggest the keel of a ship. This timber structure, combined with the omission of display walls (most exhibits are free-standing), allows a close visual connection between the objects and the setting outside the building. By combining new technology (such as post-tensioned pre-cast concrete) with traditional techniques, the Sea Folk Museum has achieved a sense of durability and simple strength within the constraints of a strict budget.

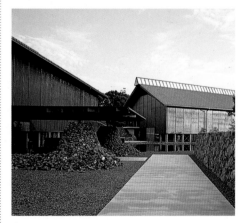

^
01

01> The two exhibition halls for permanent display.

02> Site plan showing the relationship between repository, exhibition and external spaces.

Key

1 Entrance room
2 Exhibition Wing A
3 Exhibition Wing B
4 Main entrance
5 Water plaza
6 Courtyard

03> The tiled roofscape looking north-west.

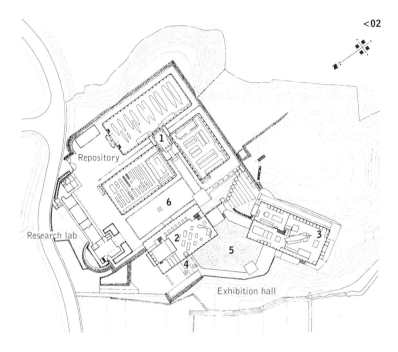

<02

Repository

Research lab

Exhibition hall

^
03

04

04> A view between the two timber-clad exhibition halls across the water court towards the concrete repository buildings.

05> North elevation.

06> Section through Exhibition Wing A, accommodating a change in level and showing the timber construction.

07> The timber roof structure of one of the exhibition halls incorporating a roof light.

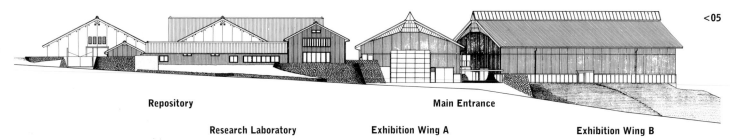

<05

Repository

Research Laboratory

Main Entrance

Exhibition Wing A

Exhibition Wing B

<06   07>

NAME OF BUILDING
Paper Church

Client/owner
Takatori Catholic Church

Date completed
September 1996

Occupier
The local community

Gross area
150m²

Location
Nagata, Kobe, Japan

Construction cost
N/S

Architect
Shigeru Ban

Climatic zone
Mediterranean

BUILDING ENERGY FEATURES

Orientation of main façades
N/A

Solar control systems
Fixed external; motorized/variable external

Natural ventilation: Approx. percentage of gross floor naturally ventilated
100%

Daylighting Approx. percentage of net floor area needing artificial lighting during daylight hours
0%

Night-time ventilation provision
Natural

Energy-saving controls for artificial lighting?
No

Thermal transmission of building envelope
High

Other
—

Utilization of building mass thermal storage as part of energy strategy?
No

HVAC SYSTEMS

Fuel/approx. % use
Mains electricity 100%

Mechanical ventilation
None

Boiler type
None

Air conditioning type
None

Heating system
None

Heat recovery
No

ENERGY PERFORMANCE

Total
N/A

Heating
N/A

Artificial lighting
N/A

Total estimated carbon dioxide output
N/A

Refrigeration cooling
N/A

Mechanical ventilation
N/A

ENVIRONMENTAL/HEALTH FEATURES

Materials/components selection strategy to reduce embodied and transport energy?
Yes

Special water conserving installation
No

Use of recycled materials
Paper

Natural organic sewage treatment
No

Use of timbers from managed sources
Softwood

Measures to encourage use of public transport
No

Paper Church and Paper Log House
Nagata, Kobe, Japan

The architect Shigeru Ban has developed both a new architectural language and a radical engineering technique through his use of large tubes made of recycled paper as a primary construction material. Initially he used them internally, as in his installation for an Alvar Aalto exhibition. He then developed the technique further, using the tubes structurally for temporary buildings and then to construct permanent buildings.

With his experience of providing emergency shelter, Ban visited the site of the Kobe earthquake in January 1995. Amongst the destruction, he found a community of Catholic Koreans and Vietnamese whose homes and church had been destroyed. He offered his help in replacing the church.

The construction comprises an oval formed of 58 industrial-grade paper tubes, 330mm (13 inches) in diameter, supporting a stressed membrane roof of Teflon-coated fabric. This is contained within a rectangular box measuring 150 square metres (1,614 square feet), made up of hinged louvre panels in clear plastic on a lightweight steel frame. The resulting single-room structure has an innate grace and buoyancy – serving its purpose most effectively as a community hall and temporary place of prayer.

The architect found himself responsible for funding the project, designing it and constructing it. Funding was the most exacting task, with the bulk of the money coming from individual donations. There were also donations in kind for the construction. The building was erected, in the main, by architectural students over a period of five weeks. It opened exactly eight months after the disaster.

As well as the church, Shigeru Ban was responsible for constructing a number of emergency homes after the earthquake. These use a generic plan and are designed to be erected quickly, without specialist skills and with minimum resource. At Kobe, each of these paper log houses is square in plan, measuring 4 x 4 metres (13 x 13 feet). The floor, walls and roof trusses are all constructed from 108mm (4¼ inch) diameter paper tubes. The base of each building comprises sand-filled beer crates, to which the superstructure of the building is tied. The roof comprises a double layer of Teflon-coated fabric, and incorporates a ventilation flap at one of its gable ends.

The use of paper tubes originated as an aesthetic response to a particular requirement, but developed into an expression of both social and ecological concern without losing its very distinctive stylistic attributes. This is a notable example of the use of standard, low-energy components, not intended for building purposes, being adapted to pressing social and ecological needs.

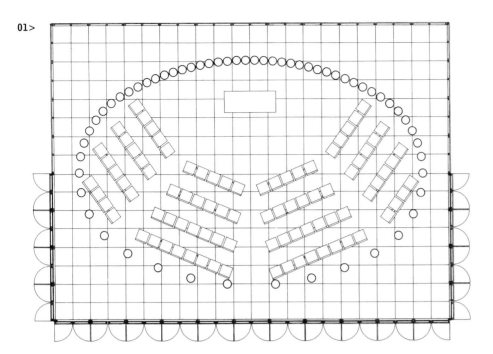

167

^
02

Pavilions / Paper Church and Paper Log House

<03

Chapter Four / Architecture and the Environment

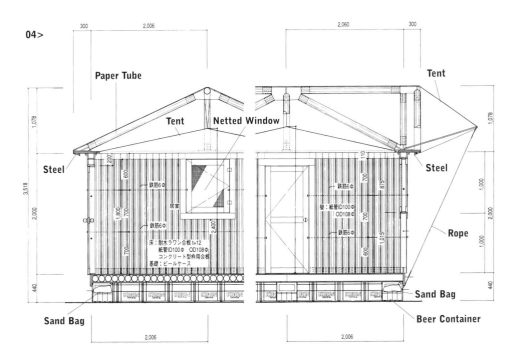

04>

Paper Tube

Tent

Tent   Netted Window

Steel

300   2,006

1,078

3,518

2,000

Steel

200

600

鉄筋6Φ

1,800
700

居室

鉄筋6Φ

700

2,400

床：耐水ラワン合板t=12
紙管ID100Φ OD108Φ
コンクリート型枠用合板
基礎：ビールケース

440

Sand Bag

Sand Bag

2,006

2,060   300

1,078

Steel

Rope

110

700

875

壁：紙管ID100Φ
OD108Φ

鉄筋6Φ

700

1,015

600

鉄筋6Φ

1,000

2,000

1,000

440

Sand Bag

Beer Container

2,006

03> The space between the paper tube colonnade and the lightweight screens allows for a gentle transition between inside and outside.

04> Elevation and section through a square emergency home. Tubes comprise the walls and roof structure. The roof finish is a membrane tied down to the base of the building and incorporating a ventilation flap.

05> Emergency houses in use.

169

^
05

Pavilions / Paper Church and Paper Log House

NAME OF BUILDING
Hall 26, Hanover Messe

Client/owner
Deutsche Messe AG

Occupier
Various

Location
Hanover, Germany

Architect
Herzog & Partner

Date completed
1996

Gross area
25,400m²

Construction cost
N/S

Climatic zone
Temperate

BUILDING ENERGY FEATURES

Orientation of main façades
North and south

Natural ventilation: Approx. percentage of gross floor naturally ventilated
0%

Night-time ventilation provision
Forced

Thermal transmission of building envelope
Standard

Utilization of building mass thermal storage as part of energy strategy?
No

Solar control systems
Fixed external; solar control glazing

Daylighting Approx. percentage of net floor area needing artificial lighting during daylight hours
10%

Energy-saving controls for artificial lighting?
N/S

Other
–

HVAC SYSTEMS

Fuel/approx. % use
N/S

Boiler type
N/S

Heating system
Heated air and heat reclaim

Mechanical ventilation
None

Air conditioning type
VAV (total cooling capacity 4.450kW)

Heat recovery
Yes

ENERGY PERFORMANCE

Total
N/S

Artificial lighting
N/S

Refrigeration cooling
N/S

Mechanical ventilation
N/S

Heating
N/S

Total estimated carbon dioxide output
N/S

ENVIRONMENTAL/HEALTH FEATURES

Materials/components selection strategy to reduce embodied and transport energy?
No

Use of recycled materials
No

Use of timbers from managed sources
N/S

Special water conserving installation
No

Natural organic sewage treatment
No

Measures to encourage use of public transport
N/A

Hall 26, Hanover Messe
Hanover, Germany

Hall 26 is an exhibition space of 25,400 square metres (273,410 square feet) located within the enormous Deutsche Messe AG trade fair complex at Hanover, which the architects were also asked to master plan. The exhibition space comprises three 70-metre (230-foot) bays with service cores at either end of each bay. The roof is suspended from four steel 'A'-frame structures and the walls are of glass curtain walling with timber cladding on the concrete service pods. The roof membrane is constructed from prefabricated timber panels.

The space relies for comfort on displacement ventilation. The air, however, is not introduced from the floor but from large glazed ducts that run along the line of the supporting structure, 4.1 metres (13½ feet) from the floor. The glazed walls of the duct ensure a sense of spatial continuity. The fresh air flows downwards distributing itself evenly over the floor. The air is then borne slowly upwards by the heat generated within the space itself and expelled through continuous openings in the ridge of each zone. The openings are controlled by adjustable flaps. For heating purposes, the ventilation system can be switched to a mode whereby pre-heated air is injected horizontally via adjustable long-range nozzles. A proportion of the heated air can be recirculated.

Natural lighting within the hall is introduced via large north lights along the main structural supports and via light grids in the roof at the lowest points of the suspension bays. Light-deflecting elements channel daylight into the underside of the suspended roof and down into the public areas.

Supplementary and full artificial lighting follow the same principles.

The various passive and active systems that Hall 26 employs are thoroughly integrated and mutually supporting. The result is a building that is both elegant and practical.

^
01

01> The end façade of the hall shows the 'A'-frame structure and high-level shading element.

02> Schematic explaining the structural principles.

03> The contrasting suspended roofs and rectangular service pods.

<02

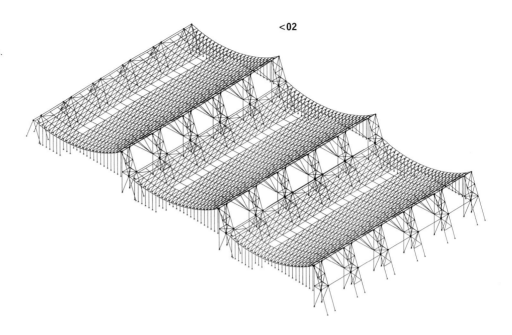

^
03

Pavilions / Hall 26, Hanover Messe

04 > The building's distinctive roofscape.

05 > The glazed walk-through air-supply trunking with directional diffuser nozzles.

06 > The glazed air-supply trunking allows the full volume of the hall to be read visually without interruption.

07 > Schematic sections.

^
04

^
05

07A > Mechanical and natural ventilation

Cooling operation:
1 Natural air supply via flaps in façade
2 Glass ventilation duct with cool-air outlets in floor of duct
3 Thermal up-currents from internal heat sources
4 Natural ventilation via ridge flaps
Heating operation:
5 Mechanical distribution of heated air via long-range nozzles
6 Air extract via ventilation plant at sides

07B > Daylighting system

1 Direct sunlight
2 External sunscreening
3 Triple glazing with daylight grids; reflected sunlight
4 Diffused daylight
5 Louvres for light deflection
6 Mirror soffit

07C > Artificial lighting system

1 Glass duct with light fittings at sides
2 Indirect lighting via mirror soffit
3 Suspended lighting strip

^
06

07 >

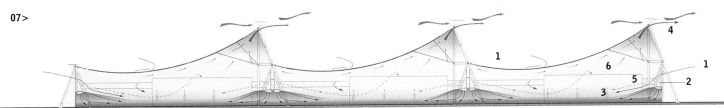

A

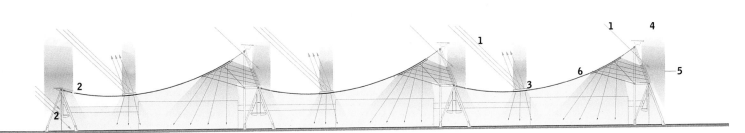

B

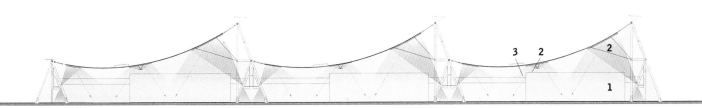

C

Pavilions / Hall 26, Hanover Messe

NAME OF BUILDING
Museum of Wood

Client/owner
Hyogo Prefecture

Date completed
April 1994

Occupier
–

Gross area
2,695m²

Location
Mikata-gun, Hyogo, Japan

Construction cost
N/S

Architect
Tadao Ando

Climatic zone
Temperate

BUILDING ENERGY FEATURES

Orientation of main façades
Multiple

Solar control systems
Building fabric

Natural ventilation: Approx. percentage of gross floor naturally ventilated
N/A

Daylighting Approx. percentage of net floor area needing artificial lighting during daylight hours
N/A

Night-time ventilation provision
N/A

Energy-saving controls for artificial lighting?
N/A

Thermal transmission of building envelope
Standard

Other
–

Utilization of building mass thermal storage as part of energy strategy?
N/A

HVAC SYSTEMS

Fuel/approx. % use
Mains electricity

Mechanical ventilation
N/S

Boiler type
–

Air conditioning type
N/S

Heating system
None

Heat recovery
No

ENERGY PERFORMANCE

Total
N/S

Heating
N/S

Artificial lighting
N/S

Total estimated carbon dioxide output
N/S

Refrigeration cooling
N/S

Mechanical ventilation
N/S

ENVIRONMENTAL/HEALTH FEATURES

Materials/components selection strategy to reduce embodied and transport energy?
Yes

Special water conserving installation
No

Use of recycled materials
N/S

Natural organic sewage treatment
No

Use of timbers from managed sources
N/S

Measures to encourage use of public transport
No

Museum of Wood
Mikata-gun, Hyogo, Japan

'In these times of apprehension over the crisis of our earthly environment and the deterioration of our spiritual culture, it is important that we seek a new beginning – in new understandings of our environment, and in a new appreciation of forests and the culture of wood, for these can bring richness to the heart of man' (Tadao Ando). This museum sets out to present all aspects of wood and the traditions and culture that its use has inspired. The precursor of the structure was the Japanese pavilion designed by Tadao Ando for the Seville Exposition in 1992. It was initially intended that when the Expo closed the pavilion would be shipped to Japan to celebrate National Arbor Day. This plan had to be abandoned, however, due to legal and technical complications. A new building was therefore designed to take its place.

The site is located in a secluded spot among the mountains of Hyogo Prefecture. This is a heavily wooded area, and the ring-shaped building is inserted into the scenery with minimal interruption to the natural setting. At the centre of the building is a void in which a pool has been set. Water sprays have been placed on a grid within the pool. The walls of the court are constructed of faceted and lapped timber planks which rise vertically, reaching up to a circular patch of sky. The building thus dramatically makes the connection between skies above and water below.

The museum comprises a one-room, ring-shaped space, 18 metres (59 feet) high. Pillars stand aligned on a circular arc within this space, which displays the characteristic power of space formed by wooden pillar and beam construction. Here, items related to cultures of forest and wood are exhibited, along a curvilinear ramp winding through the interior. An inclined bridge penetrates the building, crossing the pond and leading to the annexe. It offers views of the rich enclosing forest.

Visitors to the museum experience both the profound wealth of the deep forest and, in the powerful space produced by the building, a man-made representation of that sylvan heritage. They are then released into the interval between purified sky and water. In this way, the museum provides the instrument for experiencing the profound relationship uniting human culture with nature. The building's woodland location, its construction and the elemental nature of the display emphatically connect place, nature and resource.

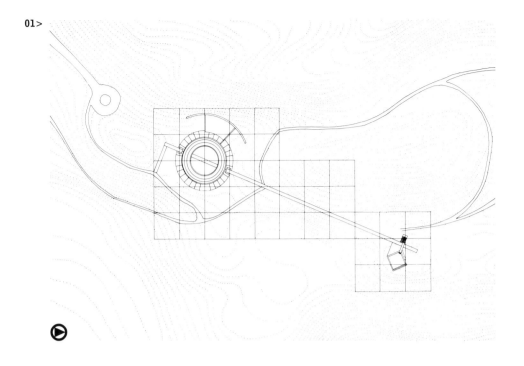

01> Site plan.

02> Aerial view of
the museum set within
the forest.

175

02

Pavilions / Museum of Wood

03>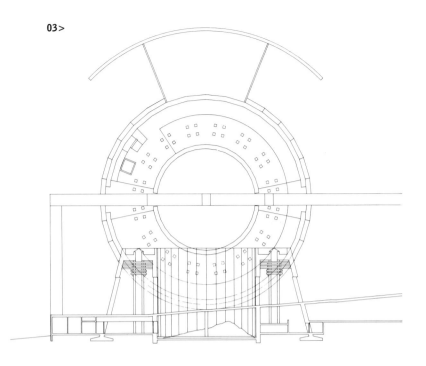

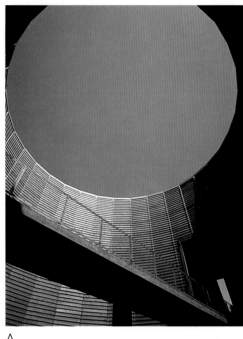

^
04

^
05

Chapter Four / Architecture and the Environment

03> The section overlaid on the plan of the main display space.

04> The ramp passing through the central circular court with sky above and water below.

05> The entrance conservatory at tree-top level takes visitors to the timber-clad exhibition drum.

06> The timber 'forest' set within the display space.

177

NAME OF BUILDING
BRE (Building Research Establishment) Office of the Future

Client/owner	**Date completed**
BRE	December 1996
Occupier	**Gross area**
BRE	2,000m²
Location	**Construction cost**
Garston, Hertfordshire, UK	£3 million
Architect	**Climatic zone**
Feilden Clegg Architects	Temperate

BUILDING ENERGY FEATURES

Orientation of main façades	**Solar control systems**
South	Motorized/variable external; internal blinds/louvres
Natural ventilation: Approx. percentage of gross floor naturally ventilated	**Daylighting Approx. percentage of net floor area needing artificial lighting during daylight hours**
100%	5%
Night-time ventilation provision	
Natural	**Energy-saving controls for artificial lighting?**
Thermal transmission of building envelope	Yes
Above standard	**Other**
Utilization of building mass thermal storage as part of energy strategy?	–
Yes	

HVAC SYSTEMS

Fuel/approx. % use	**Heating system**
Mains electricity 28%; photovoltaics 5%; passive solar and daylight 22%; natural gas 45%	Low-pressure hot water with underfloor heating and perimeter radiators
Boiler type	**Mechanical ventilation**
Low-nox lead condensing gas and standard low-nox gas	Extract fans in WCs
	Air conditioning type
	N/A
	Heat recovery
	No

ENERGY PERFORMANCE

Total	**Heating**
83kW/h/m²/y	47kW/h/m²/y
Artificial lighting	**General electric usage**
9kW/h/m²/y	23kW/h/m²/y
Refrigeration cooling	**Total estimated carbon dioxide output**
2–3.5kW/h/m²/y	31kg/m²/y
Mechanical ventilation	
0.5kW/h/m²/y	

ENVIRONMENTAL/HEALTH FEATURES

Materials/components selection strategy to reduce embodied and transport energy?	**Special water conserving installation**
Yes	Low-flush WCs
Use of recycled materials	**Natural organic sewage treatment**
Concrete and brickwork for hardcore; timber block floor	No
Use of timbers from managed sources	**Measures to encourage use of public transport**
No	No

BRE Office of the Future
Garston, Hertfordshire, UK

The Office of the Future is located at the Building Research Establishment (BRE) in the suburban outskirts of Watford. It is situated in the temperate south of England, in an area with minimal noise or air quality problems. With a combination of leading-edge energy-reducing features, the office demonstrates state-of-the-art energy use in the UK and acts as a testbed for environmental research by the BRE.

The offices are arranged on three storeys, aligned close to east/west, with open-plan and cellular offices, plus seminar rooms. The plan is asymmetric with a 7.5-metre (25-foot) space fronting the south façade, a central corridor zone, and a 4.5-metre (15-foot) space fronting the north façade. The building envelope is well insulated, with low emissivity argon-filled double glazed openable windows making up about 50 per cent of the main façades. These have external motorized glass louvres on the south side to screen the office-space from the sun (trickle ventilation is provided by BMS control of high-level windows, with manual trickle vents on the top floor).

The floor-to-floor height of 3.7 metres (12 feet) is considerably higher than that of a conventional office. The undulating concrete floor slab incorporates raised access floor panels to provide a flat top surface and to accommodate services; large low resistance voids for air movement; and panels of underfloor heating and cooling pipes in a floor screed. Outside air, controlled by BMS-operated windows can enter the rooms directly (at 'high points' in the slab) or enter the voids in the structure (at the slab's 'low points').

The south façade has five ventilation stacks which are glazed and may provide solar assistance; they have low velocity propeller fans to assist stack-effect ventilation in hot, still weather conditions. In intermediate seasons the building is ventilated by opening windows. In cold weather it is heated by underfloor pipes and perimeter radiators fed by a combination of a lead condensing boiler and a low-nox boiler, with fresh air supplied through the BMS-controlled high-level windows. The windows provide supplementary ventilation and night-time cooling in hot weather. Further cooling of the floor slab is provided by water supplied from an on-site borehole.

The high frequency fluorescent lighting using new T5 lamps is dimmable and designed to be controlled by the building's occupants. Photosensors (managed by the BMS) are also incorporated, in order to keep artificial lighting requirements to a minimum.

The building is also an example of good practice in environmental design. Ninety-six per cent of the structure of the building that previously occupied the site was recycled. In the new building recycled bricks were used and recycled aggregate from a demolished concrete panelled building was also used for structural concrete in the foundations, ground slabs and much of the superstructure concrete – a first in the UK.

The energy systems are elaborate for a modestly sized office building, but significant findings should result over the next few years which will help inform the next generation of bioclimatic office buildings.

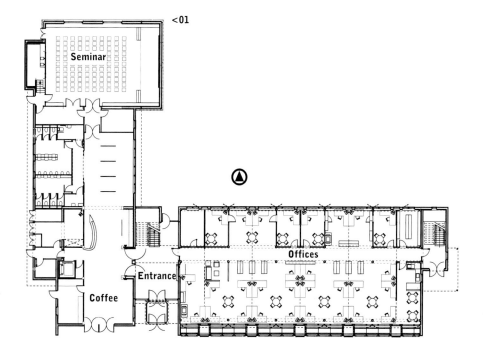

01> Ground-floor plan.

02> The south façade showing the ventilation stacks and the outboard glass louvre system. A late addition is the introduction of a small grid-connected photovoltaic array fixed vertically adjacent to the main entrance.

Seminar

Offices

Entrance

Coffee

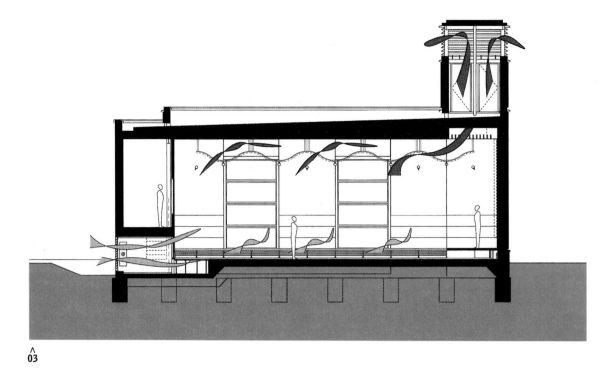

∧
03

∧
04

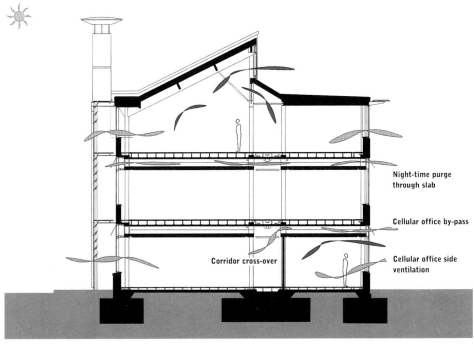

Night-time purge through slab

Cellular office by-pass

Corridor cross-over

Cellular office side ventilation

03 > Section through the seminar room showing the natural ventilation strategy.

04 > External glass louvres shown in horizontal alignment are used for solar control.

05 > Section through the office wing showing air movement.

06 > View of the office space with the undulating ceiling soffit. Cellular offices are on the right.

181

Pavilions / BRE Office of the Future

NAME OF BUILDING
Seed House and Forestry Centre

Client/owner
Ministry of the Walloon region

Occupier
Forest and Nature Dept

Location
Marche-en-Famenne, Belgium

Architect and engineers
Samyn & Partners

Date completed
November 1995

Gross area
1,144m²

Construction cost
£812,240

Climatic zone
Temperate

BUILDING ENERGY FEATURES

Orientation of main façades
East and west

Natural ventilation: Approx. percentage of gross floor naturally ventilated
0%

Night-time ventilation provision
Forced

Thermal transmission of building envelope
Below average

Utilization of building mass thermal storage as part of energy strategy?
Yes

Solar control systems
Solar control glazing

Daylighting Approx. percentage of net floor area needing artificial lighting during daylight hours
17%

Energy-saving controls for artificial lighting?
No

Other
–

HVAC SYSTEMS

Fuel/approx. % use
Mains electricity; mains gas

Boiler type
N/S

Heating system
Radiant panels

Mechanical ventilation
Ducted extract system

Air conditioning type
N/A

Heat recovery
No

ENERGY PERFORMANCE

Total
N/S

Artificial lighting
N/S

Refrigeration cooling
N/A

Mechanical ventilation
N/S

Heating
N/S

Total estimated carbon dioxide output
N/S

ENVIRONMENTAL/HEALTH FEATURES

Materials/components selection strategy to reduce embodied and transport energy?
Yes

Use of recycled materials
No

Use of timbers from managed sources
Yes

Special water conserving installation
No

Natural organic sewage treatment
No

Measures to encourage use of public transport
N/A

Seed House and Forestry Centre
Marche-en-Famenne, Belgium

The public administration of the Walloon area in southern Belgium has been anxious to encourage local ecology. When a silviculture (forestry) centre was proposed, therefore, they insisted that it should be an imaginative demonstration of the potential of timber.

The centre consists of an elongated dome 12.5 metres (41 feet) high and 43 metres (141 feet) long. Timber has been used to build up a matrix of ribs, comprising two layers in the transverse arches and three in the longitudinal arches. All the transverse arches are of equal radius (permitting repetition of components) while the longitudinal arches have radii varying according to their position in the dome. The arches cross at right angles, forming a frame to support a roof of 1,691 laminated glass panels. The timber is generally square in section and was steam-bent to the necessary curvature. Inside the dome are two longitudinal structures in blockwork, housing offices and other functions. The much higher space in-between is used for machinery. The project is a *tour de force* in the contemporary structural use of timber. The internal space it creates is strikingly beautiful, although the prosaic activities seem a little out of place in such an impressive volume.

The energy strategy has not been thought through so carefully, however. There is in effect no insulation and little shading of the interior in summer, and consequently a large amount of mechanical extract ventilation is required to cool the building in the warmest months. In winter large radiant heaters are used; it is now proposed to add a horizontal translucent membrane to reduce the volume and cut the heating load.

The roof covering forms a carapace that resembles a giant woodlouse. All entrances are at ground level and no service pipes pass through the shell; this may become a restriction on adaptability in the future. Despite some shortcomings, however, the building represents an inspired exploitation of a renewable natural resource.

^
01

01> The sylviculture centre located in its forest clearing.

02> Plan of the building showing the pure external shape with subsidiary accommodation within.

03> At night the internal illumination glows through the glass panels.

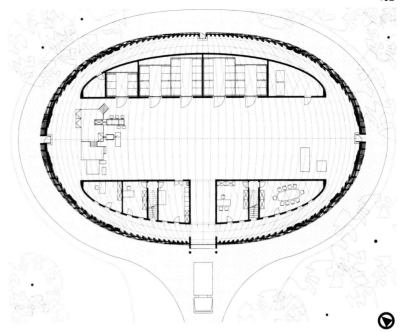

^
03

05>

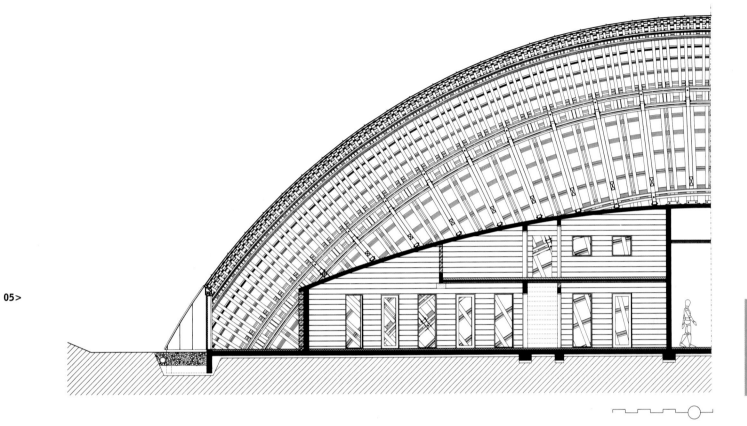

185

04>The space between the external timber framework and the blockwork structure housing offices. The large proportion of glazed area to timber structure is indicated by the pattern of sunlight.

05>Longitudinal section through the end of the building. Prefabrication of the timber structure has been greatly simplified by making all the transverse arches the same radius.

06>The building sits on the ground like a giant woodlouse. The complexity and precision of the timber structure is evident. The external skin is of laminated glass panels.

^
06

NAME OF BUILDING
Toyo Village Mason Museum

Client/owner/occupier	**Date completed**
Toyo Village	December 1993
Location	**Gross area**
Kumamoto Prefecture,	830m²
Japan	**Construction cost**
Architect	£1.8 million
Yasufumi Kijima & Yas	**Climatic zone**
and Urbanists	Temperate

BUILDING ENERGY FEATURES

Orientation of main façades	**Solar control systems**
Multiple	N/A
Natural ventilation: Approx. percentage of gross floor naturally ventilated	**Daylighting Approx. percentage of net floor area needing artificial lighting during daylight hours**
100%	80%
Night-time ventilation provision	**Energy-saving controls for artificial lighting?**
None	N/A
Thermal transmission of building envelope	**Other**
Standard	–
Utilization of building mass thermal storage as part of energy strategy?	
Yes	

HVAC SYSTEMS

Fuel/approx. % use	**Mechanical ventilation**
N/S	N/S
Boiler type	**Air conditioning type**
N/S	Air heat pump
Heating system	**Heat recovery**
N/S	No

ENERGY PERFORMANCE

Total	**Heating**
N/S	N/S
Artificial lighting	**Total estimated carbon dioxide output**
N/S	N/S
Refrigeration cooling	
N/S	
Mechanical ventilation	
N/S	

ENVIRONMENTAL/HEALTH FEATURES

Materials/components selection strategy to reduce embodied and transport energy?	**Special water conserving installation**
Yes	No
Use of recycled materials	**Natural organic sewage treatment**
–	No
Use of timbers from managed sources	**Measures to encourage use of public transport**
–	No

Toyo Village Mason Museum
Kumamoto Prefecture, Japan

This museum celebrates the stonemason's craft. Toyo is a small village in southern Kyushu. At one time, many masons came from this village. Called the Taneyama masons, they constructed many magnificent stone bridges, mainly in Kyushu. They were also responsible for the stone bridge in the Palace of Tokyo.

The architect has made the building itself an integral component of the museum display. The walls exemplify the stonemasons' traditional techniques, complemented by the roof which comprises a traditional Japanese timber structure. The success of the building depended on the expertise of the masons. In the village, however, few were left and masons had to be imported from China where the skill has been retained. Collaborating with masons from Toyo, they reinterpreted and developed the tradition, covering all aspects of the trade from cutting the stone to laying it.

Another aim of this project was to reinterpret the construction technique of the local timber roof structure into a rationalized contemporary process. Timber has declined in popularity in Japanese contemporary architecture, partly because of its 'primitive' connotations but also because of the complexity of detail that traditional Japanese structures require. In this case, computers came to the aid of the architects. They measured each log and input all the necessary information for structural calculations in the computer program. By applying innovatory structural logic to the recorded data they found that in a particular assembly logs are

highly suited to forming a dome. The result is a building that dramatically expresses timber and stone structures in combination.

∧
01

01> The museum is set in the exquisite landscape of the Kyushu Valley.

02> Site plan.

03> The exterior of the museum is characterized by the use of various stone-walling techniques.

^
03

05>

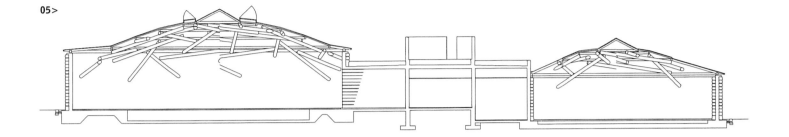

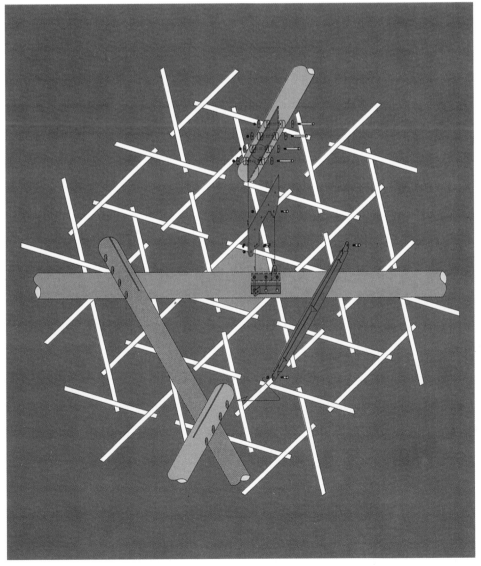

04> The roof of the main exhibition space is a complex timber construction. The central feature is a stone arch with supporting timber falsework.

05> Section through the exhibition spaces.

06> Schematic showing the principles of the roof structure.

∧
06

NAME OF BUILDING
EDF Regional Headquarters

Client/owner
Electricité de France

Occupier
Electricité de France

Location
Bordeaux, France

Architect
Foster and Partners

Date completed
July 1996

Net area
7,230m²

Construction cost
£7.1 million

Climatic zone
Mediterranean

BUILDING ENERGY FEATURES

Orientation of main façades
East and west

Natural ventilation: Approx. percentage of gross floor naturally ventilated
(mixed mode)

Night-time ventilation provision
Natural

Thermal transmission of building envelope
Standard (transparent insulation and low E glass)

Utilization of building mass thermal storage as part of energy strategy?
Yes

Solar control systems
Fixed external

Daylighting Approx. percentage of net floor area needing artificial lighting during daylight hours
50%

Energy-saving controls for artificial lighting?
Yes

Other
–

HVAC SYSTEMS

Fuel/approx. % use
Mains electricity
100%

Boiler type
Heat pump

Heating system
APELSA water mats in floor

Mechanical ventilation
Fan coils with central exhaust

Air conditioning type
Cooled/heated; reduction in hygromery only

Heat recovery
No

ENERGY PERFORMANCE

Total
65 kW/h/m² (base load)

Artificial lighting
8kW/h/m²/y

Refrigeration cooling
31kW/h/m²/y

Mechanical ventilation
13kW/h/m²/y

Heating
13kW/h/m²/y

Total estimated carbon dioxide output
Low (electrical generation is nuclear or hydro)

ENVIRONMENTAL/HEALTH FEATURES

Materials/components selection strategy to reduce embodied and transport energy?
Yes

Use of recycled materials
No

Use of timbers from managed sources
Yes

Special water conserving installation
No

Natural organic sewage treatment
No

Measures to encourage use of public transport
No

EDF Regional Headquarters
Bordeaux, France

This new regional headquarters in Bordeaux for the state electricity company gathers together various departments previously scattered throughout the city. The building was intended as a showpiece for the innovative use of electricity. Thanks to the ingenious application of natural ventilation and other energy-saving devices appropriate to the warm climate of southern France, the four-storey, electricity-powered building is expected to have an energy consumption approximately 30 per cent less than buildings of a similar type in France. For efficiency, it can compete with gas-powered buildings.

The building envelope minimizes heat gain and loss (as well as reducing traffic noise from the busy road on the west side). To prevent solar gain the elevations are fitted with bleached cedarwood louvres, the most prominent exterior feature. The louvres are fixed and provide shade without unduly obscuring views out. Internal heat gain is minimized by restricting heat-producing office equipment to a central air-conditioned zone.

Natural ventilation is used wherever possible. The thermal mass of the exposed concrete ceiling soffits helps to maintain comfortable interior temperatures during the day. At night the windows on the east and west sides open automatically, allowing air to cool the concrete.

The energy-efficient water-based heating and cooling system is run by an electric heat pump that works off a centralized exhaust stack. The water-cooled floor is kept at the ambient temperature of 20°C in summer and 22°C

in winter. Natural lighting is employed as much as possible; the target daylight factor is 200 lux in the entrance atrium and 450 lux in offices.

Bright colours contrast with the natural hues of the timber screens: the internal circulation areas are painted in vivid yellow, while externally the blue-painted concrete structure is visible behind the brise-soleil. An avenue of indigenous trees has been planted along the entrance axis, echoing the geometry of nearby Château Raba.

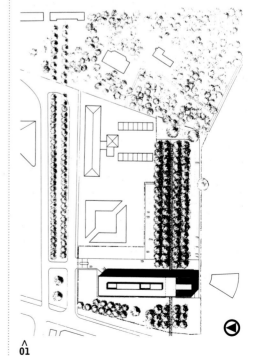

^
01

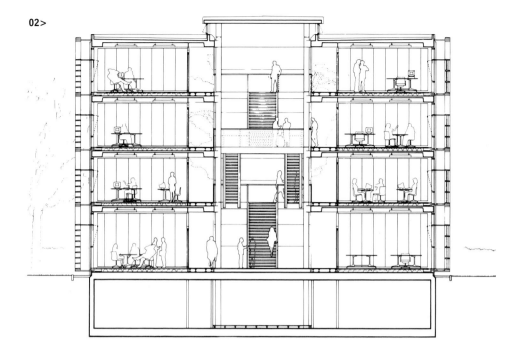

01> Site plan. The building is designed to relate to the geometry of nearby Château Raba. An avenue of trees leads to the entrance.

02> A cross-section shows the arrangement of cellular offices and seminar rooms around a central circulation area. Heat gain is the main problem in the Bordeaux climate; electric office equipment is kept in the central, air-conditioned area. The building envelope provides high insulation, and fixed-louvre brise-soleils reduce solar gain on both the main façades.

03> The exterior from the south-west. The louvres across the west façade are designed to allow views from the building. The smaller block on the right contains trade union offices and the staff restaurant.

191

^
03

Pavilions / EDF Regional Headquarters

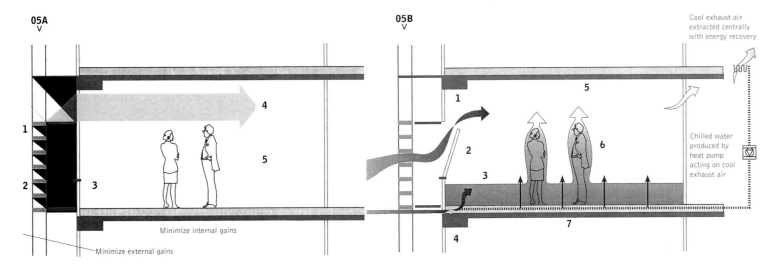

05A
∨

1

2 3

4

5

Minimize internal gains

Minimize external gains

05B
∨

1

2

3

4

5

6

7

Cool exhaust air extracted centrally with energy recovery

Chilled water produced by heat pump acting on cool exhaust air

Key

05A> Reduction of Energy Requirements

1 Transparent insulation and reflector panel to optimize daylighting
2 Fixed sun-shading to minimize solar gain
3 High-performance building envelope cuts down ambient heat gains
4 Daylighting reduces heat load from artificial lighting
5 Heat-producing equipment moved from office to support space

05B> Recycling of Energy and use of Natural Cooling

1 Night cooling of concrete structure
2 Opening window shuts off floor fan
3 Layer of cool fresh air
4 Floor fan and humidity control
5 Night cooled slab reduces the need for mechanical cooling
6 Fresh air rises around users
7 Floor cooled by water-chilled mats

04> The main entrance to the office building. The two blocks are separated by a chasm spanned by a bridge at the upper level.

05> Schematics illustrating energy-saving strategies. Natural ventilation and lighting are used wherever possible. The thermal mass of the concrete ceilings helps to keep the interior temperatures constant in daytime, and water-filled floors are part of an efficient cooling and heating system.

06> Detail of the fixed cedarwood louvres on the east façade. The louvres are different from those on the west front.

∧
06

NAME OF BUILDING
Westminster Lodge

Client/owner	**Date completed**
Parnham Trust	April 1996
Occupier	**Gross area**
Parnham Trust	190m²
Location	**Construction cost**
Dorset, UK	£165,000
Architect	**Climatic zone**
Edward Cullinan Architects	Temperate

BUILDING ENERGY FEATURES

Orientation of main façades
Multiple

Solar control systems
Fixed external

Natural ventilation: Approx. percentage of gross floor naturally ventilated
100%

Daylighting Approx. percentage of net floor area needing artificial lighting during daylight hours
0%

Night-time ventilation provision
Natural

Energy-saving controls for artificial lighting?
No

Thermal transmission of building envelope
Above standard

Other
–

Utilization of building mass thermal storage as part of energy strategy?
No

HVAC SYSTEMS

Fuel/approx. % use
Mains electricity 100%

Mechanical ventilation
None

Boiler type
None

Air conditioning type
None

Heating system
Electric storage heaters

Heat recovery
No

ENERGY PERFORMANCE (per month?)

Total
0.0686kW/h/m²

Heating
0.055kW/h/m²

Artificial lighting
0.0136kW/h/m²

Total estimated carbon dioxide output
N/S

Refrigeration cooling
N/A

Mechanical ventilation
N/A

ENVIRONMENTAL/HEALTH FEATURES

Materials/components selection strategy to reduce embodied and transport energy?
Yes

Special water conserving installation
No

Natural organic sewage treatment
No

Use of recycled materials
No

Measures to encourage use of public transport
No

Use of timbers from managed sources
Yes

Westminster Lodge
Dorset, UK

Westminster Lodge is to be a residence for students following training courses at the Hooke Park College. The College, which is at present established at nearby Parnham House, was set up to research and demonstrate the use of timber products, particularly thinnings (young green saplings too slender for conventional construction). Its buildings have themselves been demonstrations of innovative timber technology. They provide for an ecological community in a wooded area of rural Dorset, which has a coastal temperate climate with cold winters and mild summers.

This building is the first on the site in which roundwood thinnings have been used to construct a cellular space. Thinnings have little shear strength, so there is an advantage in using them 'in the round'. The poles are not cut in section so the whole strength of the pole can be utilized.

The building is set on a platform supported on timber struts on pad foundations, and comprises four pairs of double rooms surrounding a central living and dining space. The saucer-shaped roof is constructed from thinnings formed into a double lattice, covered with insulation and a turf roof. A round rooflight illuminates the central area. Partition walls are also constructed from roundwood thinnings. The result is a delightful house floating above the bluebells in sylvan surroundings.

∧
01

01> The central meeting area. The roof is supported by thinnings, bent over dividing walls and engineered into a double lattice.

02> Section through the timber frame and grass roof. A skylight ensures light and ventilation.

03> View of the south side. The building is supported on stilts on a platform above the forest floor. The roof is a grass-topped, curving canopy.

<02

^
03

NAME OF BUILDING
Water Temple

Client/owner
Hompukuji

Occupier
Hompukuji

Location
Tsuna-gun, Hyogo, Japan

Architect
Tadao Ando

Date completed
September 1991

Gross area
417m²

Construction cost
N/S

Climatic zone
Temperate

BUILDING ENERGY FEATURES

Orientation of main façades
Multiple

Natural ventilation: Approx. percentage of gross floor naturally ventilated
N/S

Night-time ventilation provision
N/A

Thermal transmission of building envelope
Low

Utilization of building mass thermal storage as part of energy strategy?
N/S

Solar control systems
N/A

Daylighting Approx. percentage of net floor area needing artificial lighting during daylight hours
N/A

Energy-saving controls for artificial lighting?
N/A

Other
–

HVAC SYSTEMS

Fuel/approx. % use
N/S

Boiler type
N/S

Heating system
N/S

Mechanical ventilation
N/S

Air conditioning type
N/S

Heat recovery
N/S

ENERGY PERFORMANCE

Total
N/S

Artificial lighting
N/S

Refrigeration cooling
N/S

Mechanical ventilation
N/S

Heating
N/S

Total estimated carbon dioxide output
N/S

ENVIRONMENTAL/HEALTH FEATURES

Materials/components selection strategy to reduce embodied and transport energy?
N/S

Use of recycled materials
N/S

Use of timbers from managed sources
N/S

Special water conserving installation
No

Natural organic sewage treatment
No

Measures to encourage use of public transport
No

Water Temple
Tsuna-gun, Hyogo, Japan

In the Buddhist birth-myth of Creation, water was the first element. Water gave birth to the lotus, and the lotus flower is the symbol of Buddha's spiritual awakening. This new main hall (Mizumido) for Hompukuji – a temple of the Shingon sect – is set into the ground immediately below an oval-shaped lotus pool measuring 40 x 30 metres (130 x 98 feet). It is screened to the south-east by two 6-metre (20-foot) high in-situ concrete walls, one straight and the other curved. The temple is situated on a bluff on the small island of Awaji, and commands sweeping views of Osaka Bay.

The route to the Mizumido ascends along a white sand path and passes through the outer straight wall. The visitor is then confronted by an inner curved wall on either side of which the ocean can be seen. Behind this wall the path leads up a ramp back to the central axis. From this point a staircase leads down through the pool to the main hall below.

The prayer room is set asymmetrically below the dish-shaped under-surface of the pool. Its geometry is based on the circle and the square, comprising a square grid of timber screens and panelling set within a similarly constructed drum. The spaces are appropriately simple, serene and contemplative. Daylight enters from the north-west where the hillside falls away from the pool towards the Gulf. The walls are vermillion and when the sun shines in, the room is suffused in a reddish glow. The temple is a sublime orchestration of the elemental and the spiritual. The intricate route to the

sanctum assists in casting off the turmoil of the day to day, prepares the mind for contemplation, and gently absorbs the pilgrim into a transcendental space of harmony and repose.

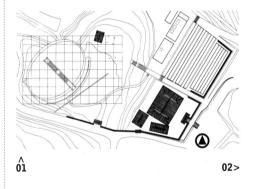

∧
01

02>

01> Site plan. The new temple overlooks Osaka Bay.

02> View across the lotus flower pool to Osaka Bay.

Pavilions / Water Temple

<03

03> The descent, through the pool, to the Mizumido hall.

04> An elevation and two cross-sections through the temple, showing the pool/roof and the manner in which it is set into the hillside.

04>

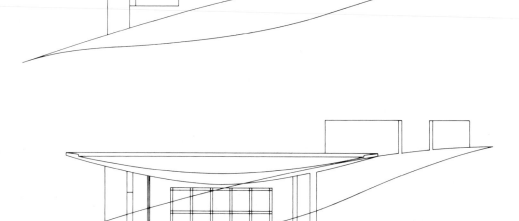

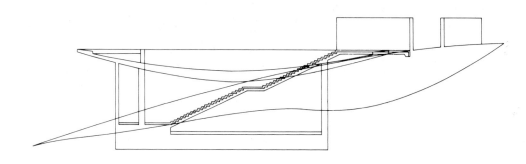

'Men come together in cities in order to live: they remain together in order to live the good life.'

(Aristotle, quoted by L. Mumford, *The Culture of Cities*, 1938)

Fruili, Italy (1935), built as a garden city on an old Roman site.

Mankind has dreamt of ideal cities: medieval artists painted them bright and gem-like in their manuscript illuminations, Renaissance princes created them as expressions of order and beauty, the architects of the Modern movement designed them for a brave new world of technology. But there has always been an ambivalence. The city is the setting for civilized life, yet often life there is a grim economic necessity. Cities are constantly in flux, continually adapting to changing economic and social circumstances. In a world of accelerating change, making provision for new services, new means of transport, new housing, while at the same time creating civilized urban spaces, cutting environmental degradation and relating to the city texture inherited from the past, is delicate, difficult and essential.

NAME OF BUILDING
Eastgate

Client/owner
Old Mutual Properties

Occupier
Mixed development

Location
Harare, Zimbabwe

Architect
Pearce Partnership

Date completed
April 1996

Gross area
44,650m²

Construction cost
Z$350 million

Climatic zone
Tropical

BUILDING ENERGY FEATURES

Orientation of main façades
North and south

Natural ventilation: Approx. percentage of gross floor naturally ventilated
–

Night-time ventilation provision
Forced

Thermal transmission of building envelope
Roof: 1.5w/m²°C; walls: 2.3w/m²°C; windows: 5.9w/m²°C

Utilization of building mass thermal storage as part of energy strategy?
Yes

Solar control systems
Fixed external

Daylighting Approx. percentage of net floor area needing artificial lighting during daylight hours
60%

Energy-saving controls for artificial lighting?
Daylight level light sensor equipment used to control level of artificial light required

HVAC SYSTEMS

Fuel/approx. % use
Mains electricity 100%

Boiler type
None

Heating system
Electrical perimeter heaters

Mechanical ventilation
Passive cooling ventilation. Full forced supply with natural exhaust by chimney stack effect.

Air conditioning type
None

Heat recovery
–

ENERGY PERFORMANCE (average per month)

Total
9.1kW/h/m²

Artificial lighting
4.1kW/h/m²

Refrigeration cooling
N/A

Mechanical ventilation
0.8 kW/h/m² (day);
0.6 kW/h/m² (night)

Heating
4.2kW/h/m²

Total estimated carbon dioxide output
N/S

ENVIRONMENTAL/HEALTH FEATURES

Materials/components selection strategy to reduce embodied and transport energy?
Minimum use of glass and aluminium; mainly local materials used. Locally grown timber used to support roof tiles

Use of recycled materials
No

Special water conserving installation
Borehole sunk in basement to supply water to plantings

Natural organic sewage treatment
No

Measures to encourage use of public transport
City location

Eastgate
Harare, Zimbabwe

This remarkable project uses many established principles to dramatically reduce energy consumption. The climate of Harare is particularly pleasant, warm and dry, with only a short season that is hot and humid. Nights are cool and clear throughout the year, permitting buildings to lose heat by convection and radiation overnight, ready for the next day.

Eastgate is the largest mixed office and retail development in Zimbabwe. Two narrow blocks of 150 metres (500 feet) in length have been aligned side by side, running from east to west (the best orientation to minimize heat gain). Between the two is a full-height atrium forming a street and containing stairs and bridges for circulation within the complex.

The upper seven floors of the blocks contain offices, while the ground and first floors house shops and car parking. Between the first and second floors is a large plenum into which fans draw air from the street (at first floor level) and distribute it via large vertical ducts (16 per block) to the offices above. The air then passes through a double floor in each office containing a maze of precast concrete elements to increase heat transfer, and emerges through perimeter grilles below the window-sills. The relative coolness of the building structure reduces the temperature of this incoming air. Warmer air, particularly around the light fittings, is then drawn off at ceiling level, opposite the windows, and is induced to travel upwards by stack effect, finally leaving the building through chimneys. During the day small fans provide two air changes per hour which is adequate ventilation to the office spaces and adequate to absorb heat loads without an excessive temperature rise. At night when the air is cooler, larger fans are used to produce ten air changes per hour in order to reduce the temperature of the building mass in readiness for the heat of the next day.

Thoughtful design has reduced the amount of sun penetration and optimized the surface areas within to help to absorb heat from lighting and other sources. Inside air temperature normally ranges from 21°C to 25°C (70°F to 77°F) for external ambient temperatures ranging from 5°C to 33°C (41°F to 91°F). However, for ten days in October when there was high humidity and high dry bulb temperatures, often with cloudy night skies, 28°C was recorded by the architects for two hours on three separate days. Annual saving on energy running costs compared with a fully air-conditioned building in Harare has been calculated at £250,000, depending on the efficiency of the air-conditioning plant. Credit for this excellent and appropriate project goes not only to the architect and engineer but to the far-sighted client who initiated the design philosophy.

01> The internal street or atrium contains shops, and stairs and bridges for circulation within the complex. There is a rich array of articulated metal balconies and balustrades which contrast with the heavier, more solid concrete structural elements.

02> View of the façade showing the heavily modelled reinforced concrete elevational treatment and the exhaust stacks of the forced air ventilation system.

^
01

^
02

NAME OF BUILDING
Central Market of Athens

Client/owner
Municipality of Athens

Date completed
1997

Occupier
Merchants

Gross area
3,216m²

Location
Athens, Greece

Construction cost
400 million ECU

Architect
N. Fintikakis – Synthesis and Research Ltd

Climatic zone
Mediterranean

BUILDING ENERGY FEATURES

Orientation of main façades
North-east

Solar control systems
Fixed external; motorized/variable external; solar control glazing; deciduous planting

Natural ventilation: Approx. percentage of gross floor naturally ventilated
0%

Daylighting Approx. percentage of net floor area needing artificial lighting during daylight hours
10%

Night-time ventilation provision
Forced

Thermal transmission of building envelope
Standard

Energy-saving controls for artificial lighting?
No

Utilization of building mass thermal storage as part of energy strategy?
Yes

Other
–

HVAC SYSTEMS

Fuel/approx. % use
Mains electricity 100%; photovoltaics; indirect solar

Mechanical ventilation
Yes

Boiler type
None

Air conditioning type
–

Heating system
Earth to air heat exchanger; solar air heaters

Heat recovery
–

ENERGY PERFORMANCE (predicted)

Total
41kW/h/m²

Heating
12kW/h/m²

Artificial lighting
17kW/h/m²

Total estimated carbon dioxide output
N/S

Refrigeration cooling
N/A

Mechanical ventilation
12kW/h/m²

ENVIRONMENTAL/HEALTH FEATURES

Materials/components selection strategy to reduce embodied and transport energy?
No

Special water conserving installation
N/A

Use of recycled materials
No

Natural organic sewage treatment
N/A

Use of timbers from managed sources
No

Measures to encourage use of public transport
City location

Central Market of Athens
Athens, Greece

The old Central Market in Athens is a magnificent example of nineteenth-century architecture. It also constitutes a vital part of the socio-economic life of the city; it caters predominantly for the lower-income citizens and has been in continuous operation since it was built. In 1995 it was decided to renovate and refit the building. The approach adopted used environmentally conscious measures in a comprehensive and well-integrated manner.

The four towers at the corners of the building are used as 'air chimneys' for supply and extraction, and waste heat recovery units have been installed to assist heating in winter. Filtering has also been introduced to ensure protection from pollution. Solar control glazing has been installed in the roof to allow more daylight, while reducing heat gain, and deciduous planting above the glazing provides additional screening in summer.

Thermostatically controlled louvres and 'air curtains' at the main entrances, allowing doors to be kept open without heat loss, are also new features. The automated elements (such as the louvres) are powered by photovoltaic arrays. A hybrid system for cooling and heating has been used. This consists of an air-to-air heat exchanger (earth pipe), an air collector (a series of solar air heaters), and an air distribution plant.

When the building is reopened, these measures will transform what was previously a draughty space in the winter and a polluted, stuffy one in the summer into a market place that, throughout the year, is clean, well-lit and comfortable with economical running costs.

^01

01> Computer visualization of the completed market interior.

02> Section through the market hall illustrating the ventilation strategy.

03> Schematic showing lighting, ventilation and heat reclaim strategies for winter operation.

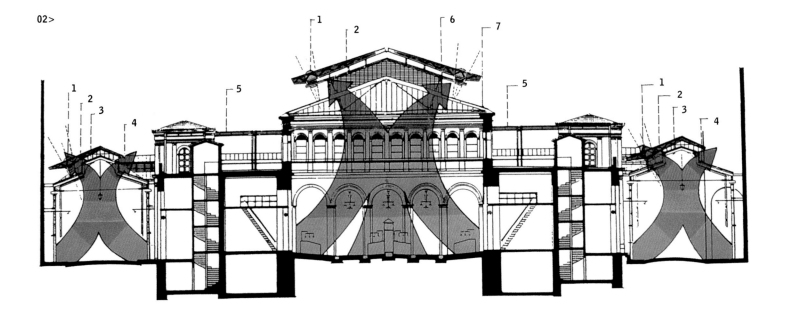

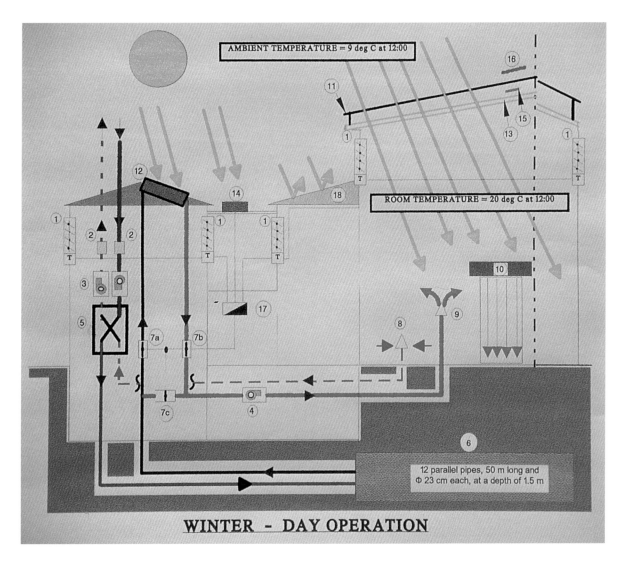

AMBIENT TEMPERATURE = 9 deg C at 12:00

ROOM TEMPERATURE = 20 deg C at 12:00

12 parallel pipes, 50 m long and
Φ 23 cm each, at a depth of 1.5 m

WINTER - DAY OPERATION

02>Key

1 Fresnel lenses device
2 Environmental panels
3 Glass roof
4 Dampalon panel
5 Pergola
6 Louvres
7 Non-transparent roof
panel

203

03>Ambient temperature
= 9°C (48°F) at 12.00
Room temperature =
20°C (68°F) at 12.00
12 parallel pipes, 50m
(164 ft) long and each
23cm (9in) in diameter,
at a depth of 1.5m (5ft)

NAME OF BUILDING
Helicon

Client/owner
London and Manchester
Insurance

Occupier
Marks & Spencer

Location
London, UK

Architect
Sheppard Robson

Date completed
October 1996

Gross area
20,530m²

Construction cost
£29 million

Climatic zone
Temperate

BUILDING ENERGY FEATURES

Orientation of main façades
East and west

Natural ventilation: Approx. percentage of gross floor naturally ventilated
0%

Night-time ventilation provision
None

Thermal transmission of building envelope
Standard

Utilization of building mass thermal storage as part of energy strategy?
Floor void used as air plenum

Solar control systems
Solar control glazing on top floor and to atrium; fully active retractable blinds within ventilated cavity

Daylighting Approx. percentage of net floor area needing artificial lighting during daylight hours
30% (office space)

Energy-saving controls for artificial lighting?
Yes

Other
–

HVAC SYSTEMS

Fuel/approx. % use
Mains electricity for cooling; mains gas for heating

Boiler type
Gas-fired

Heating system
Perimeter heating tubes

Mechanical ventilation
Displacement air system

Air conditioning type
Chilled ceilings and floor supply

Heat recovery
From air systems (recirc.)

ENERGY PERFORMANCE

Total
(base load including fans, lifts and pumps)
237kW/h/m²/y

Artificial lighting
34kW/h/m²/y

Refrigeration cooling
25kW/h/m²/y

Mechanical ventilation
36kW/h/m²/y

Heating
70kW/h/m²/y

Total estimated carbon dioxide output
N/S

ENVIRONMENTAL/HEALTH FEATURES

Materials/components selection strategy to reduce embodied and transport energy?
No

Use of recycled materials
No

Use of timbers from managed sources
Yes (doors and door frames)

Special water conserving installation
No

Natural organic sewage treatment
No

Measures to encourage use of public transport
City location

Helicon
London, UK

The Helicon building occupies an entire block in the City of London. It comprises six storeys of office space over five of retail, two of which are below ground. Retail environments, with their multiplicity of signs and high demand for goods and refuse access, are generally thought to detract from prestige office space. Here, the developers were fortunate in attracting a single retailer, Marks & Spencer, whose presence does not overly intrude on the offices above.

The building's exterior makes extensive use of metal and glass and does not suggest a particular sympathy towards environmental sustainability. A closer look at the energy strategy for the offices, however, shows a more thoughtful and effective approach compared to the 'gas-guzzler' developments of the 1980s. Instead of resorting to blanket air conditioning, the building uses a sophisticated 'mixed mode' approach combining a well-insulated and solar-screened building envelope with sensitive air treatment.

The building has no opening windows and uses a combination of a displacement air system and chilled ceilings. Water-chilled (15°C/60°F) panels are fixed to a metal suspended ceiling and air is extracted at high level through the light fittings. Air is supplied through a raised floor via diffusers set within it. 'Free cooling' is provided by the introduction of filtered outdoor air. In winter, fresh air is mixed with filtered return air. If necessary, extra heat can be supplied by perimeter finned tubes.

The architects wanted the external walls to be highly transparent; they are accordingly constructed of a triple-skinned floor-to-ceiling glazing. The east and west façades each comprise external single glazing bolt-fixed to internal mullions, a 900mm (35½ inch) wide accessible cavity, and internal double glazing. Perforated aluminium venetian blinds are located in the cavity, their deployment and tilt controlled by a sophisticated automated actuating system. The cavity is ventilated to further reduce solar gains. There is a central atrium for the office floor which introduces daylight into the centre of the building and through which air is extracted, thereby reducing the need for large extract ducts in the office ceilings.

Energy conservation for buildings in the heart of the city is difficult since interiors require good protection from dirt and noise. Low-energy solutions, consequently, tend to require a higher level of sophistication than that needed for their out-of-town counterparts. Helicon is just such a case. The success of the energy strategy will depend to a considerable extent on its management.

01> Plans of the ground, third and seventh floors and roof.

02> View towards the entrance of the store.

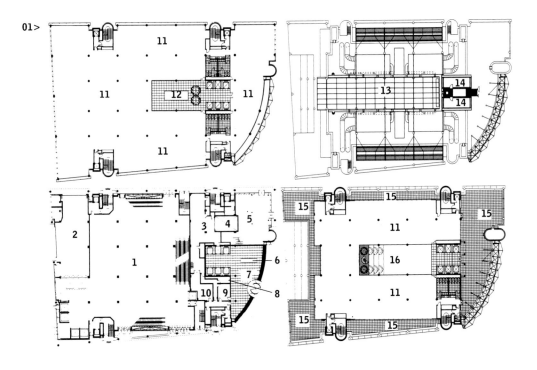

01>

<02

Key

1 Retail store
2 Retail loading bay
3 Loading bay
4 Car lift
5 Bank
6 Pool
7 Entrance foyer
8 Services
9 Security
10 Refuse store
11 Office
12 Atrium pool
13 Atrium roof
14 Cooling tower
15 Terrace
16 Atrium

Chapter Four / Architecture and the Environment

03 > The east and west façades have a 900mm (35½ inch) wide cavity in which venetian blinds are located. Cool air is passed through the cavity to combat the heat of the sun.

04 > The six-storey office atrium has a glazed barrel vault roof. Clear untinted glass ensures maximum natural daylight.

05 > Schematic showing the forced ventilation and cooling strategy designed by Ove Arup & Partners.

05 >

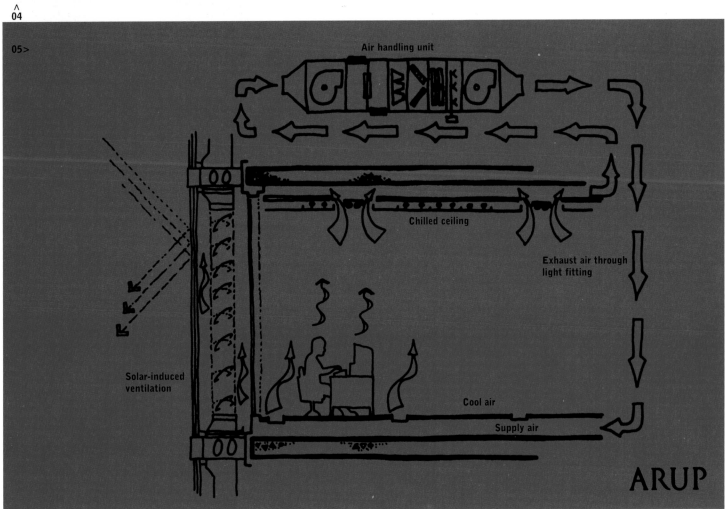

Air handling unit

Chilled ceiling

Exhaust air through light fitting

Solar-induced ventilation

Cool air

Supply air

ARUP

NAME OF BUILDING
Yasuda Academia

Client/owner
The YASUDA Mutual Life
Insurance Company

Occupier
Yasuda Insurance

Location
Tokyo, Japan

Architect
Nihon Sekkei Inc.

Date completed
March 1994

Gross area
33,609m²

Construction cost
£103.4 million

Climatic zone
Temperate

BUILDING ENERGY FEATURES

**Orientation of main
façades**
Multiple

**Natural ventilation:
Approx. percentage of
gross floor naturally
ventilated**
N/S

**Night-time ventilation
provision**
N/S

**Thermal transmission
of building envelope**
Standard

**Utilization of building
mass thermal storage as
part of energy strategy?**
No

Solar control systems
Solar-control glazing;
blinds/louvres

**Daylighting
Approx. percentage of
net floor area needing
artificial lighting during
daylight hours**
N/S

**Energy-saving controls
for artificial lighting?**
—

Other
—

HVAC SYSTEMS

Fuel/approx. % use
Mains electricity 100%

Boiler type
Heat pump

Heating system
N/A

Mechanical ventilation
Exhaust and ventilator;
air duct

Air conditioning type
Interior air conditioning
unit; perimeter fan coil unit

Heat recovery
—

ENERGY PERFORMANCE

Total
0.063kW/h/m²

Artificial lighting
0.020kW/h/m²

Refrigeration cooling
0.029kW/h/m²

Mechanical ventilation
0.014kW/h/m²

Heating
N/A

**Total estimated carbon
dioxide output**
N/S

ENVIRONMENTAL/HEALTH FEATURES

**Materials/components
selection strategy to
reduce embodied and
transport energy?**
No

Use of recycled materials
No

**Use of timbers from
managed sources**
No

**Special water conserving
installation**
Recycling of waste water

**Natural organic sewage
treatment**
Yes

**Measures to encourage
use of public transport**
City location

Yasuda Academia
Tokyo, Japan

Yasuda Academia is a training centre for Yasuda Insurance. According to the architects the underlying themes of the building are 'intelligence', 'sensitivity' and 'health'; its purpose is to provide a setting that will help contribute to the development of each facet of a trainee's character and help them realize their full potential. The building reflects an important aspect of Japanese corporate culture whereby the company not only offers the wherewithal for a lifetime career, but plays a major part in each member's social life and the well-being of them and their families.

The building is not dissimilar to a hotel, providing both residential accommodation and training and recreation facilities. The bedrooms are located on the upper floors. On the third floor is a restaurant; the training facilities are on the first and second floors; and the reception spaces occupy the ground floor. In the basement there is a gymnasium and an assembly hall for 900 people.

The building is essentially an 'extruded' section – two blocks facing on to a central atrium – aligned north/south on a city block. The architects have managed to avoid the sense that this is a length of accommodation chopped off to suit the dimensions of the site, however, by making the atrium oval in plan. This vast space holds the building together, provides a central focus for all activities, and thus reinforces the corporate message of development of the individual for the benefit of the common good.

The atrium is naturally ventilated. In warm weather air enters at ground and intermediate levels, rises in the atrium through natural buoyancy, and is expelled through the atrium roof. The central section of the glazed roof slides back to allow air to pass through. The surrounding bedrooms on the upper floors are cross ventilated, drawing air from outside and allowing it to pass into the atrium space. A heat reclaim plant is located at the top of the atrium, allowing the heat of the air being expelled to assist in keeping the building warm. The training facilities, restaurant and basement are air conditioned.

Both east and west façades, at the upper levels, are shaded by a system of catwalks. These are unable to protect the rooms from low morning and evening sun, however. The rooms are therefore protected by windows which incorporate heat-reflecting glass and blinds.

The building is located on reclaimed industrial land in a suburb of Tokyo. Together with the adjacent public spaces it is a key initiative in the plan to regenerate that part of the city.

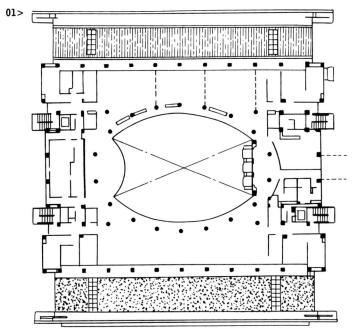

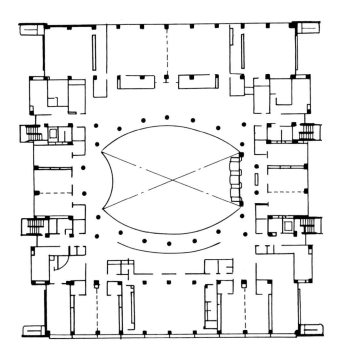

01> Lower and upper-
level floor plans.

02> View from the west
façade.

209

^
02

Metropolis / Yasuda Academia

03> Aerial view showing the oval of the atrium reflected in the pattern of rooflights.

04> Cross-section through the building showing the natural ventilation strategy. Heat reclaim is incorporated at roof level.

05> The lifts seen from the heavily planted atrium.

∧
03

<04   05>

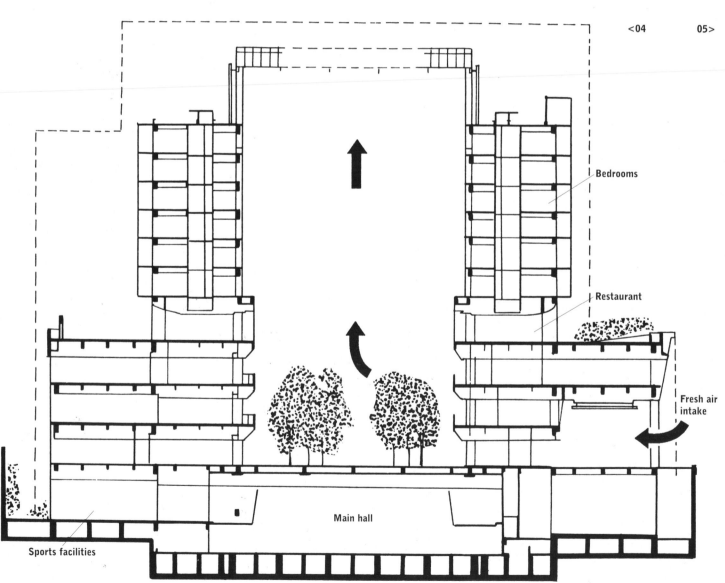

Bedrooms

Restaurant

Fresh air intake

Main hall

Sports facilities

NAME OF BUILDING
Viaduct Refurbishment

Client/owner	**Date completed**
SEMAEST	1995
Occupier	**Gross area**
Various	12,600m²
Location	**Construction cost**
Paris, France	£7.3 million
Architect	**Climatic zone**
Patrick Berger	Continental

BUILDING ENERGY FEATURES

Orientation of main façades	**Solar control systems**
N/A	N/A
Natural ventilation: Approx. percentage of gross floor naturally ventilated	**Daylighting Approx. percentage of net floor area needing artificial lighting during daylight hours**
N/A	N/A
Night-time ventilation provision	**Energy-saving controls for artificial lighting?**
N/A	N/A
Thermal transmission of building envelope	**Other**
N/A	–
Utilization of building mass thermal storage as part of energy strategy?	
N/A	

HVAC SYSTEMS

Fuel/approx. % use	**Mechanical ventilation**
N/S	N/S
Boiler type	**Air conditioning type**
N/S	–
Heating system	**Heat recovery**
N/S	No

ENERGY PERFORMANCE

Total	**Heating**
N/A	N/A
Artificial lighting	**Total estimated carbon dioxide output**
N/A	N/A
Refrigeration cooling	
N/A	
Mechanical ventilation	
N/A	

ENVIRONMENTAL/HEALTH FEATURES

Materials/components selection strategy to reduce embodied and transport energy?	**Special water conserving installation**
No	No
Use of recycled materials	**Natural organic sewage treatment**
No	No
Use of timbers from managed sources	**Measures to encourage use of public transport**
No	City location

Viaduct Refurbishment
Paris, France

What can one do with 1.4 kilometres (1,500 yards) of disused elevated railway line, and its supporting arched structure, running through the middle of a bustling city? This was the question faced by Parisian planners when examining the potential of the Bastille railway viaduct, which extends from the new opera house eastwards to the Gare de Reuilly.

Built in the middle of the last century but disused since 1969, the railway arches had become run down and were home to a motley collection of small businesses. Demolition of the viaduct was considered but rejected, as it would have left exposed an untidy jumble of gable ends, yards and sheds which had been built up against the structure. The architect's solution was to allow the use of the arches for small businesses and shops, provided that they conform to strict guidelines regarding external features such as glazing and signs, and convert the area occupied by the railway lines themselves into a linear garden or *promenade plantée*.

The finished project has proved popular with Parisians and tourists alike, for a number of reasons. The original edifice was of fine architectural quality, with stone vaults, piers and arches, and red brick spandrels, all surrounded by a bold stone cornice and blocking course. It was noble in scale, as befits a capital city, and this integrity has been respected. New elements, such as the shop-fronts, have been treated as secondary to the original structure. As for the promenade above, various devices have been used to integrate it sensitively into the city fabric – new trees, for instance, have been planted

exactly on the axes of existing columns. The promenade offers the visitor a tantalizing reinterpretation of the city: it cuts through the city fabric, sometimes offering surprising urban views, at other times entering a cutting surrounded by new greenery.

The project shows how an imaginative and thoughtful design approach has enabled a fine historic structure to become a new, exciting element in the modern city.

01> The route of the viaduct from the Bastille Opera House towards the Gare de Reuilly (above). Perspective view of part of the viaduct (below).

02> The newly planted viaduct acts as a raised promenade, almost like a pier, passing through this densely built-up area of eastern Paris.

01>

^
02

03> The arches within the viaduct make excellent spaces for shops and ateliers.

04> The fine quality and grand scale of the original structure has been enhanced by the careful design of the shop façades.

^
03

214

^
04

'Towered cities please us then,
And the busy hum of men.'

(John Milton, *L'Allegro*)

4.6
Towers

The clusters of high-rise towers that mark
the centres of today's cities are not just a
symptom of high land value. Their verticality
gives shape and direction to the townscape
physically, intellectually and emotionally.
Religious inspiration drove the upward-striving
spires of cathedrals and gravity-defying
minarets of mosques; today it is Mammon.
But all towers aspire to the heights. Indeed
Babel's tower-builders and their punishment
has made towers, above all other architectural
forms, the symbol of human hubris. From
the towers that crowd the skyline of San
Gimignano to the serried office blocks
of twentieth-century cities, they express the
pride and rivalry of nations and cities,
families and corporations.

The famous 13th-century
towers of San Gimignano,
Italy.

NAME OF BUILDING
RWE AG Headquarters

Client/owner Hochtief AG	**Date completed** December 1996
Occupier RWE AG	**Gross area** 35,000m²
Location Essen, Germany	**Construction cost** £90 million
Architect Ingenhoven, Overdiek Kahlen und Partner	**Climatic zone** Temperate

BUILDING ENERGY FEATURES

Orientation of main façades Circular plan	**Solar control systems** Motorized/variable external; solar control glazing (Optiwhite Climaplus)
Natural ventilation: Approx. percentage of gross floor naturally ventilated 70%	**Daylighting Approx. percentage of net floor area needing artificial lighting during daylight hours** 30%
Night-time ventilation provision Natural	
Thermal transmission of building envelope Above standard	**Energy-saving controls for artificial lighting?** Yes
Utilization of building mass thermal storage as part of energy strategy? Yes	**Other** –

HVAC SYSTEMS

Fuel/approx. % use Mains electricity 99%; photovoltaics 1%	**Mechanical ventilation** Air ventilation; water cooling systems
Boiler type None	**Air conditioning type** Supported ventilation and chilled ceilings
Heating system District heating	**Heat recovery** Yes

ENERGY PERFORMANCE

Total 0.278kW/h/m²	**Heating** 0.072kW/h/m²
Artificial lighting 0.011kW/h/m²	**Total estimated carbon dioxide output** N/S
Refrigeration cooling 0.020kW/h/m²	
Mechanical ventilation 0.015kW/h/m²	

ENVIRONMENTAL/HEALTH FEATURES

Materials/components selection strategy to reduce embodied and transport energy? Yes	**Special water conserving installation** Yes
Use of recycled materials No	**Natural organic sewage treatment** No
Use of timbers from managed sources Yes	**Measures to encourage use of public transport** Yes

RWE AG Headquarters
Essen, Germany

This cylindrical office tower, overlooking a lake and park, comprises 30 storeys set on a one-storey plinth. The tower, which is 163 metres (535 feet) high, is encased in a double glass skin. Outside is a single layer of strengthened safety glass, while the inner glazing is heat-insulated Climaplus white glass, allowing daylight to be maximized. A 50-centimetre (20-inch) void between the layers of glass acts as a thermal buffer. All office windows have sliding panels and can be opened for ventilation. Except under extreme weather conditions (which might occur 20 per cent of the time) the building is naturally ventilated.

Central to the design are several specially developed, innovative features designed to minimize energy demand. The 'fish-mouth' elements placed between glazing layers are there to integrate devices for sun and glare protection with an air-exchange system. Their electronically controlled aluminium lamellae provide protection from the sun, while optional power-operated internal textile blinds shield against glare. Air baffle plates control the inflow and outflow of air in the glass corridor.

Environmental conditions are managed by Building Management Systems (BMS) technology, with a single control panel in every room enabling light, temperature, façade and sun protection to be adjusted to individual requirements. Integrated ceiling elements set into the concrete soffits are also multifunctional, incorporating low-energy lighting and a water-flushed pipework system for cooling, as well as smoke alarms and sprinkler systems.

The energy strategy exploits the heat storage capacity of the concrete ceilings. Heating can be augmented from the district heating system.

Some of the building's energy (0.1 per cent) is generated by photovoltaic panels; these are situated on adjustable fixings incorporated into specially designed elements on the roof-level loggia.

^
01

01> The junction of the lift tower passage to the main building. The electronically controlled lamellae to protect against solar gain are part of an integrated and flexible system.

02> Cross-section. The building has a double glass skin for insulation, incorporating a specially designed natural ventilation system. The offices are naturally ventilated: windows can be opened.

03> The cylindrical tower, 163 metres (535 feet) high, is a new landmark for Essen.

02>

217

^
03

Towers / RWE AG Headquarters

Chapter Four / Architecture and the Environment

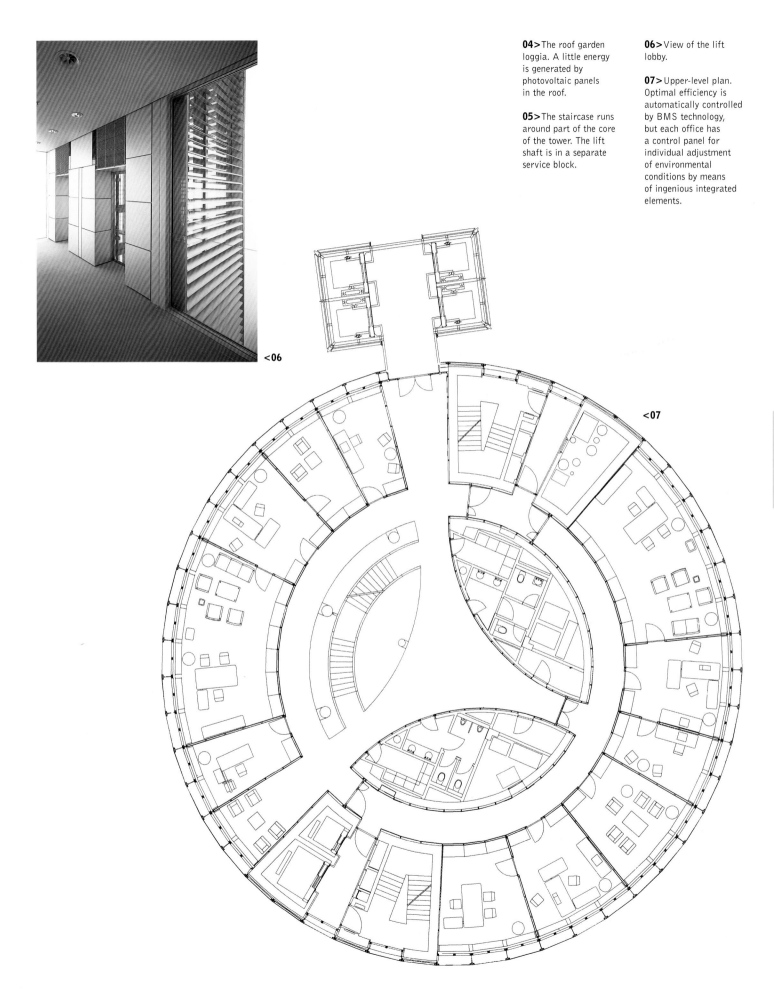

04> The roof garden loggia. A little energy is generated by photovoltaic panels in the roof.

05> The staircase runs around part of the core of the tower. The lift shaft is in a separate service block.

06> View of the lift lobby.

07> Upper-level plan. Optimal efficiency is automatically controlled by BMS technology, but each office has a control panel for individual adjustment of environmental conditions by means of ingenious integrated elements.

<06

<07

219

Towers / RWE AG Headquarters

NAME OF BUILDING
The Thames Tower

Client/owner	**Date completed**
Thames Water	Autumn 1995
Occupier	**Gross area**
N/A	N/A
Location	**Construction cost**
Shepherd's Bush, London, UK	N/S
Architect	**Climatic zone**
Brookes Stacey Randall Fursdon	Temperate

BUILDING ENERGY FEATURES

Orientation of main façades	**Solar control systems**
Multiple	N/A
Natural ventilation: Approx. percentage of gross floor naturally ventilated	**Daylighting Approx. percentage of net floor area needing artificial lighting during daylight hours**
N/A	N/A
Night-time ventilation provision	**Energy-saving controls for artificial lighting?**
N/A	N/A
Thermal transmission of building envelope	**Other**
N/A	–
Utilization of building mass thermal storage as part of energy strategy?	
N/A	

HVAC SYSTEMS

Fuel/approx. % use	**Mechanical ventilation**
N/A	Forced ventilation for breathing during maintenance access
Boiler type	
N/A	**Air conditioning type**
Heating system	N/A
N/A	**Heat recovery**
	N/A

ENERGY PERFORMANCE

Total	**Heating**
N/A	N/A
Artificial lighting	**Total estimated carbon dioxide output**
N/A	N/A
Refrigeration cooling	
N/A	
Mechanical ventilation	
N/A	

ENVIRONMENTAL/HEALTH FEATURES

Materials/components selection strategy to reduce embodied and transport energy?	**Special water conserving installation**
No	Recycling
Use of recycled materials	**Natural organic sewage treatment**
No	No
Use of timbers from managed sources	**Measures to encourage use of public transport**
No	No

The Thames Tower
Shepherd's Bush, London, UK

The Thames Water Tower, located on a roundabout in west London, is an integral part of the new 80-kilometre (50-mile) City ring main. The tower houses one of three large diameter pipes which rise above ground to accommodate water surges in the water main. It is not a building intended for occupation, but it combines an engineering purpose with environmentally inspired sculptural effect.

The tower concept arose as the result of an 'ideas competition' won by students Damien O'Sullivan and Tania Doufa. The architects, Brookes Stacey Randall Fursdon, were subsequently commissioned to design, consider and advise on the feasibility of constructing it as a public barometer. The idea was to create a structure that would communicate effectively the varying climatic pressure levels.

The tower, which measures 16 metres (52½ feet) in height, is subdivided into five sections. Any change in climatic pressure is detected by an electronic barometer which sends a signal (via a control panel) to activate sprays of blue water at the required level within the tower. The sprayed water forms a thin film on the inside face of the toughened glass cylinder. Barometer and controls are powered by solar power obtained from photovoltaic panels mounted on top of the tower. The barometric pressure is calibrated by stainless steel grillages set within the tower at 2-metre (6½ foot) vertical centres and supported on stainless steel castings. The castings also provide cantilevered support for the suspended glazed enclosure. Water enters the tower via risers located within the polished stainless steel core cladding, and then passes through a series of horizontal water rings and out through spray nozzles.

A number of issues had to be resolved during the design process. The adhesion of the water to the glass had to be tested, as did water flow rates. The architects developed a special organic-dyed water with anti-freeze, anti-algae and UV-stabilizing properties. The amount of water used to convey atmospheric pressure is minimal, and is recirculated.

The Thames Tower is a working model of responsive structure. The architect has sought to design the assembly in such a way as to encourage the play of light as it penetrates the glass and the translucent blue film of water. This simple communication of weather conditions and the prospect of change is a useful and stimulating addition to the urban landscape.

01> The upper part of the tower with the circular tubes and nozzles of the spray mechanism. The platforms indicate the measure of barometric pressure.

222

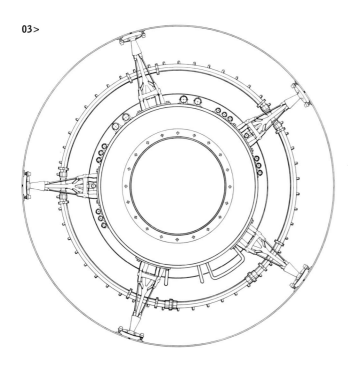

02> The tower
surmounted by the
photovoltaic array.

03> Upper-level plan.

04> Section through
the tower.

Key

1 Glazing
2 Surge pipe
3 Glazing fixing
4 Glazing support arm
5 Accessible services zone
6 Core cladding
7 Access grillage
8 Glazing joint
9 Glass enclosure
10 Recirculation tank
11 Base cladding
12 Base cladding
(openable)
13 Base door
14 Base support bracket

04>

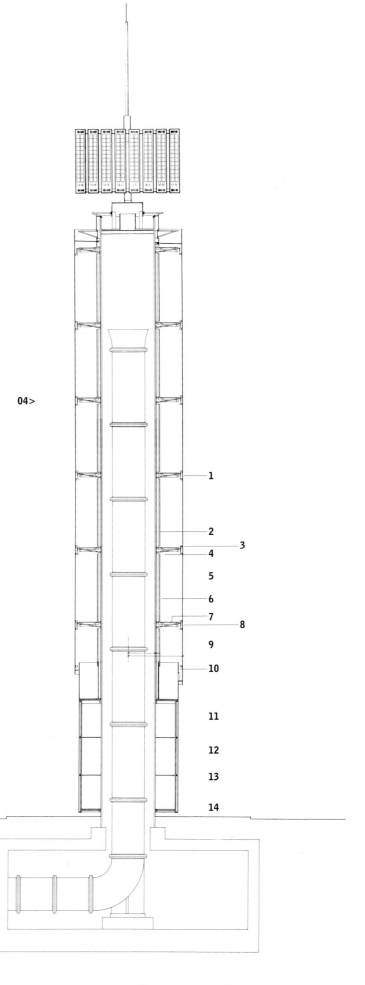

NAME OF BUILDING
City Gate

Client/owner
GbR Düsseldorfer Stadttor mbH

Occupier
–

Location
Düsseldorf, Germany

Architect
Petzinka, Pink und Partner

Date completed
August 1997

Gross area
40,000m²

Construction cost
£46 million

Climatic zone
Temperate

BUILDING ENERGY FEATURES

Orientation of main façades
Multiple

Natural ventilation: Approx. percentage of gross floor naturally ventilated
0%

Night-time ventilation provision
Natural

Thermal transmission of building envelope
Above standard

Utilization of building mass thermal storage as part of energy strategy?
Yes

Solar control systems
Internal blinds/louvres

Daylighting Approx. percentage of net floor area needing artificial lighting during daylight hours
15%

Energy-saving controls for artificial lighting?
Yes

Other
Daylight-sensitive lighting

HVAC SYSTEMS

Fuel/approx. % use
N/S

Boiler type
–

Heating system
Heated ceilings

Mechanical ventilation
–

Air conditioning type
Outside air supply, combined with cooled/heated ceilings

Heat recovery
–

ENERGY PERFORMANCE

Total
115kW/h/m²

Artificial lighting
14kW/h/m²

Refrigeration cooling
–

Mechanical ventilation/ Heating
115kW/h/m²

Total estimated carbon dioxide output
N/S

ENVIRONMENTAL/HEALTH FEATURES

Materials/components selection strategy to reduce embodied and transport energy?
N/S

Use of recycled materials
N/S

Use of timbers from managed sources
N/S

Special water conserving installation
No

Natural organic sewage treatment
No

Measures to encourage use of public transport
City location

City Gate
Düsseldorf, Germany

Located on the edge of the Rhine Park and built over the busy entrance to the Rhine Embankment Tunnel, this office block is intended as a new landmark for the city and as a showpiece of flexible, low-energy architecture.

Constructed on a rhomboid ground plan, it comprises two 16-storey towers separated by an atrium and surmounted by a three-storey bridging structure. The entire building is surrounded by a glass envelope. Within this the towers are double glazed with heat-protective glass in wooden frames. Between the single and double glazing an accessible balcony, 0.9–1.4 metres (3–4½ feet) wide, acts as an acoustic and thermal buffer. Electronically controlled blinds within the windows provide shade on sunny days and also create a buoyancy which draws warm air out of the corridor.

The most important element in the natural ventilation system is the specially designed ventilation boxes which are set above and below each window in the façade. These are 60 centimetres (2 feet) high and fitted with sensitive aerodynamic shutters, which are electronically controlled to make optimal use of the climatic conditions and prevent wind noise.

The glazing and natural ventilation are sufficient when outside temperatures are between 5°C (41°F) and 20°C (68°F). For more extreme conditions an environment-friendly air-conditioning system is provided. This comprises a twofold air-exchange system using a combination of sorption and adiabatic

cooling in the ceilings, and exploiting the cool groundwater present below the riverside site. No CFC coolants are used. The ceilings can also be heated using the local district heating system.

When external temperatures are between -12°C (10°F) and +28°C (82°F) the building requires no additional heating or cooling energy. Building maintenance costs are slightly higher than normal but these are offset by much lower running costs.

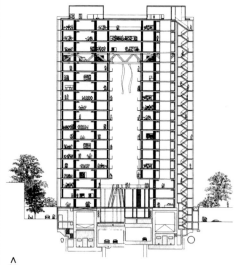

∧
01

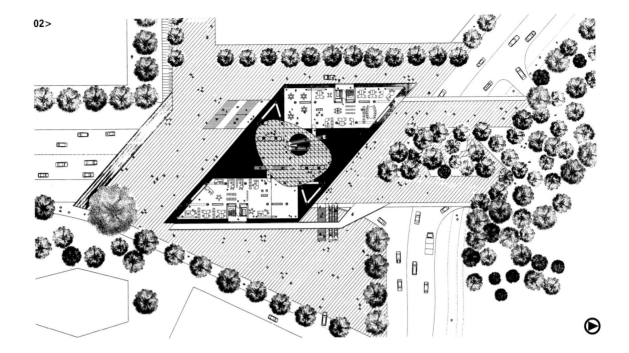

01> Cross-section.
The archway, which
is built over the entrance
to a busy road tunnel,
consists of two sixteen-
storey towers with a tall
glazed atrium between
them. The towers are
linked by a three-storey
bridging element.

02> Site plan showing
the location of the
building over the tunnel
entrance on the edge of
the new Rhine Park.

03> The archway
under construction.
It is intended to become
a new city landmark
for Düsseldorf.

225

^
03

Towers / City Gate

Chapter Four / Architecture and the Environment

04 > Detail of the façade. The natural ventilation provided by the specially designed ventilation boxes above and below each window is sufficient when outside temperatures are between 5 and 20°C (41° and 68°F). An environment friendly, sorption-based air-conditioning system using ground water is also provided.

05 > A model shows the atrium with the office towers on either side. The whole building is encased in a glass envelope, with a double layer of glazing for the offices.

06 > Diagram of the ventilation boxes. Their electronically controlled shutters make optimal use of climatic conditions. The space between the outer glass envelope and the inner glazing acts as a thermal and acoustic buffer.

∧
05

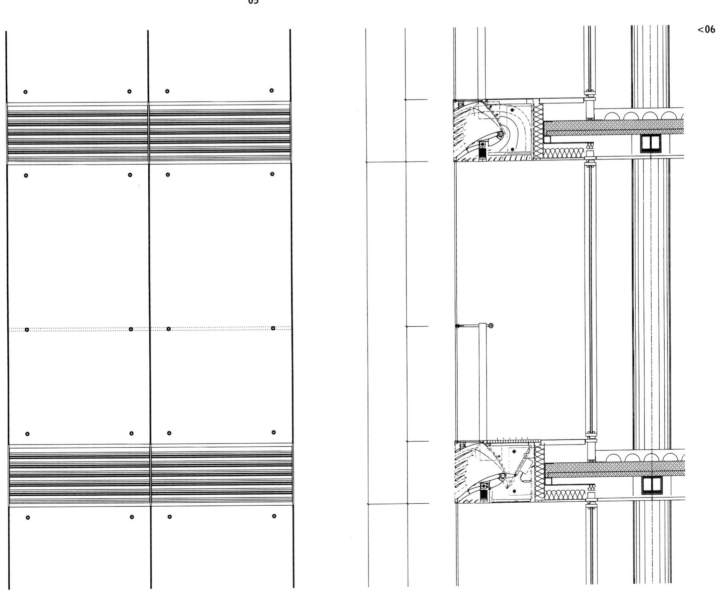

< 06

227

NAME OF BUILDING
Commerzbank Headquarters

Client/owner	**Date completed**
Commerzbank	June 1997
Occupier	**Gross area**
Commerzbank	130,000m²
Location	**Construction cost**
Frankfurt, Germany	£220 million
Architect	**Climatic zone**
Foster & Partners	Temperate

BUILDING ENERGY FEATURES

Orientation of main façades	**Solar control systems**
Multiple	Motorized vertical blinds
Natural ventilation: Approx. percentage of gross floor naturally ventilated	**Daylighting Approx. percentage of net floor area needing artificial lighting during daylight hours**
100% (+A/C)	0% (target)
Night-time ventilation provision	**Energy-saving controls for artificial lighting?**
Natural	Timers and movement detectors
Thermal transmission of building envelope	**Other**
N/S	–
Utilization of building mass thermal storage as part of energy strategy?	
Free night cooling	

HVAC SYSTEMS

Fuel/approx. % use	**Mechanical ventilation/ Air conditioning type**
N/S	Minimum fresh air, chilled ceiling
Boiler type	
Heat exchanger	
Heating system	**Heat recovery**
Water radiation; perimeter heating	Heat recovery in central plant; only 2–3 air changes needed due to 'cool ceilings'

ENERGY PERFORMANCE (predicted)

Total	**Heating**
185kW/h/m²/y	36kW/h/m²/y
Artificial lighting	**Total estimated carbon dioxide output**
16kW/h/m²/y	N/S
Refrigeration cooling	
115kW/h/m²/y	
Mechanical ventilation	
18kW/h/m²/y	

ENVIRONMENTAL/HEALTH FEATURES

Materials/components selection strategy to reduce embodied and transport energy?	**Special water conserving installation**
N/S	Sludge water from cooling towers used for WCs
Use of recycled materials	**Natural organic sewage treatment**
No	For catering waste
Use of timbers from managed sources	**Measures to encourage use of public transport**
Yes	Minimum parking available; city location

Commerzbank Headquarters
Frankfurt, Germany

This 60-storey tower is the centrepiece of Commerzbank's new headquarters in central Frankfurt. At 298 metres (977 feet) it is Europe's tallest building, and is claimed to be the world's first ecological high-rise office block.

The plan is an equilateral triangle with sides 60 metres (197 feet) long. These surround a central atrium and curve outwards to provide more office space. The three corners contain lifts, staircases and services. To maximize the use of natural lighting and ventilation, the sides of the tower are interrupted every eight storeys by four-storey winter gardens. These are arranged in a spiral formation, so that on any floor two sides are occupied by offices and one by a garden. Besides enabling all inward-facing offices to have natural sunlight, the gardens are also places where staff can eat and relax. The tower is divided vertically into five 12-storey 'villages'.

All windows can be opened manually with a tilt action; an external pane of glass outside each window, with gaps above and below for ventilation, prevents penetration by wind and rain. On the occasions when weather conditions make natural ventilation impossible, all windows can be closed by central control and a full air-conditioning system can be used. The gardens are protected by the fixed outer layer of glazing alone. The atrium acts as a ventilation chimney for the interior offices. Glass partitions at 12-storey intervals enable the rising hot air to be drawn off through the gardens to the outside and prevent excessive up-draughts.

The steel construction, with pairs of vertical supports at each corner supporting eight-storey Vierendeel trusses, enables offices and gardens to be free of columns.

Building this high has a very significant demographic impact and involves the use of large quantities of materials with high 'embodied' energy. It will be instructive to see how far possible adverse neighbourhood impacts and resource deficits can be offset against the creation of a stimulating and responsive office space and low energy consumption.

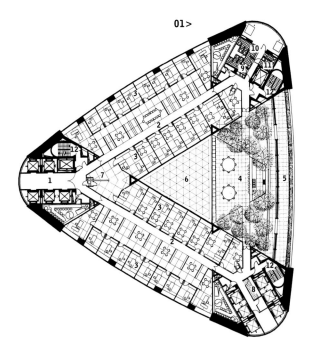

Key

1 Lift lobby
2 Office area
3 Office
4 Sky court
5 Terrace
6 Atrium
7 Document hoist
8 Kitchen
9 Women's WC
10 Men's WC
11 Disabled WC
12 Fire escape

01> Plan of a typical storey. On each floor, only two sides of the triangle are occupied by offices; the third is a winter garden, allowing light into the centre of the building. Lifts and services are at the corners.

02> The tower's commanding height as well as its unusual form, with winter gardens spiralling up its 60 storeys, has given Frankfurt a new landmark.

229

∧
02

Towers / Commerzbank Headquarters

<04

03> A view up one of the faces of the tower through the glass roof of the reception area. The offices have two layers of glazing and all windows can be opened manually.

04> The winter gardens are glazed with a single layer of glass and open into the central atrium. They are planted with a variety of vegetation and provide space where the staff can eat and relax. The use of Vierendeel beams leaves the interiors free of supporting structure.

05> A vertical section through the tower. The central atrium is interrrupted by glass partitions, dividing the building into five twelve-storey 'villages'. Each four-storey cluster has its own winter garden.

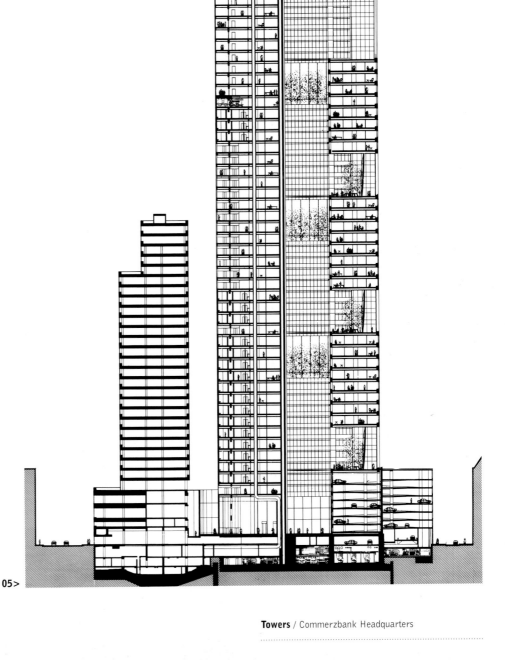

<03

05>

231

NAME OF BUILDING
Menara Mesiniaga

Client/owner	**Date completed**
Mesiniaga Sdn. Bhd.	August 1992
Occupier	**Gross area**
–	12,346m²
Location	**Construction cost**
Selangor, Malaysia	£5.9 million
Architect	**Climatic zone**
T.R. Hamzah & Yeang	Subtropical

BUILDING ENERGY FEATURES

Orientation of main façades
North, south, east

Natural ventilation: Approx. percentage of gross floor naturally ventilated
10%

Night-time ventilation provision
No

Thermal transmission of building envelope
Standard

Utilization of building mass thermal storage as part of energy strategy?
No

Solar control systems
Fixed external; solar control glazing; internal blinds/louvres

Daylighting Approx. percentage of net floor area needing artificial lighting during daylight hours
30%

Energy-saving controls for artificial lighting?
No

Other
–

HVAC SYSTEMS

Fuel/approx. % use
Mains electricity 100%

Boiler type
None

Heating system
None

Mechanical ventilation
Supply and extract to ancillary spaces

Air conditioning type
Centralized chilled water system; AHU (CHW) on floor plant; one unit per floor

Heat recovery
–

ENERGY PERFORMANCE

Total
0.062kW/h/m²

Artificial lighting
0.016kW/h/m²

Refrigeration cooling
0.038kW/h/m²

Mechanical ventilation
0.008kW/h/m²

Heating
N/A

Total estimated carbon dioxide output
N/S

ENVIRONMENTAL/HEALTH FEATURES

Materials/components selection strategy to reduce embodied and transport energy?
No

Use of recycled materials
No

Use of timbers from managed sources
No

Special water conserving installation
No

Natural organic sewage treatment
No

Measures to encourage use of public transport
No

Menara Mesiniaga
Selangor, Malaysia

Menara Mesiniaga is a headquarters building for an electronics and business machine company (IBM's Malaysia agency). Both external and internal design features use a bioclimatic approach to configure the built form and to produce an operationally low-energy building that makes the most of the hot-humid tropical ambient climate.

The most striking design feature is the planting which is introduced into the façade and the 'skycourts', starting from a three-storey-high planted mound and spiralling up the face of the building. Triple-height recessed terraces towards the upper part of the building are also planted. These atriums allow a cool flow of air to be channelled through the building's transitional spaces, while the planting provides shade and an oxygen-rich atmosphere. Curtain-wall glazing is used only on the north and south façades so as to moderate solar gain. All the window areas facing the hot east and west faces have external aluminium fins and louvres to provide sun shading. Glazing details allow the light green glass to act as a ventilation filter protecting the interior without totally insulating it. Terraces are provided for all the office floors, and have sliding full-height glass doors to control the extent of natural ventilation (when required). Lift lobbies, stairwells and toilets are naturally ventilated and sunlit. The lift lobbies do not need pressurization for fire protection.

The rooftop sun terrace is covered with a sunroof of trussed steel and aluminium; this both shades and filters light on to the swimming pool and the curved gymnasium roof (it also provides space for the possible future fixing of solar cells). Internally, enclosed rooms are placed as a central core rather than being situated at the periphery. This ensures good natural lighting and views out for the peripherally located workstations. The building's circular plan means that there are no dark corners. A range of automated systems are employed to reduce energy consumption by equipment and the air-conditioning plant.

This is perhaps the best known of a series of towers that Ken Yeang has designed in the Far East. In each he attempts a sensitivity towards the environment and the use of energy, despite a building form and local climate that do not encourage this approach.

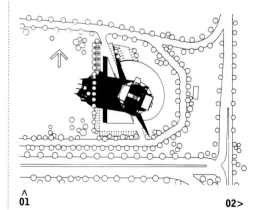

^
01

02>

01> Site plan.

02> View up the tower showing solar shading panels and the 'sky courts' which offer outdoor retreats for office staff.

03 > The main entrance lobby.

04 > Schematic showing environmental features.

05 > The tower is tied to the ground by planted elements and trained climbing plants.

< 03

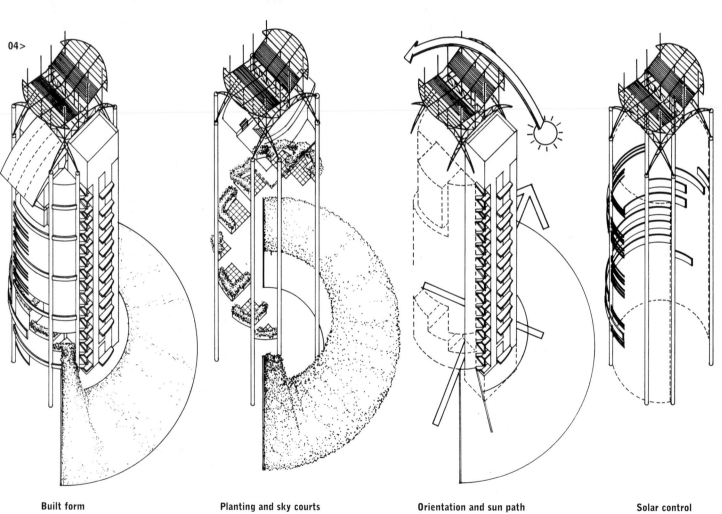

04 >

Built form

Planting and sky courts

Orientation and sun path

Solar control

235

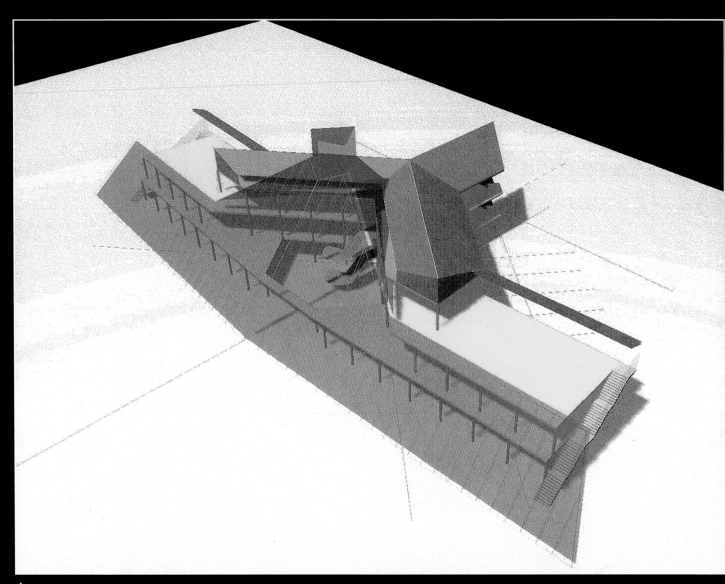

01> Early schematic
of the Solar Offices,
Doxford International
Business Park,
Sunderland, UK.

When reviewing the health of a nation, culture or society, commentators tend to stress the criticality of its position. It is described in starkly black and white terms: how things could go either way depending on the timely mobilization of beneficial or harmful forces. Often, evoking the knife edge in this way has more to do with engaging the attention of the reader than portraying things as they actually are. In the case of our environmental predicament, however, all indicators suggest that we are indeed balanced on a knife edge.

Figures collected by the Munich Reinsurance Company, one of the largest in the world, show that losses from weather-related disasters totalled more than $200 billion between 1990 and 1996 – four times as much as in the whole of the 1980s. With records showing that carbon dioxide – the primary cause of global warming – reached a new record in 1996, most climatologists place the blame for these disasters on atmospheric pollution.

Our present predicament recalls that which the world faced at the height of the Cold War, when human existence was held at the mercy of a politician's thumb as it hovered over the nuclear button. Today the world may not be poised on the brink of apocalypse but, if we continue on our present course, the end result could be very similar. Our choice, therefore, is either to continue to behave profligately and irresponsibly or to transform our political, economic and cultural way of life rapidly to sustainable practice. The aspect of sustainability dealt with in this book is the built environment, and it is within this sphere,

as we have seen, that the debate is being conducted between what might be called the 'Reversionaries' and the 'Progressives'.

Edward Goldsmith, author and founding editor of *The Ecologist,* and his camp argue in favour of resisting the process of urbanization on the authority of historical precedent, citing Aristotle's dictum that the size of a city should be determined by the number of people who could comfortably gather in the marketplace of Athens: not more than 5,400. In contrast, Norman Foster, again evoking historical precedent, suggests that during its early development most vernacular architecture was at the cutting edge of technology within the society in which it was produced (4th European Conference on Architecture, Berlin, 1996); and Richard Rogers, in pointing out that half the world's population now lives in cities and that this proportion will increase to three-quarters by the year 2025, concludes that the social needs of the community can only be met by the exploitation of modern science and technology (Reith Lectures, 1995).

There are clearly truths and fallacies within both stances. The gentle ruralist formulas of some members of the Reversionist camp seem hopelessly inadequate to resolve the issues of sustainability confronting the teeming cities of the Pacific Rim, India and South America; and yet their brand of bottom-up, proselytizing self-sufficiency and their adversarial defence of natural habitat will continue to promote change. Conversely, the Progressives' faith in the power of technology to solve complex social problems is often antithetical to the provision of humane and environmentally

sensitive settings. Without technical innovation in such fields as building-integrated power generation, climatically responsive building shells and building control systems, however, we have no chance of eradicating extravagant energy use in buildings.

During the next few years, grass-roots pressure and technological innovation will come together respectively to force and expedite change. Indeed, evidence suggests that this is already taking place. When white goods manufacturers turned down Greenpeace's German initiative for the development of an ozone-friendly refrigerator using CFC-free insulants (on the grounds that consumers would not be prepared to pay the extra cost), Greenpeace took it to the market themselves. Contrary to manufacturers' expectations, demand outstripped supply and the industry had to follow this example. If that was an instance of the 'agitproppers' bringing conventional industry into line, the reverse is true with photovoltaics. Major conglomerates such as BP, Shell, Siemens and Sanyo had developed photovoltaics as a spin-off from computer and space technology and were tentatively marketing it as a building-integrated energy resource. But it was only when Greenpeace, understanding its potential, produced a pamphlet and planted modules on the new Department of the Environment building in London that the wider public (in Britain at least) began to grasp its significance.

A review of the projects in the previous chapter not only illustrates the wide diversity of nature-sensitive buildings, but also

^
02

a growing confidence in the disposition and interpretation of measures to conserve energy and the environment. With a few notable exceptions, buildings designed around a comprehensive Green agenda have, until recently, displayed the ungainliness and self-consciousness of all prototype products. Solar chimneys have been over-enthusiastically flaunted and photovoltaic modules strapped on seemingly as an afterthought; the exploitation of thermal mass has led to oppressive, underlit spaces; and the inadequate detailing of 'right-on' Green materials and products, such as planted roofs, timber thinnings, trombe walls, and recycled car tyres (for walls), has produced tacky results. As architects become better acquainted with the authentic requirements of bioclimatic design, these will become absorbed into the overall stock of building design strategies. In a few years the incorporation of bioclimatic features will become as habitual to architects as the measures needed to ensure buildings stand up.

Although reference is constantly made to architects in this book, the Greening of buildings is having a profound effect on the roles of the design team as a whole. Conventional professional demarcation lines are being dissolved. Buildings, from a bioclimatic perspective, have to be conceived as comprising a number of interactive constituent parts, some of which are mutually supportive, while others are in direct conflict. A judgement has to be made as to the right balance – the optimum reconciliation for any particular set of circumstances. In order

to make this judgement, the architect, environmentalist, building services engineer, structural engineer and (in the UK) quantity surveyor have to understand each other's business thoroughly and be able to move across professional boundaries without arousing rancour.

Issues of heating, cooling and lighting are once again as much to do with the design of the building's fabric as with its engineering; the development of structural systems have as much to do with the integrity of façade design as with ensuring that the building does not fall down; and the financial investment in a building is as much to do with life-cycle estimates, often involving judgements relating to people's quality of life and the long-term protection of the environment, as with calculating construction costs. This comprehensive understanding of issues, together with a vision (which could be contributed by just one member of the team) is essential for the creation of a well-integrated, responsive and noteworthy building; and one which stands as a credit to sustainable principles.

This final part of the book looks to the future – albeit not very far into it. The chapter focuses on what will, or is likely, to happen in the next few years in respect of bioclimatic architecture (not to society, politics or economics, although changes in all these fields will impact on buildings). In order to do this, we will consider three buildings which are currently on the drawing board or under construction. They represent an approach to bioclimatic architecture in three

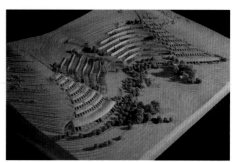

^
03

different settings: the wilderness, the suburb and the city.

The Wilderness

The first project is a retreat for the Samye Ling Tibetan Buddhist community, located on Holy Island, a tiny island off the south-west coast of Scotland. The commission followed an international architectural competition. Andrew Wright Associates and his multidisciplinary consultant team, who were shortlisted in the competition, were subsequently selected to develop their proposals. The Centre is non-sectarian and non-denominational and is dedicated to bringing religions together. All visitors will be welcomed.

The team's objective was to design a complex which would allow the community to live in harmony with the island and to capitalize on its natural attributes. This involved gaining an understanding of the local climate, ecology, economy and culture and interweaving these findings with the requirements of the Samye

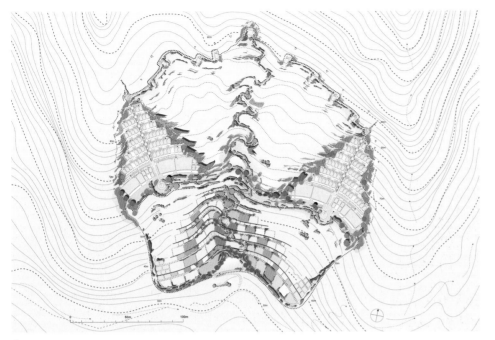

^
04

02> Aerial view of Holy Island showing the south-facing slopes on which the Retreat is to be built.

03> Competition proposal, overall view.

04> The layout of the community with the female accommodation to the west and the male to the east. The terraced farming and horticulture is placed centrally and below the buildings, while the Lama's House is located above them.

05> Section through a cell. All the accommodation is dug into the side of the southern slope and each has a small conservatory space to assist heating and insulate against heat loss. The roof is turfed but accommodates ventilation extract cowls and light 'scoops'.

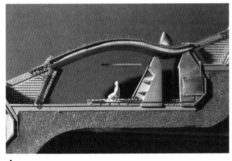

^
05

Ling community. The result is curvaceous terracing covering 4.4 hectares (10.9 acres) of the lower slopes of Mullach Mori. The complex is divided into two separate buildings, one for men and the other for women on retreat. The buildings are placed on south-facing spurs of land to make the best use of available sunlight. The accommodation is arranged in half-buried cells to the east and the west of the terraced area, with intensive farming and horticulture occupying the sheltered land below and to the centre. The Lama's House further up the slope overlooks the community.

The development aims to minimize impacts on the existing setting and to ensure that any impact it does have supports and enhances the topography, ecology and character of the island. The target is for the community to be self-sufficient in terms of water, waste, food and energy. Water is collected from rain run-off and distributed via gravity; waste water is treated using reed beds and used for irrigation; and crops, fruit,

vegetables and other produce will be cultivated on the terraces.

The buildings are sunk into the hillside and are designed to use very low levels of energy. Modelling and calculations show energy consumption of about 32 per cent of a typical domestic complex on such a site. Electrical power will be generated by wind turbines. This project falls within the tradition of 'ideal' community planning as advocated by Ebenezer Howard in *Garden Cities of Tomorrow* (1902) and Raymond Unwin in *Town Planning in Practice* (1880). It is located on beautiful virgin land where such holistic and idealized strategies are possible and, indeed, essential. The sensitivity brought to the scheme, its careful analytical basis and its undemonstrative appearance will make it a model for other community developments.

The Samye Ling project will undoubtedly serve its immediate purpose with success. Its more lasting value, however, may be as an inspirational model for future sustainable resort development around the world. In the last decade, growth in the tourist industry has been phenomenal. It now lies third in the ranking of international industries behind those of arms and oil. Since, by its nature, it tends to be focused on the most attractive, historic and fragile locations around the world, enormous damage has been caused by indiscriminate tourist development.

Only now is the industry tentatively responding to pressure from advocates of sustainability to clean up its act. Much effort will need to be made in order to reverse the

damage caused by existing developments. In the meantime, coastlines, lake sides, mountain valleys and natural wildernesses are being despoiled and the indigenous communities being exploited, deprived of rights and sidelined. The sustainable principles that underpin the Samye Ling Retreat need to be applied to many tourist developments.

The Suburb

The second project is an office building set within a business park. The phenomenon of the business park was to the 1970s and 1980s what the city suburbs were to the 1920s, 1930s and 1940s. They both have the same goal: an approximation of rural surroundings with a high level of convenience and service. Both are predicated on good public transport – to get in and out of the city or to and from the business park – and both rely on a high degree of personal mobility – to get to shops, the office, friends and real countryside.

Although the business park corrals the office buildings into a single 'estate', each building is a separate entity, surrounded by echelons of parked cars. An architect involved in designing one of these office buildings must follow planning and specification formulas deriving from entrenched real estate values. These cover efficient use of space, flexibility of subdivision, versatility of servicing, durability of fabric and the evocation of a sense of prestige. The architect must also give the building sufficient individuality for the occupiers to identify it as their own. Despite the prescriptive requirements of the business park office building, a surprising degree of

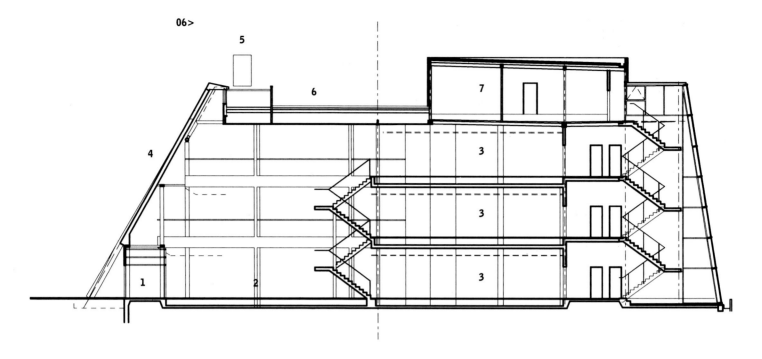

06>

5

6

7

4

3

3

3

1

2

07
v

innovation, at least among a few far-sighted developers, has taken place. The majority of low-energy office buildings illustrated in this book are located in business parks. Innovation in these buildings includes the development of the atrium space – space which does not fit neatly into either 'gross' or 'net' categories of office space, but provides a physical focus and potential economies in energy use (net office space can be let, whereas the gross includes non-rentalized landlord space and space taken up by the building's structure). The buildings also reflect rationalization of and innovation in construction and procurement processes, and significant advances in energy conservation, protection of the environment and provision for the health and well-being of the occupants.

The Solar Offices at Doxford International Business Park, located near Sunderland in the north of England, are designed by Studio E Architects for Akeler Developments PLC. In terms of energy use, this scheme makes the leap from building-as-consumer to building-as-consumer-*and*-provider which, as was noted in Chapter Two, is the approach that must be generally adopted if any real impact is to be made on the drive for sustainability in the built environment. The aims of the project are to provide a distinctive building containing versatile and responsive office space; to ensure that the building makes minimal impact on the global and local environment; and to integrate within its fabric the means to generate a worthwhile proportion of its energy needs. The building will be the first speculative office development in the world to do this. Energy will be provided by directly converting

Chapter Five / Architecture and the Environment

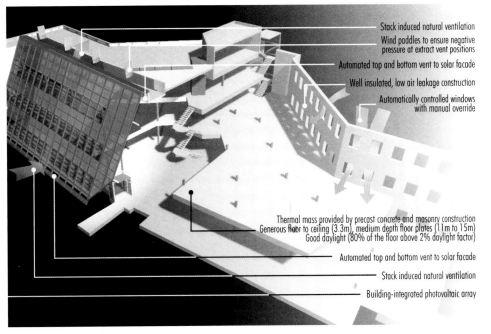

Stack induced natural ventilation

Wind paddles to ensure negative
pressure at extract vent positions

Automated top and bottom vent to solar façade

Well insulated, low air leakage construction

Automatically controlled windows
with manual override

Thermal mass provided by precast concrete and masonry construction
Generous floor to ceiling (3.3m), medium depth floor plates (11m to 15m)
Good daylight (80% of the floor above 2% daylight factor)

Automated top and bottom vent to solar facade

Stack induced natural ventilation

Building-integrated photovoltaic array

^
08

06> Section through the centre of the Solar Offices showing: 1 the main entrance; 2 atrium; 3 office space; 4 solar façade; 5 wind paddles; 6 wind trough; and 7 plant room.

07> Model of the offices with, to the right, the inclinced solar façade topped by the wind trough and paddles.

08> The cutaway perspective shows the integration of low-energy features – which minimize the demand for power – with the photovoltaic array which generates about one-third of the electricity needed clearly, silently and at the point of use.

09> A computational fluid dynamic (CFD) diagram shows resultant temperatures across one of the wings of the Solar Offices based on meteorological data from a typical summer (1986) and relying entirely on natural ventilation.

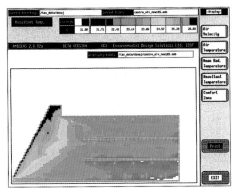

^
09

the sun's rays into electricity through the use of photovoltaic (PV) arrays. These are made up of 'modules', typically flat panels of laminated glass within which a grid of PV 'cells' is laid out. The solar cells are about the size of a saucer and are made from a very thin layer of semi-conductor material (usually silicon). This is doped with impurities (other elements) on both sides. As a result, one side acquires a negative charge and the other a positive one. When sunlight falls on the material, electrons are forced from one side to the other by its radiative energy. This produces electrical voltage, and thus direct current at the terminals.

Cells and modules are all wired up, and the electricity is stored (either in batteries or, more usually, in a building-integrated application), converted to alternating current and connected to the national grid. This allows any surplus power generation to be used by others and, when there is a shortfall, it enables power to be drawn from the grid

for the building's use in the normal way. The amount of current generated depends on the efficiency of the cells, their number, their orientation in relation to the sun, their temperature and the amount of sunlight the building receives.

The PV modules, being impervious and flat, lend themselves to incorporation within the building envelope. If carefully designed they can take the place of other components such as glazing, spandrel panels, sun screens, rain screen elements and canopies. The technology of building-integrated PV is, however, in its infancy. At the moment just 10 to 15 per cent of the sun's energy falling on the cells is converted into electricity. A further 10 to 15 per cent is reflected off the modules and the remainder is converted into heat. This means that in order to generate a useful amount of electricity, large areas of PVs have to be introduced. And to compound the problem, the modules are, in comparative building component terms, very expensive. Increased demand, more widespread subsidies and incentives and commercial competition, however, are expected to drive generating efficiencies up and bring prices down.

The incorporation of photovoltaics will have the same impact on buildings as, say, the elevator did in the mid-nineteenth century. The invention of the elevator coincided with the development of steel frame construction and the dramatic rise in city-centre real estate values. This resulted in the urban high rise. The combination of photovoltaics, the requirement for energy efficient, environmentally sensitive buildings, and a

move away from the city centres will produce a very different building type. The Solar Offices at Doxford provide an insight into the form this might take.

The City

If sustainability is to be substantially realized on a global scale, however, it is the city that has to be tackled, and this means working within an existing framework that is profligate and damaging. So far, sustainable models for the city context have been few in number and generally unconvincing. The third project offers a pointer to how bioclimatic building might aid urban reclamation. It is a professional training centre for the Ministry of the Interior of Nordrhein-Westfalen (Fortbildungsakademie), Germany, designed by Jourda and Perraudin Architects with HHS Planer + Architekten BDA.

The project was a winning entry in an architectural competition held in 1992. It is a latter-day reworking in microcosm of Buckminster-Fuller's project for placing a geodesic dome over a large part of Manhattan, thereby creating a more favourable local climate, cutting energy consumption and controlling emissions. The proposition on which this scheme is based, however, is the containment of new buildings and landscape designed for the modified environment that the enclosure will provide, not the covering of existing buildings designed to stand in the open.

The building occupies reclaimed parkland on the site of the old pithead around which,

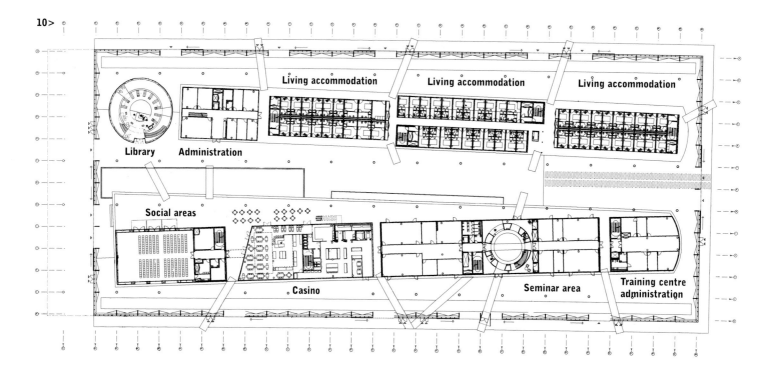

10

Living accommodation   Living accommodation   Living accommodation

Library   Administration

Social areas

Casino

Seminar area

Training centre administration

since the beginning of the century, the town of Herne-Sodingen has grown. The enclosing envelope will cover a 13,000-square-metre section of the park and will create a temperate, year-round micro-climate, the product of carefully controlled natural ventilation, humidifiers, sun screens and planting. Like the Solar Offices at Doxford, the building will also provide some of its own energy needs by means of thermal solar collectors and photovoltaics.

The gigantic greenhouse is designed on the basis of industrialized warehouse technology, but the supporting structure is largely of low embodied energy timber construction. Two long wooden buildings within this new ecological setting house the training and accommodation facilities. The protected temperate climate means that many of the requirements of buildings designed for normal climate can be relaxed or dropped altogether: the 'buildings' no longer have to keep wind, rain and snow out; thermal insulation provision can be reduced; solar control can be dispensed with; and heating is largely obviated. Critical to the success of the project will be the effectiveness of cooling provided by natural air movement. With this level of freedom, the internal enclosures take on the characteristics of furniture rather than buildings. While the shells of the internal buildings have to provide for aural and visual privacy, and still have to stand up and be plumbed in, it is easy to imagine a modular approach of lightweight components and packaged servicing units which could be relatively simply reconfigured, exchanged and adapted as and when required. A building

∧
11

scenario such as this would be truly organic. The outer carapace would respond to or, using the latest neural technology, anticipate climate change, while simultaneously providing the bulk of the energy requirement. The distinction between vegetation and artefact, between inside and outside, would be replaced internally by degrees of privacy, assembly and servicing.

Many commentators have pointed out that to talk of sustainability is to talk of the city, and that a move towards sustainability requires radical change in urban form, structure and society. As with the design

of a single building, this transformation has to be tackled on two fronts: changing consumption habits and providing localized non-polluting power generation. Attempts to change consumption habits – the routine expenditure of non-renewable resources – are often frustrated by 'chicken-and-egg' scenarios. Three examples illustrate this. Firstly there is the need to reduce the number of private cars on the roads. As well as consuming energy unnecessarily, private transport exacerbates atmospheric pollution, thereby endangering health. Since in many countries public transport is inefficient and undercapitalized, there is little incentive for

∧
12

people to leave their cars at home. Consequently, demand for a better service is half-hearted, and pressure on governments to invest in public transport is insufficient. Secondly, there is the contemporary reliance on air-conditioning which in many cities is the only means of providing clean, uncontaminated air. The fact that the majority of occupied buildings in these cities now have air-conditioning undermines efforts to combat air pollution.

The third example concerns food supplies. Much of the food needed by those who live in the city is flown half-way round the world. Because citizens have been persuaded that out-of-season, standardized fare is an essential part of their diet, and because of the realpolitik of powerful farming interests, there is little encouragement for cities to develop localized food production or to persuade their citizens of the efficacy of doing so. In order to transform these vicious

circles into virtuous ones, sustained grass-roots pressure and political action are necessary. In addition, corporations need to be convinced that changes will bring long-term commercial benefits. So far such efforts have been at best sporadic. With regard to the issue of energy supply, it has been pointed out by Bruce Anderson *(Solar Building Architecture,* 1990), and Dean Hawkes that in all the world's principal population centres, the surfaces of buildings receive many times more ambient energy than they consume in all their processes and operations. Paradoxically, even the most effective 'solar' buildings tap just a tiny fraction of this, and most buildings consume delivered energy in order to reject it. Accordingly, modern cities are sustained by a far-flung energy hinterland and a worldwide infrastructure. If the technical transformation can be achieved which would allow energy falling on all these buildings to be converted more efficiently, it is feasible that buildings, and the cities of which they are constituents, could become net producers of energy, rather than profligate consumers. The complex framework of sustaining hinterland and infrastructure would collapse to be replaced by a new order of self-sufficiency and sustainability. This transformation could be as significant to the city as was its historical metamorphosis from a place of protection and fortification to a place of commerce and culture.

These formulas for change are grossly oversimplified, but if change is to be brought about, simple, clear goals will need to be pursued. There have been numerous instances

of carefully constructed sustainable objectives being countered by short-term political or commercial interest. Politicians will happily support Green ideals involving regulations that happen to coincide with the demands of the Exchequer, but they remain conspicuously silent when these same ideals conflict with their programme for re-election. If progress towards sustainability is confounded by the ebb and flow of expediency at governmental levels, how can architects, engineers, designers, builders and traders make a difference? The fact is that in the long run it is they alone who can make a difference. Our man-made environment is the product of the dreams and workmanship of precisely these groups; they are the people who, through a combination of sociological perceptiveness, design flare, technological skill and commercial understanding, promote and translate the ideals and instincts of society into actuality.

When environmental calamity strikes; when an industrial process threatens life or health, it is usually a sign of a failure of creativity or forethought, not an act of malice or political calculation. Seen from this perspective, there is clearly scope for designers to steward and mobilize the Green Idea. It makes sense to use well-judged measures for reducing energy consumption, protecting the environment and promoting good health as stimuli for innovation and experimentation, and to take these results and develop them as the technological underpinning for inspired and instinctive responses to our natural environment here on Earth.

Chapter Five / Future Directions

APPENDIX

A Guide to Worldwide Energy-Efficient Comfort Strategies

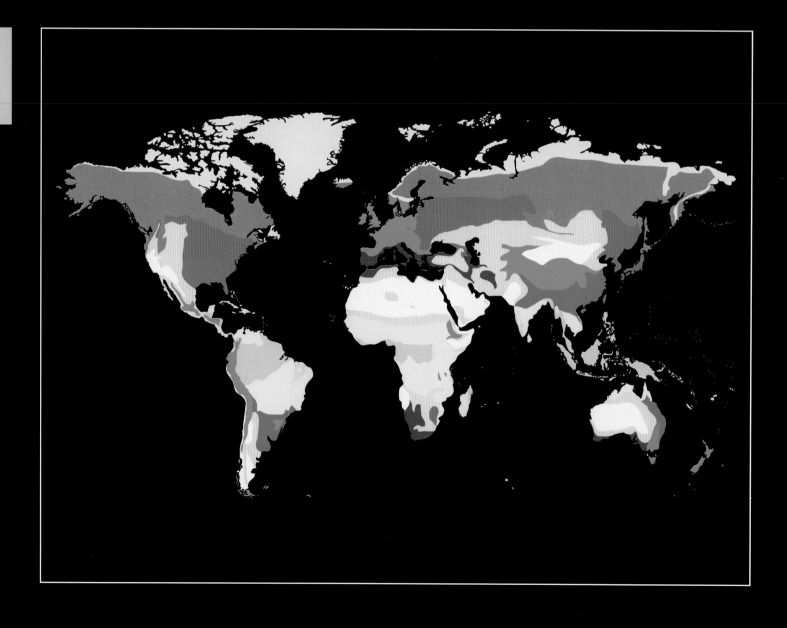

Key

Ice Caps	Subtropical
Tundra	Tropical
Uplands	Savannah
Continental	Steppes
Temperate	Desert
Mediterranean	

Strategies for providing comfort in buildings around the world vary widely according to the different types of climate. The most obvious difference is in temperature: a cold climate requires one set of measures and a hot one another. However, superimposed on temperature are a range of other factors which will also determine the type of construction, orientation and layout of a building. These include humidity, precipitation, wind, permeability, mass, ventilation and lighting.

Except in those parts of the world with very extreme climate, the contribution of 'passive' comfort measures – that is those that exploit natural forces without recourse to mechanical and electrical systems – can make a very considerable contribution to comfort if orchestrated effectively. Good bioclimatic building will always call on these measures first and extract as much benefit from them as possible. Once a strategy for passive measures has been outlined, 'active' measures can be called upon to augment and enhance them so that reasonable comfort can be established throughout the year and during day and night. The active measures include fans to assist natural air currents, cooling to lower temperatures when passive systems are inadequate, heating in the reverse situation, and artificial lighting.

Over and above the measures needed to provide comfort in an energy-efficient manner are those affecting energy consumption in construction generally. These apply regardless of climatic zone. They include embodied, grey and induced energy, renewable energy generation and efficient and responsive management of energy systems. These issues are described in detail in Chapter Two.

The chart on the following page provides an overview of the importance of different measures – both passive and active – relating to eleven different climatic zones. These are identified on the adjacent map. Clearly this can only provide general guidance. A project in any one of these zones would need to be carefully analysed and a strategy particular to its own requirements and locality developed. However, the chart shows a clear energy pattern between measures and zones.

245

Importance is rated from 0 to 7
or from pale blue to scarlet.

PASSIVE COMFORT MEASURES	ACTIVE COMFORT MEASURES	Ice Caps	Tundra	Uplands	Continental	Temperate	Mediterranean	Subtropical	Tropical	Savannah	Steppes	Desert
Natural Ventilation		0	0	1	4	6	6	7	7	7	7	7
	Mechanical Ventilation	5	5	3	3	3	4	5	6	6	6	6
Night Ventilation		0	1	2	3	5	6	7	7	7	7	7
	Artificial Cooling	0	0	0	1	1	3	5	5	5	5	6
Evaporative Cooling		0	0	0	1	2	3	2	2	5	6	7
	Free Cooling	0	0	0	4	3	5	6	6	7	7	7
Heavy Construction		3	4	4	6	5	6	2	2	3	5	6
Lightweight Construction		3	3	2	2	3	3	5	5	6	4	4
	Artificial Heating	7	7	7	7	6	4	0	0	2	4	1
Solar Heating		2	3	6	6	7	6	0	0	2	3	0
	Free Heating	7	7	7	6	6	5	0	0	0	3	0
Incidental Heat		6	6	6	5	5	4	0	0	1	2	0
Insulation/Permeability		7	7	7	7	6	5	0	0	1	3	4
Solar Control/Shading		0	1	3	4	5	6	6	6	6	7	7
	Artificial Lighting During Daytime	6	6	4	4	4	3	3	3	2	2	2
Daylight		6	6	6	6	6	6	5	5	5	4	4

246

Key

| 0 No Importance | 7 Very Important |

ENERGY-EFFICIENT MEASURES WHICH ARE CONSTANT WHEREVER THE BUILDING IS LOCATED

Embodied, Grey and Induced Energy   Comfort Management   Energy Generation

CLIMATIC ZONES

Ice Caps> Sub-zero temperatures are the norm. Very little daylight for over half the year. Heavy precipitation in the form of snow. The only building materials in plentiful supply are ice and compacted snow. **Tundra>** Sub-zero temperatures for half the year. Mild summers. Precipitation throughout the year. Strong winds. Traditional settlement is semi-nomadic with demountable buildings of timber framing and fabric or hide covering. **Uplands>** Extreme conditions. Long, cold winters with heavy snow and danger from avalanches. Fresh, mild summers with strong sun. Strong winds and sudden changes in weather. Location and orientation are critical design factors. Stone and timber are usually plentiful building materials and enable buildings to be robust and enduring. **Continental>** A climate of extremes: long, cold winters and long, hot summers. Spring and autumn are brief transitional periods. Precipitation throughout the year. Strong winds. Traditional construction is geared to providing comfort in the severe winter conditions; in summer more time can be spent out of doors. **Temperate>** The weather in these zones is particularly influenced by the beneficial effects of the neighbouring oceans. They are characterized by mild, wet winters and warm, wet summers, although greater extremes have been experienced over recent years. These zones are generally very populous. Resources of every kind are available for construction. Traditional construction varies widely in accordance with local geology and vegetation. **Mediterranean>** This zone is the closest to an ideal climate for human habitation. However, buildings must alleviate the intense heat in high summer. Building materials are abundant, but stone is particularly suitable on account of its high thermal mass; and timber, fabric, climbing plants and trees on account of their ability to provide shade. **Subtropical>** Temperatures never fall below freezing and the climate is generally comfortable throughout the year. Summers, however, are hot and humid. Cyclones and hurricanes are a particular danger. High rainfall all the year round. Traditional construction is geared to providing comfort in the more taxing conditions of summer. It is generally lightweight with a premium on good ventilation. However, construction has to be tough in cyclone-prone areas. **Tropical>** The climate is hot and humid all the year round with extremely heavy precipitation. The climate is particularly dependent on the rainforest ecology. As this is cleared, the climate is changed. Building materials are abundant; particularly timber and thatch. Construction must shed the rain effectively and dry out quickly. It should encourage natural ventilation. **Savannah>** In these zones the temperatures are fairly constant throughout the year; between 20 and 30°C. Rainfall is more variable, often related to two distinct seasons. Human kind is descended from antecedents designed for these regions. Protection from climate can be minimal: shade from the sun and the induction of natural ventilation. **Steppes>** These regions are very hot in summer, but cool in winter with very little precipitation. In many areas there is a reliable seasonal wind pattern allowing it to be harnessed to cool interiors. However, if the wind is warm the benefit will be confined to evaporative cooling. Buildings need to protect occupants from dust and sand as well as the sun. Compacted earth is often used as a primary building material in these areas. **Desert>** These regions are virtually uninhabitable during summer due to the very high temperatures. However, night temperatures can be cool and at high altitudes as low as freezing. There is negligible precipitation and water has to be drawn from subterranean aquifers. Traditional settlement is nomadic, but in countries such as Egypt and Saudi Arabia, where population growth requires permanent desert settlement, considerable resources are required to make living conditions tolerable.

PASSIVE COMFORT MEASURES

Cooling

Natural Ventilation> The ventilation and cooling of space by designing the building to make use of natural convection currents and to induce air movement by imposed pressure and temperature differentials. Strategies include single-sided ventilation, cross ventilation and stack ventilation.

Following these strategies imposes constraints on floor depths and favours generous floor heights. **Night Ventilation>** An important aspect of passive cooling when the weather is hot, but nights are cooler than the day. The benefits of night ventilation are best realized when used in conjunction with high mass building construction and when night air is allowed to pass across exposed high mass elements such as floor slabs and masonry walls. Over extended periods of hot weather the cooling cycle will become less effective as the nights get warmer. **Evaporative Cooling>** Cooling experienced when air (not necessarily cool air) passes across one's body causing evaporation of perspiration and moisture (which has to be replenished by drinking). Hot, dry air passing over water or damp surfaces and taking up moisture will also give a sense of cooling.

Thermal Inertia

Heavy Construction> The use of the permanent constructional elements of a building – walls, floors, roof – as a means of absorbing, retaining and releasing heat on a diurnal basis, but on a cycle that lags behind air temperatures. Typically, therefore, the building fabric absorbs heat during the day and releases it in the cool of the night. This phenomenon is most effective when used with night-time ventilation. **Lightweight Construction>** Where constructional elements are selected on the basis of their lack of thermal retentiveness and where no benefit derives from thermal mass. Lightweight construction is usually associated with encouragement of natural ventilation and the provision for extensively opening up the building.

Heating

Solar Heating> Using the sun to heat, or assist in heating, internal spaces. Solar heating can be enhanced passively by careful orientation and by ensuring that once the heat has entered the building it is not allowed to escape before it has transferred its energy. **Incidental Heat>** Activities and processes taking place within a building or on its surface (e.g. a photovoltaic installation) will generate heat. This can make a valuable contribution to the space heating if effectively harnessed. **Insulation/Permeability>** Highly insulated buildings will retain their internal temperatures, whether cooler or warmer than external temperatures, over much longer periods than those that are less well insulated; as will a building whose air leakage is minimized. High insulation and airtightness is therefore important where internal air temperatures are at variance with external temperatures. **Solar Control/Shading>** Shielding internal spaces from the sun is essential where they are likely to overheat. This is best achieved before solar irradiation hits the building fabric and where heat absorbed by shading devices can be dissipated without heating the building or its interior. **Daylight>** Daylight more than any other natural force relies for its success in lighting a building on the combination of qualitative and quantitative attributes. Internal spaces in all parts of the world need adequate and sympathetic natural light. The means, not the value, of achieving this will vary from region to region.

ACTIVE COMFORT MEASURES

Cooling

Mechanical Ventilation> Mechanical installations employing fans and ductwork used to ensure adequate ventilation. It is used most effectively when augmenting natural air movement. Fans can also be used as a fall back on still days or when occasional adverse wind conditions may counter designed air flow patterns. **Artificial Cooling>** Cooling of air either directly or indirectly by condensing or evaporative systems. The efficiency, controls, deployment and maintenance of the systems are key if they are to be used effectively and economically with minimal environmental impact. **Free Cooling>** Opportunities can arise where natural cool stores, such as lakes, the sea or underground aquifers, can be tapped to provide cooling to indoor spaces. This is usually executed by means of pumps and a heat exchange installation, thereby requiring auxiliary mechanical systems.

Heating

Artificial Heating and Heat Reclaim> Auxiliary heating can be provided from a wide range of radiant or conductive systems. They should be designed to augment solar and incidental heat gains. As with artificial cooling, the efficiency, controls, deployment and maintenance of the systems are key to effective and economical operation and minimizing environmental impact. Savings in heating can be made by taking heat from warm air that might otherwise have been expelled from the building. **Free Heating>** In some parts of the world (most notably Iceland) geothermal heat can be tapped and used as an energy supply for heating (or super heating) to provide space and water heating. Mechanical systems will be required to distribute and control this heat. **Artificial Lighting During Daytime>** Lighting systems are needed in daytime to augment daylight where the use of the building requires deep or internal spaces and, therefore, does not permit comprehensive daylighting of spaces, and to light in winter when days may be short. The efficiency of the lighting system, its controls, the deployment of luminaires and its management, are key to providing an effective and energy-efficient installation.

ENERGY EFFICIENT MEASURES WHICH ARE CONSTANT WHEREVER THE BUILDING IS LOCATED

Embodied, Grey and Induced Energy> Energy use in the manufacture of materials, components and systems; in their distribution and transportation; and in the construction of buildings needs to be husbanded and minimized wherever the building is located. **Comfort Management>** The management of comfort systems in a complex building and the split between central and local management and control of systems will not only affect the efficient performance of the building, but influence the occupants' identification with it, their sense of being part of it and the manner in which it delivers comfort. **Energy Generation>** Local energy generation using renewable sources – wind turbine, photovoltaics and biomass, etc. – minimizes greenhouse emissions wherever the building is located, but different regions will favour different renewable systems.

Glossary

Acid Rain> The removal (or 'washing out') of oxides of sulphur and nitrogen from the atmosphere by precipitation (rain, snow, hail, etc). Such oxides are produced in the combustion of coal and petroleum-derived fuels. The presence of these compounds dissolved in precipitation causes an increase in acidity, which may prove harmful to terrestrial flora and fauna. These compounds may also be particulates, and can fall to earth in the absence of precipitation.

Adiabatic> Of a thermodynamic process taking place without loss or gain of heat.

Air Curtain> A zone of high air movement generated by fan power and used at the openings to a building to contain internal comfort temperatures without the need for physical barriers.

Air Cycle Refrigeration> A system of providing cooling using air as a refrigerant.

Argon> An inert, colourless and odourless gas used in sealed double glazing to improve its ability to insulate.

Berm> A narrow path or ledge at the edge of a slope, road or canal, but now often used to describe a man-made embankment.

Bioclimatic> Describes an approach to building design which is inspired by nature and which applies a sustained logic to every aspect of a project, focused on optimizing and using the environment. The logic covers conditions of setting, economy, construction, building management and individual health and well-being, in addition to building physics.

Bio-degradable> Refers to a substance's ability to be broken down into harmless products by processes and organisms in the environment.

Biomass> The total amount of living organisms in a given area, expressed in terms of living or dry weight per unit area, but here used to describe a source of energy fuel.

Blinding> Material laid on top of hardcore to form a base for casting a concrete ground slab.

BRECSU (Building Research Energy Conservation Support Unit)> Part of the BRE (Building Research Establishment). Its main role is the management of technology transfer programmes in energy efficiency. It is involved in the Department of the Environment's Best Practice Programme, and the THERMIE Programme for the Commission of the European Communities.

Carbon Dioxide> A colourless, odourless, incombustible gas present in the atmosphere and formed during respiration, the decomposition and combustion of organic compounds (including fossil fuels) and the reaction of acids with carbonates. The major contributor to 'greenhouse' effect.

CFC (Chlorofluorocarbon)> This family of substances is widely used as refrigerants, aerosol propellants, coolants, sterilants, solvents, and in the production of foam insulation. CFCs are persistent in the atmosphere and are known to cause ozone depletion and global warming, some CFCs being over 10,000 times more damaging than carbon dioxide in respect of global warming. CFCs are now being phased out under the Montreal Protocol, and alternatives are being sought. An EU Regulation required the consumption and production of CFCs to cease by 01.01.95.

Co-generation Plant> Plant which generates both electricity and heat, the heat being utilized to help warm the hot water supply and/or internal spaces.

Composite> A material whose performance derives from the integral combination of two or more materials, for example reinforced concrete; in manufacturing industry the term specifically describes reinforced plastics and carbon fibre.

Condensing Boiler> A very high-efficiency boiler (efficiencies of 90 per cent compared to 80–85 per cent for conventional boilers) which uses residual heat of the combustion gases in the flue to heat water in a secondary heat exchanger. This causes the water vapour in the flue gases to condense. The condensate then has to be drained from the boiler.

Curtain Wall> A non-load-bearing wall placed as a weather-proof membrane round a structure, and usually made of glass and metal.

Damper> A mechanism for adjusting or closing down air flow in a ventilation duct or other air passage.

Displacement Ventilation> A ventilation system installed in a building whereby fresh, cool air is introduced at low level, usually through the floor, forcing the 'old' warm out of the space at high level. The air can be artificially cooled or heated, and filtered or humidified in the same manner as other air-conditioning systems.

Embodied Energy> The energy consumed in the manufacture of building materials, components and systems.

Entropy> A thermodynamic quantity that changes in a reversible process by an amount equal to the heat absorbed or emitted, divided by the thermodynamic temperature.

Fossil Fuel> Any naturally occurring carbon or hydrocarbon fuel, such as coal, petroleum, peat and natural gas, formed by the decomposition of prehistoric organisms.

Greenhouse Effect> The process in which carbon dioxide and other gases build up in the atmosphere and trap more of the sun's heat, thus leading to changes in climate.

The Grid (Electrical)> An integrated system of electricity distribution, usually covering a large area.

Global Warming> The surface temperature of the Earth is regulated by the presence of greenhouse gases in the atmosphere that trap long-wave solar radiation reflected from the Earth's surface. The main naturally produced greenhouse gases are carbon dioxide (CO_2) and methane (CH_4). The greenhouse effect is a totally natural phenomenon. The burning of fossil fuels releases carbon dioxide into the atmosphere which, along with emissions of other greenhouse gases such as CFCs, nitrous oxide (N_2O), tropospheric ozone, and methane, has caused an increase in the amount of solar radiation retained in the atmosphere. Global temperature has risen by half a degree Celsius in the last century. Climate models predict temperature rises from 1.5 to 4.5 degrees by 2050. Effects of global warming include sea-level rises and droughts, either of which could have severe consequences for the world's food production.

Halon> Halons contain bromide, which is ozone-depleting. They have been used extensively in fire-protection systems, but are now a subject of the Montreal Protocol and an EU Regulation. Substitute products and systems are being developed and marketed. Consumption and production of Halon within the EU ceased on 01.01.94. In future, only recycled Halon will be available and in decreasing quantities.

HCFC (Hydrochlorofluorocarbon)> A family of compounds used as refrigerants in place of CFCs. Their ozone depletion potential is up to two orders of magnitude below that of the CFCs. HCFCs are also less potent greenhouse gases than both the CFCs and HFCs, but are still hundreds of times more damaging than carbon

dioxide. An EU Regulation requires consumption and production to cease within the EU by 2015, but their use will be increasingly restricted and the phase-out date is likely to be brought forward.

HFC (Hydrofluorocarbon)> Refrigerants which have been used to replace CFCs, as they have zero ozone-depleting potential due to the absence of chlorine in their structures. They are less damaging than CFCs in terms of global warming, but are hundreds to thousands of times more damaging than carbon dioxide. There are also fears that these compounds can break down in the troposphere to produce toxic compounds.

Heat Reclaim> The transference of heat from hot air (or other medium) going to waste to heat the fresh air (or other medium) being introduced by the building.

HVAC System> Heating, ventilation and air-conditioning systems.

Kilowatt-hour (kW/h)> One thousand watts acting over a period of one hour. The kW/h is a unit of energy. 1 kW/h = 3600kJ.

Low Emissivity (Low E) Glazing> Glass treated with a special coating to increase its insulating properties.

Montreal Protocol> This protocol, entitled 'The agreement on substances which deplete the ozone layer' was signed in September 1987 by 60 governments. It aimed initially to reduce CFC consumption by 50 per cent before 2000, but introduced periodic revisions on the basis of new scientific predictions. It was subsequently agreed to bring to zero the consumption of CFCs, Halons and carbon tetrachloride by the year 2000.

Mushrabeyeh> Screens found in Islamic countries in the Middle East and made of small, turned, geometrically interconnected pieces of wood formed around upper-level windows.

NOx> A term used to include nitric oxide (NO) and nitrogen dioxide (NO2). Anthropogenic emissions of NOx are greatly exceeded by natural emissions, but tend to be more concentrated. NOx arises from fossil fuel combustion, including motor vehicles, and causes a number of respiratory problems. NOx can also cause acidic deposition.

Ozone Depletion> The layer of ozone gas in the stratosphere protects the earth's inhabitants from the harmful effects of ultra-violet (UV) radiation, exposure to which is known to increase the incidence of certain types of skin cancer, to cause cataracts and to suppress the immune system. The presence of ozone-depleting gases, such as CFCs and Halons, in the atmosphere has caused destruction of this layer to such an extent that a hole in the ozone layer over Antarctica was discovered in 1984. The Montreal Protocol aims at reducing the consumption of CFCs and Halons.

Peak Watts (Wp)> The amount of power produced by a photovoltaic cell or module in nominal irradiation conditions.

Permaculture> Or 'Permanent Agriculture': the concept of a self-supporting system of agriculture whereby the organization of plants and animals enables continued recycling of nutrients and energy within the system, which is ultimately sustained by input of solar energy. It is possible to remove organisms from the system for human use, but this must be sustainably managed in order to prevent the system from collapsing.

Photovoltaic (PV) Array> An interconnected system of photovoltaic panels that functions as a single electricity-producing unit.

Photovoltaic (PV) Cell> The semi-conductor element within a PV module which instantaneously converts light into electrical energy (DC voltage and current).

Photovoltaic (PV) Module> A panel comprising an assembly of PV cells wired together and usually laminated between two rigid layers of material – the outer one usually a sheet of glass – delivering a known electrical output at 'peak' conditions.

Recycling> The conversion of waste material or substance into a usable form. This is distinct from re-using, where no treatment is required. There are two types of recycling, open- and closed-loop. In the former waste is recycled a finite number of times before ultimately being disposed of; in the latter recycling is continuous. Recycling of paper and plastic is generally open-loop, as the quality of the material deteriorates, but scrap steel can be recycled in a closed-loop, as the grade of steel produced from scrap is as high as the original. There are sometimes financial benefits in recycling a material which cannot directly be reused, and environmental benefits include a reduction in the volume of waste produced, and possible conservation of embodied energy.

Reed Bed> A system of waste-water treatment which utilizes a number of gravel-based beds planted with certain species of reeds which live off the contaminants present in the water. After large solids have been removed, waste water is piped into the reed beds, which are usually arranged in a cascade system. Reed beds can be used for both domestic and some industrial applications, but the latter use may be restricted by the amount of space needed.

Renewable Energy> Renewable energy sources include solar heating (active and passive) and electricity generation, hydro power, wind power, tidal electricity generation, geothermal heating, and the use of biofuels such as RDF, wood and farm waste. In 1992 2.5 million tonnes of oil equivalent was provided by renewable energy sources, with the majority (67 per cent) coming from large-scale hydro schemes. Favourable prices for renewable energy sources are obtained through the Non Fossil Fuel Obligation (NFFO). In 1992 64 per cent of renewable energy projects were contained within this scheme, which is due to be removed in 1998.

SBS (Sick Building Syndrome)> A combination of health malfunctions which affect a significant percentage of a building's population. The effects include lethargy, headaches, respiratory infections, eye strain and dryness of the eyes, aching muscles, catarrh and asthma, which are not experienced by occupants when away from the building. There are a number of apparent causes of SBS which include air conditioning, sealed windows, recirculated air, high-density occupation, smoking, airborne micro-organisms, dust and dust-mite excrement.

Solar Chimneys> Flues constructed to exhaust air from a building using a combination of stack effect, external pressure differentials and the heating of the flue by the sun so that cooler air is drawn in to fill the vacuum.

Solar-Electric Collector> A device for collecting solar energy in the form of electricity using a photovoltaic array.

Solar Gain> The raising of temperature caused by the heat of the sun.

Solar-Thermal Collector> A device for collecting solar energy in the form of heat, usually by exposing a fluid to the sun's rays.

SOx> Refers to oxides of sulphur, the most important of which are SO_2 and SO_3. These are formed during the combustion of fossil fuels, smelting of non-ferrous ores, paper manufacture, waste incineration, and sulphuric acid manufacture. The oxides are deposited on the ground, usually many miles from their point of origin, as acid rain, causing damage to ecology. Coal burning accounts for around 50 per cent of recent annual global emissions of SO_2.

Stack Effect> The vertical movement of air caused by convection; the phenomena by which hot air rises, pulling

cooler air in to fill the vacuum. The hot air is usually expelled at high level.

Sustainability> The concept of managing the use of natural resources so that the amount of the resource is not irretrievably depleted. The development of renewable alternatives to non-renewable resources is essential, and the stock of renewables in use must be maintained. Economic development taking place in this way is termed 'Sustainable Development', and has been defined as 'Development that meets the needs of the present without compromising the ability of future generations to meet their own needs'.

Terminal Reheat> A heating element placed at the end of air ducts to raise the temperature of the supply air to the desired level.

Thermal Mass> The capacity of a material to take up heat from the surrounding space. A material of low thermal inertia, such as stone or concrete, can be used to absorb heat during the day when temperatures are hot and release it at night when it is cooler.

Trickle Vent> A small opening, usually in a window frame, fitted with a sliding shutter which allows low levels of ventilation in winter to assist in dispersing stale air.

Trombe Wall> A high thermal mass wall exposed to the sun, usually with an outer layer of glass and an inner surface of dark finish, used to absorb and store heat and release it to heat internal spaces when it is cooler.

Vernacular Architecture> Indigenous buildings developed on pragmatic bases by the peoples of a geographic region, tribe or community using materials and skills which are to hand.

Wind Towers> Towers constructed to direct wind into a building for cooling purposes.

Selected definitions reproduced from 'Environmental Code of Practice for Buildings and their Services', ISBN 086022 367 1, BSRIA 1994.

Photographic Credits

The following photographic credits are given, with page numbers in brackets:

Wayne Andrews / Esto (19 top); Arcaid / Richard Bryant (16 bottom, 21 bottom left, 22 top, 207 top); Arcaid / Niall Clutton (21 bottom right); Arcaid / Mark Fiennes (20 top right); Arcaid / Scott Frances (29); Arcaid / Mark Jones (30); Arcaid / John Edward Linden (22 bottom); Arcaid / Esto / Ezra Stoller (28); Arcaid / Alan Weintraub (116–119); Archipress / Peter Cook (73); Archipress / Michel Denance (214); Archipress / Franck Eustache (213); Courtesy of Architectenbureau Alberts & Van Huut (59 left); Architectural Association Photo Library / Archigram (49); Architectural Association Photo Library / Theo Armour (24 bottom); Architectural Association Photo Library / Bill Chaitkin (24 top); Architectural Association Photo Library / P. Collymore (27 bottom); Architectural Association Photo Library / Hazel Cook (53); Architectural Association Photo Library / Peter Cook (52 top right); Architectural Association Photo Library / David Gray (157); Architectural Association Photo Library / Erno Goldfinger; Architectural Association Photo Library / Hadden / Morphet (127); Architectural Association Photo Library / Hermione Hobhouse (107); Architectural Association Photo Library / Ulrich Kerber (55); Architectural Association Photo Library / Norman Khaled (50); Architectural Association Photo Library / Rik Nijs (56); Architectural Association Photo Library / C. Nino (27 top); Architectural Association Photo Library/Roger Sapsford (48); Architectural Association Photo Library / Timothy Street Porter (46); Architectural Association Photo Library / D. Tinero (25 top left); Richard Barnes (82–83); Ch Bastin & J. Evrard (184–185); Courtesy of

Benson & Forsyth Architects (125–126); Bibliothèque Nationale (19 bottom); Bildarchiv Foto Marbourg (23); Reiner Blunck (112–115, 121–122); Catherine Bogert (129–131); Obie Bowman (159–161); David Brazier (201); Gregory Burgess (149, 151); Comstock / George Goerster (17 bottom, 199); Courtesy of the Courtauld Institute (18 top, 20 bottom right, 25 top right, 25 bottom, 26); Jean-Pierre Cousin (52 left); Courtesy of Edward Cullinan Architects (10); Daylight / Liege (183); Philip de Bay at V&A Library (21 top left); British Architectural Library, Royal Institute of British Architects, London (16 middle, 59 right, 65, 215); Max Dupain / British Architectural Library, Royal Institute of British Architects, London (58 left); John Donat (57); Peter Durant (205, 221–222); E. T. Archive / Egyptian Museum, Cairo (33); Georges Fessy (104–106); N. Fintikakis (202); Geleta & Geleta Photo Studio (54); Courtesy of T. R. Hamzah & Yeang (234); Ryou Hata (94 top); Hedrich Blessing (88–91); Jochen Helle (103 bottom); Jorg Hempel Photodesign (75–76, 77 bottom); Courtesy of Jourda and Perraudin (242, 243); Kota Kawasaki (109–111); Kawasumi Architectural Photograph Office (209–210); Holger Knauf (216–219); Waltraud Krase (77 top); Lamb Studio (141); Ian Lambot (229–231); Dieter Leistner (136–139, 170–173); David Lloyd Jones (14 top right and left, 17 top, 34, 41); Mitsuo Matsuoka (175); Milroy McAleer (142–143); James Morris (191–193); G. Mussett (148); Naru Architecture Photograph Office (211); K. L. Ng (11, 233, 235); Courtesy of Petzinka Pink und Partner (227); Photo R.M.N. (20 top left); Mandy Reynolds (194–195); Ralph Richters / Architekturphoto (84–87, 101–103 top); Tomas Riehle / Contur (225–266); Sakamoto Photo Research Laboratory (15 bottom); Courtesy of Samyn & Associates (182); Courtesy of Sheppard Robson (206); Shinkenchiku-sha (62, 67 bottom, 68–69, 93 left, 95, 132, 134, 162–165, 167–169, 175, 176 bottom, 177, 186–188; Shinkenchiku-sha / Shigeo Ogawa (63, 145–147, 176, 177); Timothy Soar (79–81, 153–156); Courtesy of Studio E Architects (236, 240, 241); Studio Fotografico Quattrone (18 bottom); Hisao Suzuki / Archivo Eye Barcelona (133, 135); Fred Thompson (16 top right); Hiroshi Ueda (197–198); VIEW / Peter Cook (58 right, 71, 72, 97–99); VIEW / Dennis Gilbert (179–181); Tim Webster (150); Courtesy of Andrew Wright Associates (238, 239).

Project Credits

Tokyo Gas 'Earth Port' >66
Architect: Nikken Sekkei. Project team: Kiyoshi Sakurai, Kouko Nakamura, Yuki Watanabe; Tokyo Gas Urban Development Co. Ltd (supervisors). Client: Tokyo Gas. Structural engineering: Michio Keii, Hiroshi Yamamoto (in-house team). Installation engineering: Katashi Matsunawa, Fumio Nohara, Sou Takizawa (in-house team). Main contractor: Kumagai Gumi. Sub-contractors: Takasago Thermal Engineering Co. Ltd; Kandenko Co. Ltd; Kanpai, Toshiba.

John Menzies Headquarters >70
Architect: Bennetts Associates. Project team: Stephen Bates, Denise Bennetts, Rab Bennetts, Simon Erridge, David Henderson, Ray Kearney, Julian Lipscombe, Jane Willoughby. Client: John Menzies Wholesale. Management contractor: Bovis Construction. Masterplan architect: Richard Meier & Partners. Liaison architect: Campbell & Arnott. Structural engineer: Curtins Consulting. Landscape architect: Ian White Associates. Acoustics: Arup Acoustics. Quantity surveyor: Banks Wood & Partners. Mechanical installation: Vaughan Engineering. Electrical installation, including lights: Balfour Kilpatrick. Structural steelwork: Pavo Steel Specialists. Curtain wall, atrium glazing and canopy: Structal (UK). Roofing: ERP Elastomeric. Stone cladding: J.W. Smith. Suspended ceilings and dry lining: Carlton Ceilings & Partitions. Raised floors and floor finishes: System Floors. Atrium floor and ceramic tiling: The Tiling Company. Joinery and shop fitting: Swift Horsman. Blinds: Sunrite Blinds. Main entrance hall: Boon Edam. Architectural metalwork: R. Glazzard. Decorations to concrete and general decoration: Pyeroy. Audio-visual

Credits / Architecture and the Environment

fit-out: In Sight. Sculpture: Keith McCarter. Tapestries: Susan Mowatt.

J. Walter Thompson Headquarters >74
Architect: Schneider & Schumacher. Project team: Till Schneider; Michael Schumacher; Hans Pfefferkorn (project manager); Kristin Dirschl, Marcel Eckert, Karen Ehlers, Heike Heinzelmann, Beate Hoyer, Matthew O'Malia, Petra Pfeiffer, Richard Voss. Client: Michael Loulakis. Collaborators: Arup, Düsseldorf (structural engineering and technical planning). Metalwork: Magnus Müller. Lighting: Erco. Structures: Wayss & Freytag. Glass: Pilkington. Furniture: Vitra GmbH.

Ionica >78
Architect: RH Partnership. Project team: David Emond, Mike Woodbridge, Ray Chudleigh, David Doody, Jack Lewry, Kevin Myers, Tony Stevens, Paul Tyrell, Paul Wells. Client: St John's College, Cambridge. Main contractor: Wates Construction (East). Space planning: Total Office Interiors. Structural engineer: Hannah Reed Associates. Services engineer: Rybka Smith Ginsler and Battle. M&E design consultant: Battle McCarthy. Quantity surveyor: Davis Langdon & Everest. Access floor: Thorsman. Blinds: Hunter Douglas. Brickwork: Latchmore Developments. Curtain walling and windows: Velfac Windows. Entrance desk: Gatewood Joinery. Entrance screen: Colmans. Internal partitioning: Clestra Hauserman. Joinery and carpentry: P. Audus. Landscaping: Tilebrooks Landscapes. Solar shading and louvres: Colt International. Structural steelwork: Caunton Engineering. Suppliers: Milliken, Altro (floor coverings); Elementer (ironmongery); Concord, Erco (lighting).

Advanced Photovoltaic Systems (APS) Manufacturing Facility >82
Architect: Kiss Cathcart Anders Architects. Project team: Gregory Kiss (principal-in-charge); Peter Anders, Brenda November, Colin Cathcart, Keith Hone, John Loomis, Laura Kurgan, Judy Choi, Chuck Felton, Amy Nanni, Susan Gross. Client: EJC Inc. Landscape architect: Bissell & Karn. Structural / mechanical / electrical engineer: Ove Arup & Partners. Civil engineer: Bissell & Karn. General contractor: Devcon Construction, Inc.

Library and Cultural Centre >84
Architect: LOG ID. Project team: Dieter Schempp (partner-in-charge), Fred Möllring (design), Winfried Klimesch, Gerhard Steiner, Walter Gans, Eva Sedelmaier. Client: Town of Herten. Landscape architect: Jürgen Frantz (LOG ID). Main contractor: Assmann. Heating, ventilation and sanitation: PIV, Hesslinger und Baumgartner. Electrical contractor: Dohrmann.

NREL Solar Energy Research Facility >88
Architect and engineer: Anderson DeBartolo Pan, Inc. Lead designer: Jack DeBartolo Jr FAIA. Client: United States Department of Energy. Builder: G. E. Johnson Construction Company. Civil engineering: Drexel Barell. Lab design: RFD. Landscape architect: EDAW Inc. Daylighting: Architectural Energy Corporation.

Matsushita Electronic >92
Architect: Nikken Sekkei. Project team: Kiyoshi Sakura, Teruo Yokota, Kiyotaka Komuro, Mikio Kataoka, Syuzo Yamada. Client: Matsushita Electric Co. Ltd. Main contractors (Joint Venture): Kajima Corp.; Takenaka Corp.; Toda Corp.; Okumura Corp. Structural engineering: Takayuki Teramoto, Haruyuki Kiramura, Yasuhiro Tuneki (in-house team). Installation engineering: Katashi Matsunawa, Ryoshuke Hashiura, Hiroshi Iizuka (in-house team). Collaborator: Toshihiro Katayama (ground-floor landscape). Sub-contractors: Takasago Thermal Engineering Co. Ltd; Dai-Dan Corp.; Toyo Netsu Kogyo Kaisha; Sankou Air Conditioning Co. Ltd (air conditioning and plumbing installation); Kinden Corp.; Kandenko Co. Ltd; Toko Electrical Construction Co. Ltd (high electricity); Futaba Denki Tsushin (low electricity); Masatoshi Izumi (stonework).

Barclaycard Headquarters >96
Architect: Fitzroy Robinson. Project team: Robin Booth,

John Vincent, Blaise Coonan, Michael Winter, David Weston-Thomas, Simon Tucker, Martin Scott, David Peak, Pam Walton. Client: Barclays Property Holdings Ltd. Structural engineer: WSP Kenchington Ford. Quantity surveyor: Hart Gilmore Associates. Services engineer: Troup Bywaters & Anders. Landscape designer: Whitelaw Turkington. Acoustic consultant: Hann Tucker Associates. Modelmaker: Kandor Modelmakers.

Science Park Gelsenkirchen >100
Architect: Kiessler & Partner. Project team: Uwe Kiessler, Hermann Schultz, Vera Ilic, Stefanie Reithwiesner, Ursula Baptista, Thomas Brilling, Konstanze Elbel, Andreas Gierer, Klaus Jantschek, Achim Jürke, Markus Link, Klaus Löhnert, Christoph Mayr, Andreas Plesske. Client: Wissenschaftspark und Technologiezentrum Rheinelbe Gelsenkirchen Vermögensgesellschaft mbH. Project management: Norbert Muhlak. Structural engineer: Sailer & Stepan. Heating, ventilation and sanitation: Ingenieurbüro Trumpp. Electrical engineer: Planungsgemeinschaft Riemhofer/Zerull. Landscaping: Planungsbüro Drecker. Energy source consultant: Fraunhofer Institut für Solare Energiesysteme. Solar panels: Flachglas-Solartechnik GmbH. Façade consultant: Institut Schaupp. Office façades: Gebr. Schneider Fensterfabrik. Roof: Fa. Wewers GmbH. Tiling: Fa. H. Linnr. Floor coverings: Fa Häcker.

Vice Chancellor's Office, Académie des Antilles et de la Guyane >104
Architect: Christian Hauvette, Jérôme Nouel. Project team: Rémi Martinelli, Jacques Duflos de Saint-Armand, Lorenzo Pagiaro, Véronique Chapuis. Client: Ministry for National Education. Main contractor: SOGEA. Exterior woodwork, woodwork and casing: SOGEA Martinique. Carpentry: S.E.R.C.A.M. False ceilings: Laguarrigue. Paintwork: E.S.O. Electricity: Camelec. Landscaping: S.I.V.M.A.N.O.

Akira Kusumi's Guest House >108
Architect: Awaji Workshop, Kota Kawasaki. Project team: Shin Aiba, Takuto Hiki, Kazuhiro Hosaka, Kota Kawasaki, Yasuhisa Kikuti, Siro Miura, Keisuke Tamura, Paddy Tomesen, Takeshi Yosida. Client: Akira Kusumi. Main contractor: Hanasaka Dan (Akira Kusumi, Naohiro Kamimura).

Apartment Building, Biel >112
Architect: LOG ID, Dieter Schempp. Project team: Fred Möllring, Jürgen Frantz, Ueli Schmid. Client: Stettler AG. Main contractor: ASP, H. Schmid. Landscape/glasshouses: Jürgen Frantz (LOG ID).

Palmetto House >116
Architect/Builder: Jersey Devil. Project team: Jim Adamson, Steve Badanes, Donna Walter, Fred Montgomery, Les Cizek, Tony Marciante. Client: Jim Adamson (current); Lescizek/Norma Watkins (original clients). Structural engineer: Bob Fasullo.

Marika Alderton House >120
Architect: Glenn Murcutt. Client: Marika Alderton.

Temple of Time or Divided House >124
Architect: Benson and Forsyth. Project team: Gordon Benson, Alan Forsyth, Annabelle Henderson. Client: Fujie San, Arata Isozaki, Local Authority Architects. Sub-contractor: Nabetakogyo Co. Ltd. Building trader: The Zenitaka Corporation. Organizers: Urban Factory Ltd (Tokyo); Life Network Research Institute Ltd (Toyama). Heavy timber: Takahatakogyo Co. Ltd. Glass fibre reinforced cement: Dai-ichi Kouei Co. Ltd.

Women's Humane Society Animal Shelter >128
Architect: Susan Maxman Architects. Project team: Susan A. Maxman (principal); Jeffery Hayes (project architect); Kate Cleveland, Robert Hotes, Rob Rudloff. Client: Women's Humane Society. General contractor: Irwin & Leighton. Structural engineer: Ortega Consulting. Landscape architect: Lager-Raabe Landscape Architects. Civil engineer: MGL Inc. Mechanical engineer: Bruce E. Brooks & Associates, Inc. Electrical engineer: Donald F.

Nardy & Associates, Inc. Heating/air conditioning: Energy Products Company. Energy recovery system: Semco. Lighting: Litecontrol; Zumtobel Lighting Inc.; Sim-Kar Lighting Fixture Co.; Lithonia Lighting; SPI Lighting Inc.; Architectural Lighting Systems; Columbia Lighting; Staff Lighting. Outdoor lighting: Stonco. Steel roofing: Smith Steelite. Windows: EFCO Corporation. Carpeting: Collins & Aikman. Floor tiles: GTE Engineered Ceramics. Solid linoleum: DLW – Gerbert Ltd. Floor mats: Belting Associates, Inc. Benches: Santana Products.

Ukichiro Nakaya Museum of Snow and Ice >132
Architect: Arata Isozaki and Associates. Client: Kaga City. Main contractors: Taisei; Yamamoto; Kawamuki; Kaga Setsubi Joint Venture. Installation engineer: Kankyo Engineering and Mach Facility Planning Laboratory. Structural engineer: Kawaguchi Structural Engineering Studio. Collaborators: Nomura Kogei Sha (display); Iwanami Eiga Seisakusho (film); Uejyou Studio (signage); Fujiko Nakatani (snow landscaping).

Hostel for Youth Educational Institute >136
Architect: Prof. Thomas Herzog. Project team: Thomas Herzog, Peter Bonfig. Client: Prämonstratenser-Abtei Windberg. Building planning: Walter Götz. Energy simulation consultant: Institut für Energiesysteme der Fraunhofergesellschaft (ISE). Landscape architect: Anneliese Latz. Heating and ventilation: Zimmermann Lüftungs- und Wärmesysteme GmbH & Co. KG. Timber work: Holzbau Münchsmühle GmbH. Glazing: Okalux.

The Center for Regenerative Studies >140
Architect: Dougherty + Dougherty. Project team: Betsey Olenick Dougherty (partner); Troy Fountain (project architect). Client: California State University. Phase I: Structural engineer: EQE. Civil engineer: RBF. Mechanical/electrical engineer: Store, Matakovich & Wolfberg. Landscape architect: The Peridian Group (now POD/Sasaki). Contractor: Temple Construction. Phase II: Structural engineer: Felix Martin & Associates. Civil engineer: Douglas Bender & Associates. Mechanical engineer: F.T. Andrews, Inc. Electrical engineer: Dale Karjala & Associates. Landscape architect: IDEATE Studios. Lighting consultant: Clanton & Associates. Energy efficiency consultant: The Ensar Group. Contractor: RSH Construction.

Center for Japanese Studies, University of Indonesia >144
Architect: Akihiko Takeuchi/Matsuda Consultants International Co. Ltd. Client: University of Indonesia. Collaborator: Audio-Visual System Planning. Main contractor: Taisei Corporation. Sub-contractor: Kinden Corporation (air conditioning, plumbing and electricity). Structural engineer: Inoue Structural Design Ltd. Installation engineer: ARC System Sekkei Shitsu.

Uluru-Kata Tjuta National Park Cultural Centre >148
Architect: Gregory Burgess Pty Ltd Architects. Project team: Gregory Burgess (design architect); Peter Ryan, Steve Duddy (project architects); Ian Khoo, Phillip Bigg, Robert Lock, Anna Lindstad, Alvyn Williams, Thomas Kinloch. Client: Mifijulu Community and Parks Australia – Environment Australia. Structural/civil engineer: P. J. Yttrup & Associates. Services engineer: W. O. Ross & Associates. Landscape architect: Taylor Cullity. Quantity surveyor: Anthony Prowse & Associates. Display: Sonja Peter & Associates; Form Australia. Design and fabrication of Maruku fit-out: Danton Hughes. Builder: Sitzler Brothers. Site foreman: Roger Starr.

Elizabeth Fry Building, University of East Anglia >152
Architect: John Miller & Partners. Project team: Richard Brearley, Su Rogers, Neil Harkness, Umberto Emoli, John Carpenter, Soraya Khan. Client: University of East Anglia. Main contractor: Willmott Dixon Eastern Ltd. Quantity surveyor: Stockings and Clarke. Structural engineer: F.J. Samuely and Partners. Services engineer: Fulcrum Engineering Partnership. Energy consultant: Energy Advisory Associates. M&E sub-contractor: Matthew Hall

Ltd. Windows: Swedhouse Ltd. Roofing: Gale Construction Ltd. Lecture theatre seating: Haworth (UK) Ltd. Cavity wall and roof insulation: Rockwool Ltd. Canopy glazing: Columbus. Circular windows: Fenlock Hansen. Display cabinets: Preedy Glass. Internal glazing: Wensum Glass. Glass staircase: Design-A-Glass. Antitstat carpeting: Burmatex Ltd. Vinyl tiling: Altro Hyload Flooring. Ceramic tiling: Ceramic Tiles (Contract) Ltd. Floor finishes: Anglia Flooring. Ironmongery: City Fix Architectural Supplies.

Spring Lake Park Visitors Center >158
Architect: Obie G. Bowman. Project team: Obie G. Bowman (architect and principal-in-charge); Fiona O'Neill (project architect). Client: Sonoma County Water Agency. General contractor: Christianson-Williams-Bohn. Structura consultant: Dennis Fagent Asociates. Mechanical and civil consultant: Sonoma County Water Agency. Solar consultant: Larkin & Associates. Geotechnical investigation Field Engineering. Arborist: John Britton.

Sea Folk Museum >162
Architecture and interior design: Naito Architect & Associates. Client: The Foundation of Tokai Suisan Kagaku Kyoukai. Main contractor: Kamegawa Construction Corporation. Structural engineering: Kunio Watanabe; Structural Design Group Co. Ltd.

Paper Church >166
Architect: Shigeru Ban Architect. Project team: Shigeru Ban, Shigeru Hiraki, Keishin Sakuma, Client: Takatori Catholic Church. Structural engineer: Gengo Matsui; Hoshino Structural Engineering Studio. Installation engineer: Shuichi. Collaborators: TSP Taiyou, Takiron, Taiyou Cement Industry, Matsumoto Corporation, Nishiyama.

Paper Log House >166
Architect: Shigeru Ban. Project team: Shigeru Ban, Takashi Nakagawa, Masao Suzuki, Kitayama Souzou Kenkyu Sho. Client: Nippon Shinpan. Main contractor: Nomura Kougei. Structural engineer: Gengo Matsui; Hoshino Structural Engineering Studio. Sub-contractors: Sanshin Daikin Kisetsu (air conditioning); Takeomi Industry (plumbing installation); Uemura Denki (electricity).

Hall 26 >170
Architect: Herzog & Partner. Project team: Prof. Thomas Herzog, Hanns Jörg Schrade, Sabine Erdt, Nico Kienzl, Stefan Öhler, Christian Schätzke, Bärbel Schuster, Thomas Straub, Brigitte Tacke, Stefanie Zierl. Client: Deutsche Messe AG, Hanover. Structural engineer: Schlaich Bergermann und Partner. Mechanical services: HL Technik. Aerodynamic studies, natural ventilation and energy simulation: Design Flow Solutions. Daylighting and artificial lighting: Bartenbach LichtLabor GmbH. Project planning: Assmann Beraten & Planen GmbH. Heating and cooling: Friedrich Baxmann. Sun protection: Clauss Markisen Projekt GmbH. Wood façade: Kaufmann Holzbaugesellschaft mbH. Air conditioning and ventilation: H. Krantz-TKT GmbH. Roofing: Laue Bedachungen GmbH. Carpenter: Plaumann & Bonifacius GmbH. Technical engineer: HL-Technik AG. Electronics: Höhne GmbH. Fire protection: Hosser, Hass & Partner. Building shell: E. Heltkamp GmbH. Façade: Messehalle 26 Seele-Sassenscheidt; Stahl-u. Metallbau GmbH & Co. KG. Tiling: Klaus-Peter Beverungen. Interior fittings: Rheinold & Mahla Ausbau GmbH. Steelwork: Rüterbau. Concrete: Hochtief AG.

Museum of Wood >174
Architect: Tadao Ando Architect & Associates. Client: Hyogo Prefecture. Main contractor: Shimizu Kensetsu; Maeda Kensetsu Industry; Meisei Kensetsu Joint Venture. Sub-contractors: Tajima Kinki Industry (air conditioning and plumbing installation); Shirabishi Denki (electrical); Fujitec (elevators); Tansei Sha (display); NHK-ES (hi-vision).

BRE (Building Research Establishment) Office of the Future >178
Architect: Feilden Clegg Architects. Project team: Peter

Clegg, Bill Gething, Craig White, David Noble, David Stansfield, Andrew Peters. Client: Building Research Establishment Ltd. Main contractor: J. Sisk & Son Ltd. Project management: BWA Project Services. Quantity surveyor: Turner & Townsend. Structural engineer: Büro Happold. Environmental services engineer: Max Fordham & Partners. Landscape architect: Nicholas Pearson Associates. Planning supervisor: Symonds Travers Morgan Ltd. Mechanical & electrical contractor: Norstead Building Services Engineers. Pre-cast wave floor shells and beams: Structural Concrete Contractors Ltd. Recycled concrete: R.M.C. Glass blocks: Pitsburg Corning. Ventilation stack terminals: Selkirk Manufacturing Ltd. Windows: Velfac. Louvre systems (glass and metal): Colt International. Shading gratings: Thielco Grating Ltd. Glass louvre blades: Pilkingtons. BMS/control systems: Caradon Trend. Photovoltaics: Intersolar. Lighting: Philips Lighting. Recycled brick: Solopark. Timber beams and structural deck: Triad Timber Components. Underfloor heating / cooling pipework: Hepworth Building Products Ltd. Carpets: Sommer U.K. Aluminium roofing: Stramit Industries Ltd. Ironmongery: I.G.B. Ltd.

Seed House and Forestry Centre >182
Architect: Samyn & Partners. Project team: Philippe Samyn, R. Delaunoit, D. Mélotte. Gh. André. Client: Ministry of the Walloon region. Structural specialist: SETESCO; FTI. Wood modelling: Koos & Cie sa. Woodwork: Menuiserie Fréson. Contractor: Bouny Construction sprl. Sub-contractors: Gobiet Frères sa; Henneaux sa (electricity); Frédérick sa (heating and ventilation); Duvivier sprl (plumbing); Portal sa (glass cover); Grencobel sa (refrigeration installation).

Toyo Village Mason Museum >186
Architect: Yasufumi Kijima + Yas & Urbanists / Keikaku. Project team: Hirofumi Sugimoto, Takeshi Umeda, Masato Hirose, Syunichi Matsuzaka. Client: Toyo Village. Main contractor: Sakae Kensetsu. Structural engineer: Shigeru Aoki Kenkyu Shitsu. Installation engineer: Kaihatsu Setsubi Kikaku; ME Sekkei (electricity). Sub-contractors: UEDA Shoukai (air conditioning and plumbing); Murakami Denki Kouji (electrical); Nomura Kougei Sha (display).

EDF Regional Headquarters >190
Architect: Foster and Partners. Project team: Sir Norman Foster, Spencer de Grey, Andrew Thomson, Max Neal, William Castagna, Glynis Fan, Chris Bubb, Ismael Juan Khan. Client: Electricité de France. Delegated client: EDF SEISO – Service ERCI. Site architect: Berguedieu-Brochet. Structural engineer: Ove Arup and Partners. Energy consultant: Kaiser Bautechnik. Quantity surveyor: DL&E. External works: Entreprise Malet. Metalwork: Garrigues. Roofing: Smac Acieroïd. Brise-soleil: Atelier d'Agencement. Mechanical: Elyo Océan. Electrical: Electrification Générale. Joinery: Limouzin. Partitions: Clestra Hausermann. Raised flooring: Wanner Isofi. Stone and tilework: Delvaux Combalié. Signage: Graphi-Aquitaine. Plumbing: Guysanit. Painting and decorating: Larrey SA. Dryline and plastering: Sofibat.

Westminster Lodge >194
Architect: Edward Cullinan Architects. Project team: Ted Cullinan, John Romer, Sasha Bhavan, Mary-Lou Arscott. Client: The Parnham Trust. Builder: Hooke Forest (Construction) Ltd. Structural engineer: Büro Happold. Services engineer: Büro Happold. Research: University of Bath, School of Architecture and Engineering.

Water Temple >196
Architect: Tadao Ando Architect & Associates. Client: Honpukuji Temple. Structural engineer: Ascoral Engineering Associates.

Eastgate >200
Architect: Pearce Partnership Architects. Project team: Michael Pearce, Radhan Cumaraswamy. Client: Old Mutual Properties Zimbabwe. Main contractor: Costain Sisk Joint Venture. Project management and building developer: Old Mutual Properties. Retail design consultant: Design Development Group Inc. Structural engineer: Ove Arup

& Partners Zimbabwe. Mechanical engineer: Ove Arup & Partners. Quantity surveyors: Hawkins Leshnick & Bath. Electrical sub-contractor: William Steward. Plumbing sub-contractor: Hancock & Ward. Steel sub-contractors: International Construction Zimbabwe Ltd; G. Sepe Metal Fabricators; Confab; Sullivans Engineering. Pre-cast concrete: Precast Concrete. Shopfitting and partitioning: Frederick Sage.

Central Market of Athens >202
Architect: N. Fintikakis. Research team: Synthesis and Research Ltd (Mavrotas Dionysios, Tzaveli Maria). Client: Municipality of Athens. Mechanical engineer: A. N. Sgouropoulos of Talos Engineering SA; Fraunhofer – Institut für Solare Energiesysteme, Freiburg.

Helicon >204
Architect: Sheppard Robson. Project team: Graham Francis (partner); Graham Anthony (project designer); Malcolm McGowan, Andrew Bowles (project managers); Greg Gaylor (cladding). Client: London and Manchester Insurance. Project management: MDA Project Management. Structural engineer: John Savage Associates. Mechanical and electrical engineer: Ove Arup & Partners. Quantity surveyor: Silk & Frazier. Contractors: Astec Projects Ltd (ceilings); Cain Decorators (painting and decorating); Dyer (structural steel); Gormley Marble Specialists Ltd (stonework); Haden Young (M&E); John Rawlson Eng. Ltd (misc. metalwork); Singer & James (metalwork); Thorsman & Co. (UK) Ltd (floor); The Tiling Co. Ltd (tiling); Tyndale Carpets (rubber flooring/staircases). Suppliers: Bligh Boards Ltd (timber/board materials); Elite Architectural Ironmongery (ironmongery); Hills of Shoeburyness Ltd (joinery); William Sharratt & Sons Ltd (timber).

Yasuda Academia >208
Architect: Nihon Sekkei Inc. Project team: Shigeyoshi Saito, Mikitaro Okamoto. Client: The Yasuda Mutual Life Insurance Co. Ltd. Main contractor: Fujita; Kajima; Tobishima; Goyo (Joint Venture). Artwork: Hidenori Aoki. Furniture: Motomi Kawakami. Lighting: LPA. Plant: Tase. Air-conditioning and plumbing installation: Taiki Sha. Electricity: Kanden. Sub-contractors: Hitachi, Toshiba.

Viaduct Refurbishment >212
Architect: Patrick Berger. Project team: Patrick Berger, Janine Galiano. Client: SEMAEST (Société d'Economie Mixte d'Aménagement de l'Est de Paris). Main contractor: CBC Ile de France. Collaborator: BECT.

RWE AG Headquarters >216
Architect: Ingenhoven, Overdiek, Kahlen und Partner. Project team: Christoph Ingenhoven, Achim Nagel, Klaus Frankenheim, Klaus J. Osterburg, Peter-Jan van Ouwerkerk, Imre Halmai, Martin Slawik, Elisabeth Viera, Claudia de Bruyn, Jan Dvorak, Norbert Siepmann, Regina Wuff, Martin Röhrig. Client: Hochtief Project Development. General contractor: Hochtief. Structural engineer: Hochtief AG. Consulting engineer: König & Heunisch. Technical consultants: HL-Technik AG; Ingenieurgesellschaft Kruck. Building physics: Trümper & Overath. Façade consultant: Fa Gartner. Surveyor: Dipl Ing Klein.

The Thames Tower >220
Architect: Brookes Stacey Randall Fursdon. Client: Thames Water Utilities Ltd. Main contractor: J. Murphy and Sons (Contractors) Ltd. Engineer: SMP Atelier One. Glazing and cladding: Charles Henshaws and Sons Ltd. Water specialist: Thermelek Engineering Services Ltd. Water development: Atkinson Chemicals Ltd. Solar panels: Hiltec Solar Ltd. Mast: Proctor Masts Ltd.

City Gate >224
Architect: Petzinka, Pink und Partner. Client: GbR Düsseldorfer Stadttor mbH. Building contractor: Engel Projektentwicklung und Management GmbH. Project controller and energy consultant: Drees & Sommer AG. Structural engineer and façade consultant: DS-Plan. Façade planning: E. Mosbacher. Heating, ventilation and air conditioning: Jäger, Mornhinweg & Partner. Subsoil consultant: NEK Umwelttechnik GmbH.

Credits / Architecture and the Environment

Commerzbank Headquarters >228

Architect: Foster and Partners. Project team: Norman Foster, Spencer de Grey, Ken Shuttleworth, Mark Sutcliffe, Brandon Haw, Hans Brouwer, David Nelson, Robin Partington, Graham Phillips, Stefan Behling, Winston Shu, John Silver, Paul Kalkhoven, Chris Abell, Arthur Branthwaite, Chris Eisner, Tom Politowicz, Christopher Allercamp, Giuseppe Boscherini, Simon Bowden, Thomas Braun, George Brennan, Caroline Brown, Eckhardt Burling, Angus Campbell, Kei-Lu Cheong, Charles Collett, Penny Collins, David Crosswaite, Nigel Curry, John Drew, Matthew Downing, Alex Gounaris, Pauline Hanna, Ken Hutt, Nadi Jahangiri, Mike Jelliffe, Michael Jones, Joachim Kappeler, Natalie Maguire, Nikolai Malsch, Matthias Massari, Stig Mikkelson, Paul Morgan, Uwe Nienstedt, Sven Ollmann, Donia Parmasche, Stefan Ponur, Logan Reilly, Giles Robinson, Cormac Ryan, Thomas Scheel, Paul Scott, Mandy Bates, Kinna Stallard, Brian Timmoney, Huw Turner, Peter Unkrig, Ken Wai, Andreas Wolff, Robert Watson, Alan Wilkinson-Marten, Louisa Williams, Michael Wurzel. Client: Commerzbank. General contractor: Hochtief Niederlassung. Consultants: J. Roger Preston with Pettersen and Ahrends (mechanical engineering); Schad and Hölzel (electrical engineering). Project management: Weidleplan. Quantity surveyor: Davis Langdon and Everest. Space planning: Quickborner Team. Façades, radar, acoustics and building physics: Ingenieur Büro Schalm. Lighting: Lichtdesign. Landscape: Sommerlad. Structural planning: Ove Arup & Partner; Kreb and Kiefer. Mechanical and electrical engineering: Pettersson und Ahrens. Façade engineering: Ingenieurbüro Schalm.

Menara Mesiniaga >232

Architect: T. R. Hamzah & Yeang. Client: Mesiniaga. Civil and structural engineer: Reka Perunding. Mechanical and electrical engineer: Norman Disney & Young. Quantity surveyor: Baharuddin Ali & Low. Interior designer: T.R. Hamzah & Yeang Designs. Landscape architect: Lap Consultancy. Main builder: Siah Bros. Steelworks builder: Sediabena.

Bibliography

This bibliography comprises works from which the author has directly drawn, and material for further reading.

History and Theory of Architecture

S.O. Addy (1933) *The Evolution of the English House*, London

C. Alexander (1979) *The Timeless Way of Building*, New York

H.M. Baillie Scott (1906) *Houses and Gardens*, London

R. Banham (1960) *Theory and Design in the First Machine Age*, London

R. Banham (1969) *The Architecture of the Well-Tempered Environment*, London

K. Bayes (1994) *Living Architecture*, Trowbridge

P. Beaver (1970) *The Crystal Palace*, London

S. and S. Behling (1996) *Sol Power*, Munich and New York

L. Benevolo (1982) *Storia della citta*, Rome and Bari

W. Blaser (1984) *Architecture and Nature*, Basel and Boston

J-L. Bourgeois and C. Pelos (1993) *Spectacular Vernacular: The Adobe Tradition*, New York

S. Brand (1994) *How Buildings Learn*, New York

K. Butti and J. Perlin (1980) *A Golden Thread: 2500 Years of Solar Architecture and Technology*, New York and London

S. Chermayeff and C. Alexander (1963) *Community and Privacy: Towards a New Architecture of Humanism*, New York

K. Clark (1929) *The Gothic Revival*, London

C. Constant (1988) 'From the Virgilian Dream to Chandigarh: Le Corbusier and the Modern Landscape' from *Denatured Visions*, New York

Le Corbusier (1923) *Vers Une Architecture*, Paris; English translation (1927) *Towards a New Architecture*, London

Le Corbusier (1924) *Urbanisme*, Paris; English translation (1929) *The City of Tomorrow*, London

Le Corbusier (1961) *My Work*, London

Le Corbusier (1964) *The Radiant City*, London

S. Denyer (1978) *African Traditional Architecture: An Historical and Geographical Perspective*, New York

J. Farmer (1996) *Green Shift*, Oxford

H. Fathy (1973) *Architecture for the Poor*, Chicago and London

M. Fry (1969) *Art in a Machine Age*, London

J.M. Gandy (1805) *Designs for Cottages*, London

J.M. Gandy (1805) *The Rural Architect,* London

S. Giedion (1941) *Space, Time and Architecture*, Cambridge, Mass., and London

M. Goldfinger (1993) *Villages in the Sun: Mediterranean Community Architecture*, New York

E. Hadingham (1987) *Lines to the Mountain Gods: Nazca and the Mysteries of Peru*, London

D. Hawkes (1996) *The Environmental Tradition*, London

H.R. Hitchcock and P. Johnson (1932) *Functional Architecture: The International Style 1925–40*, New York and London

H.R. Hitchcock (1954) *Early Victorian Architecture*, London

H.R. Hitchcock (1958) *Architecture of the 19th and 20th Centuries*, Harmondsworth

C. Hobhouse (1937) *1851 and The Crystal Palace*, London

E. Howard (1902) *Garden Cities of Tomorrow*, London

A. Jackson (1970) *The Politics of Architecture: A History of Modern Architecture in Britain*, London

C. Jencks (1977) *The Language of Post-Modern Architecture*, London

C. Jencks (1988) *Architecture Today*, London

E. Kaufmann (1955) *Architecture in the Age of Reason*, Cambridge, Mass.

E. Kaufmann (1983) *From Ledoux to Le Corbusier*, Vienna and Leipzig

S. Kidder Smith (1950) *Sweden Builds*, Stockholm

Y. Kodama, J. Cook and S. Yannas (1991) 'Passive and Low Energy Architecture', *Process Architecture*, No. 88, Tokyo

C. Knevitt (1994) *Shelter*, London

S. Koppelkamm (1982) *Glasshouses and Wintergardens of the 19th Century*, London

W. Lam (1986) *Sunlight as Formgiver for Architecture*, Atlanta

R. Lamb (1996) *Promising the Earth*, London

M.A. Laugier (1752) *Essai sur L'Architecture*, Paris

D. Leatherbarrow (1993) *The Roots of Architectural Invention*, New York

W. Lethaby (1892) *Architecture, Mysticism and Myth*, London

D. Mackenzie (1991, 1997) *Green Design*, London

S.T. Madsen (1967) *Art Nouveau*, London

J. Malton (1798) *An Essay on British Cottage Architecture*, London

J. Meller (Ed) (1970) *The Buckminster Fuller Reader*, London

W. Morris (1878) *The Decorative Arts*, republished in *The Lesser Arts* (1822), and (1880) *The Beauty of Life*, in Collected Works, Vol. 22 (1910–15), London

H. Muthesius (1979) *The English House*, New York

G. Naylor (1971) *The Arts and Crafts Movement*, London

D.G. Noble (Ed) (1984) *New Light on Chaco Canyon*, Santa Fe

J.B. Papworth (1818) *Rural Residences*, London

P. Pearson (1994) *Earth to Spirit, In Search of Natural Architecture*, London

N. Pevsner (1936) *Pioneers of the Modern Movement*, London

N. Pevsner (1943) *Outline of European Architecture*, London

N. Pevsner (1960) *Pioneers of Modern Design*, London

N. Pevsner (1976) *A History of Building Types*, London

U. Price (1794) *Essay on the Picturesque*, London

H. Repton (1795–6) *Red Book for Blaise Castle*, City of Bristol Museum and Art Gallery

J.M. Richards (1958) *The Functional Tradition in Early Industrial Buildings*, London

J.M. Richards (1965) *Modern Architecture in Finland*, London

P.G. Rowe (1991) *Making a Middle Landscape*, Cambridge, Mass.

B. Rudofsky (1964) *Architecture without Architects: A Short Introduction to Non-Pedigreed Architecture*, London and New York

B. Rudofsky (1977) *Prodigious Builders*, London

J. Ruskin (1835) *The Poetry of Architecture*, London

J. Ruskin (1849) *The Seven Lamps of Architecture*, London

J. Ruskin (1853) *The Stones of Venice*, London

J. Ruskin (1854) *Lectures on Architecture and Painting*, London

J. Ruskin and H.W.O. Acland (1859) *The Oxford Museum*, London

V. Scully (1961) *Modern Architecture*, London

V. Scully (1962) *The Earth, the Temple and the Gods*, New Haven and London

D. Sharp (1966) *Modern Architecture and Expressionism*, London

A. and P. Smithson (1991) *Die heroische Periode der Modernen Architektur*, London

J. Summerson (1949) *Heavenly Mansions*, London

M. Tafuri (1976) *Teoria e Storia dell'Architettura*, Rome

B. Taut (1914) *Alpine Architecture*, (Ed D. Sharp, 1972), New York

D. Turrant (1997) 'Time and Energy', *RIBA Journal*, London

R. Unwin (1909) *Town Planning in Practice*, London

R. Venturi (1966) *Complexity and Contradiction in Architecture*, New York

Vitruvius (trans. M. Hicky Morgan, 1914) *The Ten Books on Architecture*, Cambridge, Mass.

C.F.A. Voysey (1915) *Individuality*, London

D. Watkin (1986, 1992, 1996) *A History of Western Architecture*, London

F.L. Wright (1939) *An Organic Architecture: The Architecture of Democracy*, New York and London

F.L. Wright (1954) *The Natural House*, New York and London

F.L. Wright (1958) *The Living City*, New York and London

B. Zevi (1950) *Towards an Organic Architecture*, London

R. De Zurko (1957) *Origins of Functionalist Theory*, New York

Architectural Biography

G. Baird (1970) *Alvar Aalto*, London

D.B. Brownlee and D.G. De Long (1992) *Louis I. Kahn: In the Realm of Architecture*, New York

G. Collins (1960) *Gaudì*, London

B. Goff (1970) 'Forty-four Realizations', in David G. De Long (1988) *Bruce Goff: Towards Absolute Architecture*, MIT

P. Inskip (1979) *Architectural Monographs 6: Edwin Lutyens*, London

E. Kaufmann and B. Raeburn (1960) *Frank Lloyd Wright: Writings and Buildings*, New York

C.N. Ledoux (1874) *Architecture*, Paris

J. Lobell (1979) *Between Silence and Light*, Boulder, Colorado

M. Pawley (1990) *Buckminster Fuller*, London

C. Roland (1970) *Frei Otto: Structures*, London

J. Rosenburg (1963) *The Darkening Glass: a Portrait of Ruskin's Genius*, London

J. Steel (1988) *Hassan Fathy Monographs*, New York

S. Tarrago (1974) *Gaudì*, Barcelona

F.L. Wright (1932) *An Autobiography*, New York and London

General Theory and Philosophy

D. Albrecht (1995) *World War II and the American Dream*, Cambridge, Mass.

M. Bender (1992) *Miracle of Life: Discover Patterns of Behaviour in the Living World*, London

N. Calder (1991) *Spaceship Earth*, London

I. Calvino (1974) *Invisible Cities*, London

F. Capra (1982) *The Turning Point*, New York

R. Carson (1951) *The Sea Around Us*, Oxford

R. Carson (1965) *The Silent Spring*, Boston and New York

'Energy: Facing up to the Problem, Getting down to Solutions', Special Report, *National Geographic* (February 1981)

R.B. Fuller (1963) *Nine Chains to the Moon*, New York
R.B. Fuller (1963) *Operating Manual for Spaceship Earth*, Arkansas
R.B. Fuller and R. Marks (1973) *The Dymaxion World of Buckminster Fuller*, London
R.B. Fuller (1981) *Critical Path*, New York
J. Gleik (1987) *Chaos: Making a New Science*, New York
A. Gore (1992) *Earth in the Balance: Forging a New Common Purpose*, London
H. Greene (1976) *Mind and Image*, Lexington, Kentucky
E. Haeckl (1904) *Art Forms in Nature*, Leipzig
W.M. Harlow (1976) *Art Forms from Plantlife*, New York
P. Harrison (1993) *The Third Revolution – Population, Environment and a Sustainable World*, London
F.E. Hulme, S. Mackie, J. Glaisher and R. Hunt (1872) *Art Studies from Nature as Applied to Design*, London
F.E. Hulme (1874) *Plants, their Natural Growth and Ornamental Treatment*, London
I. Illich (1973) *Tools for Conviviality*, New York
J. Lovelock (1988) *The Ages of GAIA: A Biography of Our Living Earth*, Oxford
M.H. Nicholson (1959) *Mountain Gloom and Mountain Glory: the Aesthetics of the Sublime*, Ithaca, New York
W. Patterson (1990) *The Energy Alternative: Changing the Way the World Works*, London
F. Ritterbush (1968) *The Art of Organic Forms*, Washington
S. Schama (1995) *Landscape and Memory*, London
H.G. Schenk (1966) *The Mind of the European Romantics*, London
F. Schumacher (1974) *Small is Beautiful*, London
R. Sheldrake (1990) *The Rebirth of Nature: the Greening of Science and God*, London
M. Singh (1993) *The Sun and Myth in Art*, London
K. Thomas (1983) *Man and the Natural World 1500–1800*, London
H.D. Thoreau (1849) *A Week on the Concord and Merrimack Rivers*, Boston
H.D. Thoreau (1854) *Walden*, Boston
R. Todd (1946) *Tracks in the Snow*, London

Contemporary Architecture

M.J. Crosby (1994) *Green Architecture*, Gloucester, Mass.
T. Herzog (Ed) (1996) *Solar Energy in Architecture and Urban Planning*, Munich and New York
S. Holl (1989) *Anchoring*, New York
L. De Luca and C. Gallo (1992) *Bioclimatic Architecture*, Rome
B. and R. Vale (1991) *Towards a Green Architecture*, London
K. Yeang (1994) *Bioclimatic Skyscrapers*, London

Technology and Economics

C. Alexander and M. Jacobsen (1974) 'Specification for an Organic and Human Building System', *The Responsive House*, MIT
T.C. Barker, Pilkington (1994) *An Age of Glass: The Illustrated History*, London
Bisschop et al (1995) *Building with Photovoltaics*, Utrecht
J. Connaughton (1990) *Building Services Magazine: Life Cycle Energy Costing*, London
E. Danz (1967) *Sonnenschutz: Sun Protection*, Stuttgart
B. Edwards (1996) *Towards a Sustainable Architecture*, Oxford
H. Fathy (1986) *Natural Energy and Vernacular Architecture: Principles and Examples with Reference to Hot Arid Climates*, Chicago
A. Fruhwald and G. Wegener (1996 conference paper) *Ecological Potential for Building Timber*
J.W. Galston (1994) 'Life Process of Plants', *Scientific American Magazine*, New York
J.R. Goulding, J.O. Lewis and T. Steemers (1992) *Energy Conscious Design: A Primer for Architects*, Brussels
D. Hancocks (1973) *Masterbuilders of the Animal World*, London
T. Herzog (1977) *Pneumatic Structures: A Handbook for the Architect and Engineer*, London
N. Howard (conference paper) *Economics of Reducing Greenhouse Car Emissions*

N. Howard (1991) *Building Services Magazine: Energy in Balance*, London
N. Howard and D. Butler (1992) *Building Services Magazine: From the Cradle to the Grave*, London
N. Howard and H. Sutcliffe (1994) *Building Magazine: Precious Joules*, London
R. Howard and E. Winterkorn (1993) *Building Environmental and Energy Design Survey*, Watford
O. Humm and P. Toggweiler (1993) *Photovoltaics and Architecture: Protovoltaik und Architektur*, Basel, Boston and Berlin
M.S. Imamura, P. Helm and W. Palz (1992) *Photovoltaics System Technology*, Brussels
O. Lewis (1986) *Energy in Architecture: The European Solar Passive Handbook*, Brussels
J. Loudon (1833) *Encyclopedia of Cottage, Farm and Villa Architecture*, London
C. Lyell (1830) *Principles of Geology*, London
V. Matus (1988) *Design for Northern Climates: Cold Climate Planning and Environmental Design*, New York
A. and V. Olgyay (1957) *Solar Control and Shading Devices*, Princeton, NJ
V. Olgyay (1963) *Design with Climate*, Princeton, NJ
V. Olgyay (1963) *Design with Climate: Bioclimatic Approach to Architectural Regionalism*, New York
Pacific Domes (1971) *The Dome Book*, California
D. Pearson (1989) *The Natural House Book*, London
H. Plummer (1987) *Poetics of Light*, Tokyo
H. Rostvik (1992) *The Sunshine Revolution*, Stavanger
M. Sala and L.N. Ceccherini (1993) *Technolgie Solari*, Florence
P. Scheerbart (1919) *Glass Architecture*, (Ed D. Sharp, 1972), New York
F. Sick and T. Erge (1996) *Photovoltaics in Buildings*, London
Solar Architecture in Europe: Design, Performance and Evaluation (1991), Brussels
R. Spurgon and M. Flood (1990) *Energy and Power: A Practical Introduction with Projects and Activities*, London
The Whole Earth Catalogue (1971), London
S. Willis, M. Fordham and W. Bordass (1995) *Avoiding or Minimizing the Use of Air-conditioning*, Watford

Sociology

J. Allen (1991) *Biosphere 2, The Human Experiment*, London
W. Bordass, A. Leaman and S. Willis (1994 conference paper) *Control Strategies for Building Services: The Role for the User*
Commission of the European Communities: *Environmental Ethics* (1990) Brussels
D. Cruickshank and N. Burton (1989) *Life in the Gregorian City*, London
S. Curwell, C. March and R. Venables (Eds) (1990) *Buildings and Health*, London
S. Eber (Ed) (1992) *Beyond the Green Horizon*, Godalming
J. Fraser (1968) *Village Planning in the Primitive World*, London
P. Oliver (1969) *Shelter and Society*, London
P. Oliver (1987) *Dwellings – The House across the World*, Austin, Texas
J.J. Rousseau (1761) *La Nouvelle Heloise*, Lausanne
J.J. Rousseau (1762) *Emile, ou de l'Education*, Amsterdam

Index

Figures in italics refer to captions.
See also Glossary, pp 248–49.

253

254

255

256